THE BERITANCE

THE
BENN
INHERITANCE

The Story of a Radical Family

Sydney Higgins

Weidenfeld and Nicolson
London

For Anna,
with my love and thanks

First published in Great Britain in 1984 by
George Weidenfeld & Nicolson Limited
91 Clapham High Street, London SW4 7TA

ISBN 0 297 78524 9

Made and printed in Great Britain by Butler &
Tanner Ltd, Frome and London

CONTENTS

ILLUSTRATIONS

The Rev. Julius Benn, 1826–1883 (*Tony Benn*)

The Rev. Julius Benn's children, *c* 1890s (*Tony Benn*)

Wedgwood Benn, MP, Junior Lord of the Treasury, 1910 (*Stansgate Papers, House of Lords Record Office*)

Margaret Eadie Holmes, aged nineteen, 1919 – the year before her engagement to Wedgwood Benn (*Tony Benn*)

At the 1906 General Election, Wedgwood Benn became the youngest Member of Parliament (*Tony Benn*)

Low's cartoon of Wedgwood Benn MP, 1921 (*Tony Benn*)

Tony Benn, aged six, outside the Houses of Parliament, June 1931 (*Tony Benn*)

Tony Benn and his father sailing off Stansgate, summer 1933 (*Tony Benn*)

Tony Benn and Peggy Rutherford on the beach at Bexhill, summer 1939 (*Tony Benn*)

Air Commodore the Rt Hon. Viscount Stansgate, DSO, DFC, with his eldest son, Michael, who shortly afterwards died in an air crash, 1944 (*Tony Benn*)

Tony Benn just after obtaining his pilot's wings, March 1945 (*Tony Benn*)

On the Oxford University debating tour of America – Tony Benn with Edward Boyle and Kenneth Harris, 1947 (*Tony Benn*)

Tony Benn and Hugh Gaitskell (centre), 1 May 1955, with (left to right) Will Coldrick, Stan Awbery and Will Wilkins (*Tony Benn*)

Caroline Benn addresses a conference on 'Education into the 1970s' held in the Royal Festival Hall, January 1970 (*Tony Benn*)

Tony Benn at work in his Bristol constituency, 1974 (*Tony Benn*)

Tony Benn with Yorkshire miners' leader, Arthur Scargill, 24 February 1976 (*Tony Benn*)

Tony Benn with Neil Kinnock, Joan Lester and, in the background, a smiling Dennis Skinner at the Labour Party Conference, October 1979 (*Daily Telegraph*)

Hilary and Sally Benn with their son, Michael, and his admiring grandfather, 1982 (*Caroline Rees*)

ACKNOWLEDGMENTS

Writing the history of a family that has for so long been actively involved in public life would be extremely difficult without the co-operation of its surviving active members. This the Benn family has given me unhesitatingly and unstintingly, despite the many other demands placed upon each of them. For their encouragement and for the wealth of material that they have made available to me, I gratefully thank Lady Stansgate, Tony Benn, Caroline Benn, David Benn and June Benn. They have readily spent many hours with me during the two and a half years that I have been working on this book. It is a mark of their generosity that, although they have provided me with so much help, they have at no time tried to modify my opinions or interfere with my writing.

Many others have also supplied important information. I thank especially Olive Winch, who has been a friend of the Benns for over fifty years, Lord Brockway and Dr Stephen Norton. Then there have been the countless people with whom I have discussed aspects of the book. They include politicians from all parties, Labour Party workers in Bristol and Chesterfield, and several journalists. Although too numerous to mention, I acknowledge my debt to them.

To the kind and efficient staff at the House of Lords Record Office I give my special thanks, not only for their help but for the excellent way in which they have catalogued the fire-damaged papers of Wedgwood Benn, the first Viscount Stansgate. For access to other reference material I am indebted to the staffs of the University of East Anglia, Suffolk County Council Library, and Churchill College, Cambridge. Books quoted in the text are given in the References, but for the wealth of factual information it contains I mention specifically *Tony Benn – A Political Biography* by Robert Jenkins.

Naturally there were times when I needed encouragement. This was always provided by my agent, Anne McDermid of Curtis Brown, and my editor, Julian Watson. Although they are in no way responsible for its contents, without them there might not have been a book.

For her efficiency and accuracy, I thank Susan Stevens who typed the final draft.

INTRODUCTION

When I first met Tony Benn a couple of years ago, I was so surprised by his kindness and good-humour – qualities in marked contrast to the intolerance and extremism some of his critics had led me to expect – that, despite my intentions, I was initially far more interested in the man than his ideas. Yet the two are inseparably entwined. Tony Benn is not what he is because of what he believes; he believes as he does because of what he is.

That too was true of his father, Wedgwood Benn, the first Viscount Stansgate, who said in a broadcast in 1958:

'I have tried to think why it is that when political issues arise I find myself instinctively holding opinions of a particular mould. I have so far to be content with the explanation of the poet who declared that we do not choose our convictions but they choose us and force us to fight for them to the death.'[1]

Tony Benn has inherited many of his father's convictions. From his mother, who although now in her eighties is President Emeritus of the Congregational Federation, he has acquired a deep interest in religion. Tony Benn comes then from a family background of independent radicalism and dissenting nonconformity. When Tony Benn was born, his father was one of the most talked about political figures of the age and a few years later became, as Secretary of State for India, a member of MacDonald's second Labour Government. So politics and religion dominated Tony Benn's life right from the earliest days. In one of the many conversations I have had with him, he told me:

'As a child throughout the thirties at every meal-time we'd discuss what was going on. As a result I have the political memory of somebody who is now in their mid-seventies, because so much was spoken about at home. And that was a tremendous thing in terms of giving me familiarity with the subject. So I can talk and think about it with a dimension that wouldn't be there if I hadn't begun when I was five or six. Mother similarly with her theological interest was always giving depth to the discussion. So I'm really the inheritor of two very formidable political and religious minds. There was very little small talk and gossip that I can remember, but it was all very entertaining.'

To understand Tony Benn's beliefs and motivations, it is then essential to examine the life and character of his parents. Yet, though in recent years so much has been written about him, his parents have been all but ignored. Perhaps because of this, rumours about the Benn family are current that are false and often scurrilous. I have, for example, been told that Tony Benn is the heir to the Wedgwood china fortune, that his family owns vast estates in Essex and the West Indies, and that his father once owned the *Daily Mail*.

Such absurd notions show that there is a need for detailed information about Tony Benn's parents. Yet they cannot be properly understood without going even further back into the history of the Benns, because the family's political and religious beliefs have been established over several generations. Tony Benn's great-grandfather, the Rev. Julius Benn, was for many years the Pastor of the Old Gravel Lane Congregational Meeting House in Wapping; his grandfather was also a Member of Parliament. So there has been a Benn in the House of Commons for almost all of the last hundred years – and this seems likely to continue, for Tony Benn's second son stood, albeit unsuccessfully, as a Labour candidate in the 1983 General Election.

Throughout this time the Benn family has been a very close one. To Tony Benn's grandmother it seemed as if the universe was divided into two parts: the family, which was everything, and the rest, mere background, called the outside world. There are, of course, reasons for this closeness. For much of this century the political activities of family members have been financially supported by profits from the Benn publishing firm, founded by Tony Benn's grandfather, most of whose successors have proved either unwilling or unable to combine as he did a political and a commercial life. This dichotomy has at times produced some acrimony between the two branches of the family which has, however, remained surprisingly united. Perhaps one reason for this is the tragedy that for the last fifty years or so later generations of the Benn family have successfully kept a secret from 'the outside world'. On 4 March 1883, William Rutherford Benn, one of the Rev. Julius Benn's sons, during a moment of insanity, killed his father. The horror of the incident united the family.

So the family has been and remains vitally important to the Benns. It has provided not just solace in adversity, but a stimulating environment in which ideas are promulgated and debated. Whilst being enthusiastically involved in the radical movement, its members have developed their own beliefs, refusing to accept a prevailing orthodoxy or an expedient, unprincipled solution. It is not surprising that the heir to such a tradition, Tony Benn, has pursued with vigour and determination the implementation of his convictions, apparently regardless of personal or political advantage.

Yet such backgrounds have disadvantages as well as strengths. Tony Benn is very aware of this and has said to me, 'I think ours is like a Jewish family - a bit too close and cloying in a way.' The emotional security such a family provides can make it more difficult for a person to indulge in the covert horse-trading and skulduggery necessary to lead political movements. Like his father and grandfather, Tony Benn, although attracting public interest and support, is a political outsider and has not risen to the top echelons of the parliamentary party. Unlike them, however, he is not universally popular for, being far more interested in policies and reforms than, as they were, in causes and cases, he is viewed with suspicion both by many of his parliamentary colleagues and by the mass media, which have for so long ruthlessly vilified him. Unable to accept that personal pleasure may be found in service to a movement or that success may be measured by any standard other than material gain, many people find Tony Benn a political enigma, wrongly believing his evangelism to be humourless, smug or even dangerous.

Perhaps more illuminatingly, others see Tony Benn as 'the keeper of the Labour Party's conscience'. Rooted as he is in a radical tradition that within his family stretches back for over a hundred and thirty years, he is pre-eminently well qualified to play this role. Significantly, his ideas on such matters as Irish independence, the abolition of the House of Lords, and ways of increasing party and parliamentary democracy - all of which some critics now attack as dangerously innovatory and revolutionary - would have found a very receptive audience in the Parliament to which his father was first elected in 1906.

With the aim of better understanding both the man and his ideas, this study examines the eventful history not only of Tony Benn but also of the three previous generations, from which he inherited the strong religious and radical beliefs that have led him in his *Arguments for Democracy* to describe himself as 'a socialist whose political commitment owes much more to the teaching of Jesus - without the mysteries within which they are presented - than to the writing of Marx whose analysis seems to lack an understanding of the deeper needs of humanity'.[2]

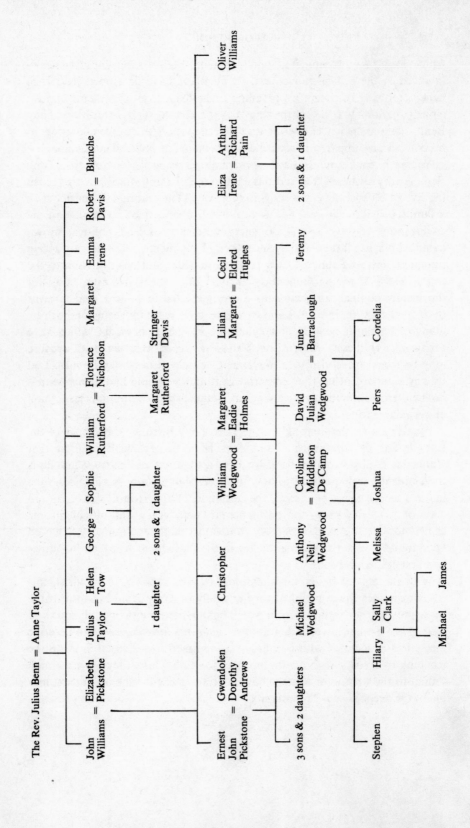

1

JULIUS AND JOHN BENN

1827–1883

On a cold, grey winter's evening in 1842, a fifteen-year-old messenger boy gazed despondently into the murky waters of the River Mersey. Penniless and miserable, Julius Benn had just trudged the thirty or so miles to Liverpool after running away from his home in Ardwick, a suburb of Manchester. This he had decided to do because he could not stand the ill-treatment of his new step-mother, whose brick-making business had given his father a prosperity he had never previously known.

Sitting on the dock-side, his feet dangling over the edge, Julius uncertainly contemplated his future. He had vaguely hoped to sail to Ireland, but that was impossible without money. The fare could, of course, be saved if he found another job. And he was not afraid of working hard. He had been doing so for years, because, when his mother was still alive, his earnings had been an essential supplement to his father's income from quilt-making which was so meagre that, when Julius was young, the family had been forced to live in the damp, foul-smelling cellar of an Ardwick slum.

But, cold and hungry in a strange town he had never even visited before, Julius concluded that there was no point in seeking a new job. There was no reason for him to stay alive. The only way to end his misery was to jump into the Mersey and drown. The decision made, he felt relief and large tears ran down his grubby cheeks. It was then that, as in a scene common in Victorian melodramas, a hand was placed on his shoulder by an aged, well-dressed man who said compassionately, 'Friend, follow me!'

The man was a rich Quaker who had that evening set out to walk along the Liverpool quayside believing that he had been directed by God to rescue a young person in distress. So he took Julius back to his palatial home and during the following months fed and cared for him. Discovering that Julius was barely literate, the kindly Quaker also taught his young protégé to read and write. Nor was that the end of the old man's kindness, for he eventually found Julius a position as an assistant in a linen-draper's business in Limerick. So, some six months after Julius had arrived so inauspiciously in

Liverpool, he sailed for Ireland a changed young man, able to look forward with enthusiasm. Yet throughout his life he retained the sensitivity and emotionalism that led him to make rash, even petulant decisions which occasionally resulted in grave misfortune.

His interest in nonconformist religion having been cultivated by his Quaker protector, Julius found in Limerick the faith that was to dominate his life. He was converted to Congregationalism by one of the most famous preachers of the day, the Rev. John de Kewer Williams, who between 1842 and 1846 was the minister at the Congregational Chapel in Limerick. With the enthusiasm of many converts, Julius Benn determined to dedicate himself to his new-found beliefs. Prevented by his lack of formal education from entering the full-time ministry, he lived his daily life by the most rigorous of principles, which led him in 1848 to object to his employer misdescribing goods to a prospective customer. As a result of this disagreement, Julius Benn packed his bags and left Limerick for good.

At the age of twenty-two, he arrived back in Liverpool, a tall man with large grey eyes, black hair, a pale face and a serious, apparently self-absorbed manner. Searching for employment as a schoolmaster's assistant he made his way to Hyde, near Manchester. Naturally he went first to the Congregational Chapel, where that week-day an evening service was being held. A hymn-book was passed to him by a nineteen-year-old girl, with whom Julius immediately fell in love. She was Ann Taylor, the vivacious, diminutive daughter of a Hyde shuttle-maker. Determined to stay in the area, he started his own school in the chapel where, on 13 February 1850, he married Ann, who helped in the school by teaching the girl scholars to sew. Exactly nine months later their first child was born, a son who, to commemorate his father's conversion by the Rev. John de Kewer Williams, was named John Williams Benn.

It was obvious that the school provided an inadequate livelihood for a growing family and so Julius Benn was delighted to receive an invitation from the London City Mission to work in the East End of London. So, late in 1851, Ann and Julius moved with their baby son to the part of London then known as St George's in the East with which the Benns were to be closely involved for many of the following sixty-five years.

In his religious and philanthropic work, Julius Benn, mindful of his own youthful experiences, concentrated on the many homeless young boys who roamed the Stepney and Wapping area. As a result, he was asked to take charge of the Institute in Stepney Causeway which was one of the first houses opened in the country to rescue children from the horrific results of the social upheaval that accompanied the industrial revolution. So successful in his work was Julius Benn that there was soon a need for larger premises, and in an old rope and sail warehouse he opened the

'Home in the East', which was soon filled with previously destitute boys.

The work was badly paid, but Ann and Julius Benn found considerable rewards in their chosen task of helping the young outcasts among the abject poverty and squalor of the East End. Their work attracted much public attention and many visitors, including Charles Dickens who said of Julius Benn that 'one could see by the expression of this man's eye and by his kindly face that Love ruled rather than Fear, and Love was triumphant'. Because of his fame and success, Julius Benn was invited by the Government, when it was decided to initiate a programme of reforming juvenile criminals, to take charge of the first Reformatory and Industrial School founded in Great Britain. It was built at Tiffield in Northamptonshire. So, in 1856, Julius and his wife moved from the East End with their three sons, for two more had been born in London. They were named Julius and William Rutherford ('Rutherford' being the maiden name of Julius Benn's mother).

At Tiffield the work was hard but satisfying and created much interest. An essay written by Julius Benn on the management of Industrial Schools won a Government prize and interested visitors included the Duke of Grafton, Earl Spencer and Lord Southampton. Unfortunately, after being at the school for a little over a year, Ann Benn, who had been actively engaged as the matron as well as looking after her own family, collapsed and for the rest of her life was to be an invalid. Rather than limiting her husband's dedication to his task, this made him work even harder. It was not that he was uncaring. Indeed he spent much time nursing his wife, to whom he was obviously devoted. But he had a commitment to the boys who had been placed in his charge which he was determined to fulfil and there is no doubt that he showered on them much loving care. On one occasion a visiting governor looking at the boys said, 'So, Mr Benn, these are the little criminals.' To this, Julius Benn replied, 'No, sir. These are the little gentlemen.' He was not then unwilling to cause offence, especially when his charges, family and religion were concerned.

As there was no Congregational chapel at Tiffield, Julius worshipped in the village church. There one Sunday he felt that his dissenting position was being attacked. The rector, while talking about the historical position of the Church of England, attacked the Reformation and said, 'Brethren, Martin Luther cannot but be regarded as an enemy of the true Church.' At this, Julius Benn rose and to the thirty or so boys from the Institute who were with him said, 'We leave the church at once. Quietly follow me, two by two.' And to the amazement of the rector and the remaining congregation the whole group marched out of the church. Later Julius Benn agreed that the school would resume attendance at the church on condition that there was no more preaching against the Reformation.

Such high-minded actions naturally upset some members of the com-

7

munity. Perhaps because of this, surprisingly little sympathy or compassion was shown when misfortune struck. In 1863, having been established at Tiffield for over five years, Julius Benn, although not well paid, had accumulated by careful living savings of £500. On the advice of a local solicitor, he invested this in an agricultural patent he was assured would make a fortune. When the venture failed, he not only lost his initial investment but was left owing a further £300. Although obviously guilty of nothing other than making a foolish decision, Julius Benn was asked by the school governors for his resignation. Characteristically, he announced, 'We leave your house tonight, sir.' And so he did.

Along the rutted country lanes, Julius Benn pushed his invalid wife in a bath-chair, accompanied by their five children, for two more (George and Margaret) had been born at Tiffield. The eldest of the five, John Williams Benn, was only eleven. The family stayed temporarily in a little cottage provided by a farmer's widow whilst the auction of their furniture and belongings was awaited.

With the small amount of money thus obtained as their only capital, the Benns returned to London. They moved first into a small toy and newspaper shop, which was also a depot for the British and Foreign Bible Society, at 1 George Terrace in the Commercial Road. The two elder boys helped their father by delivering newspapers and working in the shop, but Julius Benn was not a businessman and John, when sent for new supplies, was often told he could have nothing more until his father had paid for the previous items he had collected. He did his best to supplement his father's inadequate income by selling to other shops price-tickets he and his brother had painted on parts of toy-boxes.

But such efforts were insufficient, and Julius Benn considered himself fortunate when a visiting leather merchant's salesman offered John a job in the City at five shillings a week. So the next Monday morning, John Benn, aged eleven, wearing his mother's Sunday boots because his own were worn out, walked the two miles to Mincing Lane where he started work as an office boy at Messrs Fisher King & Co., produce merchants. Many years later he could still recall the humiliations he endured during his first day at work. He was laughed at in the coffee-shop when he began to eat the thick slices of bread-and-butter and the two apple turnovers his mother had provided for his dinner. When he went to the wash-room at work he was told to use the pail under the stairs.

Shortly after John Benn started work, his father's fortunes improved. The shop in the Commercial Road was on a site needed for a bank. With the compensation they were paid, the family moved to 7 Commercial Place, a seedy little alley, where for a short time Julius Benn ran a registry office for servants before accepting a post as city missionary with the East London

Congregational Evangelistic Association at a salary of £100 a year. Although the days of extreme poverty were over, the family (which eventually included eight children) still lived from hand to mouth, and it was not for another seventeen years that Julius Benn managed to pay off all his outstanding debts.

Yet the obvious financial problems did not make the Benn home impoverished. No zealot, Julius Benn's concern for and interest in others certainly included his own family. There was much talk to stimulate eager minds. Although the children received little schooling, they were encouraged to read, draw, think, value knowledge, and experiment with home entertainments that could amuse the family. John, as the eldest child, took the lead and his ability to amuse others – a skill he retained throughout his life – was first recognized and developed at home when he was a young boy.

John also soon found ways of augmenting the twopence a day his mother allowed him to buy coffee. For three years he ran his own part-time stamp-business and with the profits he bought clothes and was able to give money to his parents when a desperate need arose. Before he was fourteen years old he had made £80 from dealing in stamps, and that was more than his annual salary. He made further money by using a stamping-press he had bought to produce clay copies of coins that he then painted. These were so well finished that a set of them secured him an award at the Guildhall Industrial Exhibition of 1866.

A few months later he suffered an apparent misfortune that in time led not just to escape from office work but to a career that brought him fame and fortune. An employee of Fisher King & Co. left after some bitterness and set up his own business. John Benn met him shortly afterwards and informed him that a letter addressed to him had been delivered to his old firm. For passing on this information to a trade rival he was sacked on 13 July 1867. During the next six weeks he tramped around from office to office unsuccessfully seeking work. At last, T. Lawes & Co. of 65 City Road, a wholesale furniture house, employed him as a junior invoice clerk. Dealing with the paper work he was given was extremely uninteresting, but he noticed that the men who designed the furniture were well respected and much better paid than the other office workers. So, determining to become one of them, he enrolled for a technical training course on two evenings a week at the South Kensington Art School.

But before his ambition could be realized he was very nearly sent to prison. One lunch-time while walking along Broad Street he found a bunch of keys. As there was a name and address attached to them, on his return to his office he wrote to the owner saying where the keys could be collected. A few days later the man who had lost the keys, a beadle, arrived at the office and angrily demanded their return. Somewhat taken aback, young

John Benn refused to hand them over to the beadle, whom he mentally nicknamed 'Bumble', unless they were fully described and he was paid a penny for the postage of the letter he had sent. At this the man stormed out in a rage. The next day John Benn was arrested and taken before a magistrate at Worship Street. The beadle claimed that the keys had been snatched from him by 'that young rascal of a boy' who had then demanded a substantial reward. John Benn denied the story and repeated his demand for a penny compensation. He was instantly fined seventeen shillings and sixpence with the alternative of three days in prison at Coldbath Fields. Fortunately his father was able to pay the fine later in the day, but his mother was incensed by what had happened. 'Rather than that wretch of a Bumble shall triumph, I'll go and see the Postmaster General myself. That old liar shall be punished.'

So the following morning Julius Benn and his son went to St Martin's-le-Grand, the head Post Office, where a man in authority listened to the story. The beadle was summoned, reprimanded and ordered to pay the seventeen shillings and sixpence. Triumphantly the pair returned home, where as a celebration a firework representing Mount Vesuvius was lit which was so spectacular that it ruined the newly whitewashed ceiling. The incident made a deep and lasting impression on John Benn who felt deeply aggrieved by what was so nearly a grave miscarriage of justice:

> 'Is it any wonder that, later in life, I became an enemy of all Bumbledom, or that my own experience has left me with an ineradicable misgiving that not a few boys may still be having their characters sworn away by men of the overbearing official class? But for a good father I should have been sent to Coldbath Fields, and stamped as a young criminal, whereas I was, at the worst, only one of the cheeky office-boys of London.'[1]

The suspicion of lawyers and officials was also felt by John Benn's father, whose daily work was with the poor and oppressed of the East End. Their respect he earned, and in 1868 he was invited to become the Pastor of Old Gravel Lane Congregational Meeting House in Wapping, one of the poorest areas of London. It had changed little since Charles Dickens had described it as, 'A squalid maze of streets, courts and alleys, of miserable houses let out in single rooms. A wilderness of dirt, rags, and hunger. A mud-desert, chiefly inhabited by a tribe from whom employment has departed, or to whom it comes but fitfully and rarely.'

The congregation of the meeting house was so poor that it could not afford a regular stipend, but the Rev. Julius Benn, as he then became known, was content with his mission. The family moved from Commercial Place to a wooden-fronted house at 119 Stepney Green. They were still poor, but conditions were acceptable, for the three eldest boys were earning money: Julius, two years younger than John, was a Colonial Broker's clerk, and William Rutherford, another two years younger, was a clerk at East India House.

John Benn, after some setbacks, began to show a real flair for furniture design. Having been offered a junior partnership by a man called Emery, he left Lawes and started touring the country with his designs, which were made up in London as he obtained orders. It appears that at times he also worked for himself, because a trade card and circular letter have survived proudly proclaiming the business of J. Williams Benn & Co., furniture manufacturers of 119 Stepney Green. At all events it is clear that both as a salesman and as a designer he was successful, earning a sufficient income to enable him to supplement his father's meagre and uncertain stipend. His artistic skills were also used to provide elaborate entertainments at home. Having seen the popular illusion called 'Pepper's Ghost', after its inventor Professor Pepper of the old Polytechnic, he wrote his own ghost play which he presented at Stepney Green with the help of his younger brothers and a variety of 'skulls, crocodiles and other cabalistic properties'.

It was through this play that, in the summer of 1870 when he was nineteen, he met the girl he was to marry. While visiting Hyde in Cheshire, the town in which he was born, he was introduced to the Pickstones, a family of some substance which had progressed from running a profitable grocery business into becoming owners of land and property. John Benn was asked to present his 'Pepper's Ghost' at the house. This he agreed to do, requesting the help of a living person. It was then that, as he recalled later, 'Lily came bounding into the room, a compact little figure, round rather than slim, with an oval face of fresh complexion, warm autumnal brown eyes which looked shyly at me from beneath perfectly arched eyebrows and a general air of "What in the world do you want?"'

At the end of his brief visit, John Benn knew he wanted to marry Lily Pickstone. Over the next couple of years he took every opportunity he could to visit Hyde. Well aware that a man as successful as her father was not likely to be enthusiastic about his daughter marrying someone of so little fortune, he both worked extremely hard to save what money he could and pursued his courtship with great caution. A hymn-sheet in the Benn papers, dated Manchester, 16 October 1872, is marked 'Shared with Lily, the day of our betrothal'. But it was obviously a secret engagement, for it was not until 23 June 1873 that John Benn wrote formally to Lily's father asking for permission to marry his daughter. Aware that he had to prove that he had a secure future, he announced in the letter that he had agreed to return to his old firm, which had been renamed Lawes Randall & Co., as designer and manager of their bedding and feather factory at a salary of £300 a year, rising to £400. Mr Pickstone consented to the engagement, subject to a year's wait before the marriage. So it was not until 1 July 1874 that John and Lily were married at Zion Chapel in Hyde.

After a honeymoon on the east coast, the couple moved into Ferncliffe Villa, 29 Clifton Road, Dalston, which John had decorated and furnished for his bride. Some of the things provided she had chosen from drawings he had sent her during the years they had been courting.

Right from the start it was obvious that John and Lily ideally complemented each other. He was soft-hearted and yet inclined to become excited and even aggressive when opposed. She was loving, always calm, and very determined. Her family, like his, were nonconformists, teetotal, and radical. Lily had seriousness of purpose, dismissing as time-wasting all forms of worldly amusement. At a time when it was inconceivable for a married woman to pursue her own career, she saw her purpose as encouraging her husband to acquire the means to enable them to help those less fortunate than themselves. So that he could best do this, she would manage the house and bring up the family. She was to do both with great efficiency, in time mothering her husband just as enthusiastically as she did her children, the first of whom, Ernest John Pickstone, was born in 1875. A year later a second son, Christopher was born, but he lived only a few months. Always delicate, he died one evening just before his father returned from work. As John Benn had an engagement to give a lecture, which he would have cancelled if he had known, Lily bravely hid the bad news from him. On 10 May 1877 she gave birth to her third son who was called William Wedgwood, the second name being given because apparently Lily's mother was a distant relation of the famous pottery family.

By this time John Benn and his family had settled down into a comfortable but busy routine. Unlike his parents he faced problems no more severe than, as he wrote later, 'burst mains, badly-laid drains, lying gas-meters, exorbitant water-rates, German bands and piano-organs'. During the week he worked long hours, as was the custom, but Sunday was a family day. Then they worshipped at the Old Gravel Pit Chapel in Hackney where he became the Sunday School superintendent. The chapel, so named because it was built on the site of a gravel pit where dissenters had worshipped in the days of persecution, had as its pastor the Rev. John de Kewer Williams, after whom John Williams Benn had been named. So successful a preacher was he that the chapel became the recognized centre of Congregationalism. John Benn became deeply involved in the social work of the chapel, starting a Mutual Improvement Society which organized debates and talks on current affairs. At some of the meetings he gave talks illustrated by his own sketches.

As his knowledge of and interest in furniture grew, John Benn began to feel limited by his employment. In 1878 he visited the Art and Industrial

Exhibition in Paris, and on his return he gave to the Mutual Improvement Society a humorous lecture on his experiences, illustrated as he talked with crayon drawings. But he wanted a wider audience and so submitted an article on the exhibition to *The Furniture Gazette* which was then the only furniture trade journal. It was promptly accepted and so, encouraged, he devoted any spare time he had to studying examples of English furniture in the museums of South Kensington. He became fascinated by the elegant simplicity of Chippendale, which he found far superior to the clumsy elaborations of the Victorian style then at its zenith.

This belief led to a dissatisfaction with his own work, even though, having been made a junior partner, he was earning £450 a year. The long hours he worked meant that he scarcely saw his children, except on Sundays, and he began to long for the freedom he had enjoyed when he was self-employed. Yet obviously he did not want to earn less money, especially as shortly before Lilian Margaret, his fourth child, was born in May 1880 they moved into a larger house at 241 Dalston Lane.

Feeling that he might be able to make a good living by journalism, he submitted a series on Chippendale to *The Furniture Gazette*, to which had recently been appointed a new editor, Dr Dresser, who was an enthusiastic popularizer of the Scandinavian style. After a long, acrimonious interview with John Benn he rejected the articles.

This rebuff spurred John Benn to put into practice a scheme he had been thinking about for some time. With the agreement of his wife and to the astonishment of his partners when he resigned, he decided to sink his hard-earned and surprisingly large savings of £800 into starting his own illustrated monthly dealing with both the artistic and the technical aspects of furniture.

At 5 Finsbury Square he hired a room which was divided by a green baize screen, on one side of which was the trade counter and on the other the editorial space. There, helped by his two brothers Julius and Henry, he produced the first edition of *The Cabinet Maker* in July 1880. Consisting of sixteen foolscap pages, priced sixpence, it included the first of John Benn's articles on Chippendale furniture, a cabinet maker's portfolio from his old firm of Lawes Randall, and a description of furniture in the Royal Academy. Later Henry Benn recalled some of the problems they faced:

'The packing and posting of the first issue lives in my memory as a most anxious and exciting episode. Upon the delivery of the copies from the printers, the whole staff, from the editor to the office boy, rolled up its sleeves and set to work for dear life pasting and wrapping for the post. An open one-horse van was subsequently requisitioned to take this first consignment to the General Post Office, for free distribution to the whole of the furnishing houses in the United Kingdom. On the way to the Post Office, owing to the doubtful stamina of the paste and the more rapid than efficient operations of the staff, many of the copies parted company with the wrappers and had to be taken back to the office for readjustment.'[2]

With subsequent issues the misfortunes continued: a fire at Whittingham's, the printers, destroyed all his blocks and paper, none of which was insured; a subscription tout drew commission on bogus orders; and in the third issue he had to refute rumours that the journal was owned by Lawes Randall. Within a year all his savings had been spent and he could borrow nothing more. As he wrote and illustrated most of the journal himself, it was difficult to make any savings. Unless he could earn more money himself, his publishing experiment would end humiliatingly.

While toying with money-making ideas, he happened at a dinner to meet Professor Pepper and the story was told of how through 'Pepper's Ghost' John Benn had met his wife. Before the dinner was over Professor Pepper had promised to arrange for him to be auditioned as a popular lecturer at the old Polytechnic. After overcoming this hurdle John Benn gave an illustrated lecture on 'Physiognomy and Caricature' in that institute's special programme for Christmas 1880. His efforts were rapturously received and enthusiastically reviewed. As a result he received many more bookings and from this additional income was able to subsidize his journal, which was slowly becoming established throughout the furniture trade. But his life became even more hectic, and he saw less of his family than when he was an employee. From Monday to Saturday he travelled the country collecting subscriptions and selling advertising space for *The Cabinet Maker*; in the train he wrote articles for it; and many evenings he lectured to literary societies. And his illustrated talks were much in demand. Although only twenty-nine, he in fact looked much younger, and this, combined with his artistic skills, his infectious humour and his irrepressible vitality, made him exceptionally popular. His lecture subjects included 'Pickings from *Punch*', 'The Drawings of Cruikshank', 'Faces' and 'Children'. He particularly loved an audience of children and, because of the way he sometimes drew, he was known as 'The Blindfold Sketcher'. Always in search of new material for both the platform and his journal he travelled in 1882 to Italy, where not for the last time his sketching annoyed those in authority, and in the palace of King Bomba at Naples he was arrested as a spy. This and the story of how he obtained his release became the subject of yet another lecture.

Towards the end of 1882, it appeared as though his journal had become established. With the title changed to *The Cabinet Maker and Art Furnisher*, it had grown to fifty pages. At home too his family continued to grow and prosper, his fifth child, Eliza Irene, being born in February.

Living as he did in the same area, John Benn saw a great deal of his parents, whom he still helped financially, and his brothers, two of whom he employed. It was a close, loving, affectionate family, and naturally all were delighted when in October 1882, the Rev. Julius Benn received from Mr Gladstone a cheque for £50 'in recognition of his past services to the Government in relation to Reformatory Work'. The continuing religious and philanthropic work of the Rev. Julius and his children in St George's in the East made them all well known in the area. William Rutherford Benn, the third son, then aged twenty-seven, spent all his spare time working among the poor and needy of Hackney and Wapping. More academic than his brothers and sisters, he spoke a couple of foreign languages and was a successful East India merchant. For some time he had considered becoming a minister like his father, but then he met and fell in love with Florence Nicholson, who was three years his junior and an Anglican. On 16 December 1882 the couple were married at All Saints Church in Wandsworth. As both Florence's parents had died, her sister, Bessie, was her closest relation at the wedding.

The couple left immediately for a honeymoon in Paris. Then tragedy struck. William Benn had a severe mental breakdown and his unfortunate wife had to bring him back to London. For a short time his parents looked after him, but, as his condition continued to deteriorate, they regretfully agreed – for he had never before suffered from such an illness – to his being placed under care at Bethnal House Asylum.

Deeply concerned about his plight, his father and brothers visited him frequently and were relieved to observe his apparent recovery, which was so rapid that after six weeks the doctors recommended his removal for a probationary period. On Monday, 26 February 1883, the Rev. Julius Benn, having signed the appropriate papers, collected his son, and the next day went with him to Matlock Bridge in Derbyshire, where it was hoped that the fresh air and the waters would complete his cure. Late that same evening the two took rooms with Mr Marchant, a retired coachman, at 'The Cottage', Chesterfield Road in Matlock, asking that their names should not appear in the list of visitors published in the local newspapers. While in their rooms they were both very quiet and much of their time was spent walking around the district together.

At about seven o'clock on Sunday morning, Mrs Marchant heard a strange rapping sound. She got up and looked around, but as she could not find what had caused it she returned to bed. She prepared breakfast for eight o'clock, the time at which the Rev. Julius Benn and his son normally came down. As they had not appeared in half an hour, she went to their room and tapped on the door, but there was no reply. This happened again several times during the morning. When her husband returned home at 1 p.m. Mrs Marchant asked him to waken the two men. He went upstairs and knocked on the door. Eventually William Benn opened it and pointed to the bed where the obviously dead body of his father lay. Mr Marchant quickly closed the door, ushered his family out of the house, and sent neighbours for the police and a doctor.

When Dr Moxon, accompanied by his assistant and two policemen, entered the bedroom, he discovered that William Benn had a self-inflicted gash in his throat, which the doctor immediately stitched and dressed. The Rev. Julius Benn had apparently been killed, while sleeping, with a single blow on the crown of his head from an earthenware chamber-pot.

William Benn was taken in a brake driven by two horses to Derby Infirmary and, after letters to the two men had been read by a police superintendent, the Benn family was telegraphed. In Matlock the murder created a great, if temporary, sensation. The *Derby Daily Telegraph* for 6 March 1883 carried a most detailed report, commenting, with what might seem like a touch of regret: 'The event is without parallel in the memory of any of the residents, though of course the excitement is not so great as would have prevailed had the deed been committed in the height of the season.' The effects on the Benn family, however, were severe and long-lasting.

William's mother, who had for so long been an invalid, was heartbroken by the tragedy and the loss of her husband. It was left to John Benn, as the eldest son, to make all the necessary arrangements. The day after the murder he arrived in Matlock, and on Tuesday, 6 March, he attended the inquest and asked that the circumstances of his brother's release from the lunatic asylum and his normal kindly disposition should be borne in mind by the jury when they were reaching their verdict. The coroner said that this was impossible and the jury decided that William Rutherford Benn had been responsible for the wilful murder of his father. That day, John Benn visited Derby Infirmary and saw his brother, who seemed to recognize him for a moment before lapsing back into unconsciousness.

Having arranged for the body to be removed that night to London, John Benn returned there. The funeral was held two days later. A preliminary service held in the Old Gravel Lane Meeting House was conducted by the Rev. John de Kewer Williams and attended by a vast crowd, including a dozen other ministers of religion, who followed the flower-bedecked coffin to the interment at Ilford Cemetery.

Everybody in the area was deeply moved by the tragedy and within days there had been established a memorial fund for the Rev. Julius Benn's widow, who still had young children. The published circular begins: 'The

appalling calamity which has befallen the family of the above Congregational Minister has called forth the greatest sympathy in London and the
Provinces. A number of friends have suggested that the kindly feeling thus
shown should take a practical form in the shape of a money present to the
Widow and the children dependent upon her.' The circular gave a summary
of the Rev. Julius Benn's career and listed the committee members which
included thirteen ministers of religion (both Congregational and Anglican),
Samuel Morley, MP, and Dr T. J. Barnardo. The attached list of donations
made to launch the fund amounted to £136 9s. od.

One of the members of the Appeal Committee was William Mattocks
Dabbs, a builder and deacon at the Old Gravel Pit. He offered John Benn
the use of a large house he had built at 37 Kyverdale Road, Stoke Newington. And a large house was essential, for John Benn, despite all his other
commitments, had decided that his chronically sick mother and her five
unmarried children (Julius, aged thirty; Margaret, twenty-two; Henry,
twenty; Irene, eighteen; and Robert, thirteen) should live with him, his
pregnant wife and their three children. Even then, to accommodate this
huge extended family in the new house, he had to embark upon structural
changes including knocking down the wall between the front drawing-room
and the back parlour to make one large dining-room.

The aftermath of the murder deeply affected the Benn family. William
Rutherford Benn, although apparently soon recovered, was locked away in
a lunatic asylum. His mother, unable to cope with the enormity of the
tragedy, was sometimes found at night wandering through the unlit house
checking that everyone was safely in bed. Although supported by the local
community which, with more sense than some sections of our modern
society, regarded William's fit of madness as a sad misfortune rather than
a distasteful slur on the family, the Benns, already somewhat separated
from many others by their dissenting beliefs, drew even closer together.
This did not mean, however, that they isolated themselves. Indeed the
incident made them even more sympathetic to the misfortune of others and
John Benn, despite his excessive work load, still spent much time on religious and charitable work in the East End of London, the area he regarded
as his home. Always refusing to undertake paid work on Sundays he continued to be the Sunday School superintendent at the Old Gravel Pit
Chapel.

It was not then to the ordinary people but to the establishment and its
methods that the dissenting Benns became even more opposed. Other family
experiences had already produced much distrust. Investment in stocks and
shares was disliked after Julius Benn's disastrous involvement in the agricultural patent; the uncaringness of employers who had sacked Julius Benn
because of a private debt and John Benn because he gave unimportant

information to an ex-employee encouraged a desire for self-employment; and the absurdity of the legal action taken against John Benn over the keys he had found in the street made the law and its servants appear ridiculous. Now added to these was a lasting suspicion of the popular press following the way in which the murder had been reported. A family that had reasons to dislike capitalist institutions, employers, the legal system and the popular press had to be both independent and self-reliant. The Benns, supported by their strong religious beliefs, were both. John Benn added the essential quality that had eluded his father, whose life was marred by misfortune. John Benn was successful and was, therefore, able to produce the financial means by which members of the Benn family could pursue their own interests, untrammelled by petty constraints. In doing so, representatives of three subsequent generations of the family chose, not through religion but through politics, to follow the Rev. Julius Benn's example of striving to improve the lot of the less fortunate members of society.

2

JOHN AND WEDGWOOD BENN

1 1883-1903

With so many people dependent upon him, John Benn drove himself un-stintingly. While he employed three of his brothers (Julius, Henry and Robert) to look after the business side of his journal, he travelled the country speaking on public platforms. By the summer of 1885 he had completed his thousandth engagement as a lecturer, and was amazingly earning some £2000 a year.

For all this hard work there were, as he later recalled, compensations:

> 'I never regarded this platform work as more than an artistic sheet anchor and an accessory, but it brought me into contact with some of the most interesting men of the day, ranging from the Earl of Shaftesbury to the Rev. C.H. Spurgeon. It gave me a practice in public speaking which few men can get in private life.'[1]

But there were also drawbacks. He saw little enough of his family, and he developed an abdominal complaint that, because it went untreated for so long, eventually permanently damaged his health.

John Benn's two sons, although very different from each other, continued to spend much of their time together. Wedgwood Benn, or 'Will' as his parents called him, was just seven when the family moved to Kyverdale Road, but he had already developed a joyful sense of humour. His elder brother Ernest was much more serious. Although obviously aware of the sudden influx of aunts and uncles, they knew and were told little of the reason for it.

In the new house, the two boys were given their own play-cupboard in the half-basement, which like the other rooms had been newly decorated. In imitation of their father, they decided to go into business and on the white enamelled cupboard painted in black: 'Ernest and Willie Benn. Printers and Undertakers.' Having in the previous months often heard the word, they used 'undertakers' assuming that it meant someone who would under-take to do a job. This unfortunate misunderstanding led to a severe scolding from their mother and the hasty removal of the offending words.

At this time, Nurse Cliff, who had been brought up in a Barnardo's home, joined the crowded household to help look after the children. She was to stay with the family for nearly thirty years. As a dedicated teetotaller, she impressed upon the children her belief that drinking alcohol was evil, teaching them many temperance poems, including one called 'Timothy Prout' which to the end of his days Wedgwood Benn could recite in full. She also encouraged the children to present short plays, which were later, under the supervision of their father, to become spectacular Christmas presentations.

But it was their mother who was the dominant influence on the children when they were young. In *Happier Days*, Ernest Benn writes:

'My mother was the devoted slave of all of us and ruled us with a rod of love. I cannot believe that I was ever asked what I would like to have ... Bread and milk and porridge on alternate days for breakfast were followed by bread in bacon fat or, better still, bread and dripping. Mother knew what I ought to have, and should any doubt or disinclination arise on that or any other domestic matter, my father would quell all such uprisings with what he called the family motto – "What Mother says is Law." '[2]

In a broadcast he made in 1958, Wedgwood Benn, then Viscount Stansgate, also described his mother's devotion and determination. 'For her,' he said, 'the universe was divided into two parts: the family which was everything, and a mere background called the outside world. For her family she could display a courage of steel.' He recalled too that his mother was always trying to curb his natural zest:

'When I was a little boy being washed and dressed to go out to tea the last word from my mother was always, "Now remember, don't get excited at the party." I never succeeded in obeying that injunction.'[3]

Although they saw much less of their father than their mother, John Benn's own children were as delighted, amused and entertained by him as any of the boys and girls watching his lightning sketches. All too conscious of the difficulties he had been forced to face, John Benn also supplied his family with help, support and guidance. In a tribute written after his father's death, Wedgwood Benn wrote:

'It is no easy task to dissect our family life and describe my father's share in it. We are all so knit together that his influence (and my mother's too, for to us, as to themselves, they seemed one) was something inseparably essential and pervasive. My father was first a man of feeling, next a tenacious man. These are the ingredients of the fighter. They ripened with

20

experience into those wise, yet forceful qualities which made him a natural guide and protector. With him, this posture of responsibility and defence came all too early. From adolescence, even from childhood, he was a high tower to his parents and his brothers in the struggles and tragedies of their lives. To his own children, on their much easier road, he was a guardian companion.'[4]

Wedgwood greatly admired his father, with whom he had much in common, and readily followed his example and acquired his principles. One Sunday, for example, the two were walking to chapel when his father saw a man with a placard stating, 'I have suffered a great injustice.' Turning to Wedgwood, his father said, 'Will, I have suffered many injustices. Let's give him a couple of shillings.' And in the 1880s a couple of shillings was a lot of money. But it was an example that Wedgwood never forgot and in his later life much of his time and effort were to be spent in fighting injustices.

Away from the ready acceptance of their parents' authority, the children were given great freedom. Indeed they were discouraged from thinking of anyone as their natural superior or automatically accepting anyone as their master. Wedgwood did, however, have Ernest to contend with, for he took his responsibilities as the eldest son very seriously. So, when both went to a school in Jenner Street run by a Miss Johnson and had to cross Stoke Newington Common, Ernest was given the task of stopping Wedgwood walking through the puddles, something Wedgwood always tried to do, but Ernest never did. Ernest had the reputation of being a 'good' boy, while Wedgwood was always carefree and full of fun. Yet from his earliest days at school, unlike his brother, he found learning both easy and pleasurable.

It was soon felt that Wedgwood and his brother would benefit from being sent to a proper school and so, as their father's combined business and lecturing income continued to grow, it was decided in 1886 that the family should move back to the East End. The house selected was at 17 Finsbury Square, and as it had six storeys it was amply big enough to accommodate the whole Benn family. The basement was occupied by a caretaker who looked after the ground floor which was let to Sir Dundas Grant, the throat specialist. From the first floor upwards the house was occupied by the Benns, including Wedgwood's grandmother, two uncles and an aunt. The kitchen was on the third floor and the amount of cooking involved was so great that Wedgwood's mother used to buy the meat wholesale direct from Smithfield Market.

From this house Wedgwood and Ernest went to Cowper Street Middle Class School in the nearby City Road. (It is now the Central Foundation Boys' School.) As their father was a rate-payer in the parish, they were entitled to attend for half fees, and so the annual cost of their education was £5 each. The school boasted an extensive asphalt playground, but had no playing-fields and so few organized games were played. This worried neither Wedgwood nor his brother, and both when adults regarded such activities as a waste of time. Then they preferred to roam the London streets, where a favourite sport of theirs was to obtain a free ride on a horse-drawn tram-car by jumping up and holding onto the back when the conductor was busy upstairs.

In 1887, Oliver, the last of John and Lily Benn's children, was born. Shortly afterwards, Wedgwood and Ernest, from their bedroom window, watched the Colonial troops passing along the City Road in the procession which marked Queen Victoria's Jubilee. They also regularly enjoyed family outings, including an annual summer holiday. And, despite the reluctance of their mother, the children were occasionally taken to the theatre. In the 1920s, Wedgwood Benn wrote, 'I remember that in 1888 we went to see the "Armada" at the Lyceum, and what a terrible and daring adventure it seemed.' In time, Mrs Benn was forced to modify her puritanical attitudes in the face of her husband's love for the arts and the theatre.

Partially responsible for that change, but having other more far-reaching effects on the family, was a development that permitted John Benn to dedicate the rest of his working life to public service. Because his business had been established just outside the old London wall, he was not eligible to become a member of the Common Council of the City of London. It was true that as he had not made his fortune it would have been difficult for him to have given of his time, but he had reasons for wanting to serve the ordinary people of London: because of their reaction to the family's misfortune he felt he had a debt of gratitude he wished to repay; his own brushes with authority had made him aware that much of the existing administration was elitist, inefficient, and possibly corrupt; his travels around the country had shown him that many provincial cities, especially Birmingham, were far better governed than his beloved London. Most of the problem he saw as arising from the control the City of London exercised over the rest of the capital.

So John Benn was delighted when at last Westminster introduced an Act establishing the London County Council, even though its powers were unnecessarily limited. Because this new body called for new ideas and new leaders, there was formed a new alliance of radicals from the Liberals and the fledgling Labour movement. Among the first people to be approached, John Benn was asked if he would stand for East Finsbury, where his business was situated, as a candidate for the new Progressive Party. He desperately wanted to accept, but at first his wife objected until she was assured that satisfactory arrangements could be made to protect the family's financial security. It was proposed that his three brothers would run all the publishing business, which was making a steady although unspectacular profit. From this he would have sufficient funds to support his family and to run his campaign. He further agreed that if he were elected he would give up both his public lecturing and his Sunday School work. It was a courageous decision to make, for compared with most of the other candidates his means were very limited. Indeed, from then to the end of the century his income was never to exceed a £1000 a year. But in the past he had been prepared to gamble his savings on setting up his journal, and he was happy to gamble them again.

Once decided, John Benn campaigned with enthusiasm. In the election held on 17 January 1889 he topped the poll at East Finsbury. Wedgwood, aged eleven, was with his parents at the count and shared in all the excitement. It was the first of the many elections in which he was to participate.

The Progressive Party won seventy of the 118 seats and their successful candidates included Lord Rosebery, who became the first Chairman of the LCC, and John Burns, whom the newspapers always referred to as 'the Socialist'. John Benn was elected the Party's Chief Whip and set about establishing a business-like organization that was largely responsible for the long string of electoral triumphs that kept the Party in power on the LCC for the next eighteen years. Throughout this time, he was to prove one of the most tireless workers in bringing order and good government to London, so much so that when he died, after being a member of it for nearly thirty-three years, *The Times* called him 'The Father of the LCC'.

By instinct and background a radical, his political education was rapidly acquired as he and his Party strove to introduce measures, then attacked as revolutionary, which are now accepted as bringing real benefits to the nation's capital and its inhabitants, including public parks, free public libraries, and the Sunday opening of museums. Many of the battles he fought in the LCC had much in common with those waged more recently by Ken Livingstone in its successor, the GLC Against fierce opposition, John Benn worked enthusiastically and successfully to introduce subsidized municipal transport. He failed, however, to achieve local government control of the Metropolitan Police. The motion he proposed on 9 April 1889 stated 'that this Council, representing as it does the people of London, declares it to be necessary and expedient that it should, in common with all other municipal bodies in the United Kingdom, have the control of its own police'.

Political figures and their talk filled the house in Finsbury Square, and young, impressionable Wedgwood absorbed much of the excitement and enthusiasm. A life-long memory he retained was of Tom Mann, John Burns and other leaders of the Great London Dock Strike in 1889 having breakfast in the house after they had addressed the strikers who were demanding a minimum wage of sixpence an hour. (Later Wedgwood Benn and John Burns were to serve together from 1910-1914 in Asquith's Government.)

But Wedgwood's contact with this stimulating environment was about to be interrupted. His father had a friend who while on business in Paris had stayed at a small commercial hotel at 29 rue Caumartin, close to the Madeleine. The owner, Monsieur Bodson, had an English wife, and they wanted their two daughters, who were aged eleven and twelve, to stay for a year or so with a family in Britain. John Benn, feeling sure that his eldest sons would benefit from acquiring a good knowledge of French, arranged for them to be exchanged for a year with the two Bodson girls.

In the summer of 1889, Alice and Jeanne Bodson arrived at Finsbury Square. Detecting traces of perfume and face-powder, Mrs Benn insisted on scrubbing their faces and hair with soap and water. This nearly brought the arrangement to an end before it had really started, but peace was restored and, just before Christmas, Wedgwood, aged twelve, and Ernest, who was fourteen, were taken by their mother and father to Paris. For Wedgwood the highlight of his first trip overseas was being allowed by the cabman to stand with one foot on each of the pair of horses as they were driven down the rue Caumartin – it was a feat he had just seen performed at his first visit to a circus.

Until their parents left, the two boys were given a good room in the hotel; afterwards they were put in an attic. But they were well treated and began following the tasks set for them by their father. The first and most important of these was to learn French, and they were given a book in which both of them had to record when the other spoke French. Wedgwood Benn later recalled, 'Naturally Ernest obeyed the rules much more than I did. Being a real chatterbox I spoke about ten times as much English and twenty times as much French as he did.'[5] As a result he mastered the language and acquired an enduring love of the country and its people.

After about a year, John Benn arrived in Paris to collect his sons, and the three of them spent several blissfully happy days wandering around Paris. When they went to obtain tickets at the Louvre, they were delighted when the official asked, 'Trois frères?' On the way home they sang songs together, and Wedgwood, at his father's request, tried to teach his father some irregular French verbs.

But 1890, the year in which the boys had been in France, had not been a happy time for their parents. Their grandmother had died. Their father had undergone a serious internal operation without anaesthetic because the doctors wrongly thought he had a weak heart. There had been business worries too. An unemployed teacher who was given a job on *The Cabinet Maker* learnt the routines of the trade, and then left to start his own rival journal that was published at a cheaper price. This John Benn was determined to fight. He sent the children to live with their nurse in a cottage at Cambridge Terrace, Southend-on-Sea; he gave up his expensive house at 17 Finsbury Square; and he and his wife moved across the road to a small flat at the top of No. 50, from where he produced a new paper, *The Furnisher and Decorator*, which was published monthly at 2d. This undercut and eventually destroyed the competition. After six months, John Benn was able to close his cut-price journal and *The Cabinet Maker* went on from strength to strength.

So when the two boys arrived back in London they moved into their parents' flat in Finsbury Square and at the beginning of term returned to Cowper Street School.

His business worries over, their father was able to dedicate himself again to his political work. In March 1891 he was adopted as the Liberal and Radical candidate for St George's in the East and Wapping. The sitting member for what was believed to be this safe Conservative seat was the Rt Hon. C.T. Richie, the President of the Board of Trade. John Benn immediately began organizing his campaign to oust him. He rented a villa between Commercial Road and the London Docks at 203 Cable Street, renaming it Gladstone House. Because he wanted to establish himself as the resident candidate and because it was close to Cowper Street, the two eldest boys and their parents moved to Cable Street from the flat in Finsbury Square, which was retained as the firm's office. At first Wedgwood enjoyed being treated as a minor celebrity, for women in the street would point him out to their friends as he passed and say, 'That's young Gladstone!' Ernest had unhappier memories of their new home:

'Gladstone House was a bug-infested building of eight or nine rooms, and on taking possession my dear mother slaved hard to bring it nearer to her standards of cleanliness; she supervised the sealing and fumigation of each room in turn, the stripping of the wallpaper, and what was, in fact, the most thoroughgoing spring-cleaning in my experience. But even so, I have lain in bed watching the meanderings of the little creatures on the ceiling with no very clear-cut course, and wondering whether they would be able to maintain their precarious positions or succumb to greater comfort with me in my bed.'[6]

Before the election campaign began, John Benn successfully dealt with a painful personal matter. For several years he had been trying to arrange for the release from the asylum of his brother, William Rutherford, whose sanity, both he and the doctors felt convinced, had been fully restored. Rutherford's wife, a very brave woman, desperately wanted to be reunited with her husband. So John Benn approached the Tory Home Secretary and offered to be personally responsible for his brother if he were released. This undertaking was accepted and it was agreed that William Rutherford Benn, having spent nine years in an asylum, would be set free. A job was found for him with an East India merchant; a home was rented for the couple at 15 Denton Road, Balham; and to save them any further distress it was decided that they should drop the surname Benn and be known as William and Florence Rutherford.

John Benn acted, as he always did, with great compassion and a total disregard of his own situation, for if his brother had suffered from a relapse it would have been very damaging to his electoral prospects in an age when political battles were fought at an even more personal level than they are today. All those involved, especially Florence Rutherford, were most courageous, and their hopes and prayers seemed to be answered, for the couple lived happily together.

In the lull before the election, John Benn, having acquired a new workbase in London, looked round for a proper family house. In the summer of 1891 he rented Hoppea Hall in Upminster, a fine Elizabethan manor house. The cottage at Southend was surrendered, and all the children moved into the new house where each was allocated their own room on the top floor, which had old timber floors so twisted that they resembled a rolling sea. Irene, who was then nine, was delighted to be again with Wedgwood, whom she adored. She turned his room into what she called their 'Den' by making cushions of straw in muslin and cleaning up an old oil lamp they found in the stable. Ernest had his own, much larger room at the back of the house.

It was an exciting summer, the first the whole family had spent together for two years. Wedgwood brewed ginger beer that exploded and manufactured gun cotton that did not. He learned to ride a bike and was tremendously proud when he found that he could do so without holding the handle bars. He afterwards recalled:

'Ernest was much more serious than I was, and father tried hard to mould me in his pattern. When I told father, "Look, I can ride long distances without holding the handle bars," he applied his usual technique in answering: "That's all very well, Will, but supposing I go to Mr Cohen (Mr Cohen was a furniture manufacturer whose advertising in *The Cabinet Maker* was of enormous importance to our finances) and say, 'I want you to employ my boy, Mr Cohen,' Mr Cohen will say, 'What can he do?' and, Will, it really won't be sufficient for me to explain to Mr Cohen that you can ride your bicycle without holding the handle bars." '[7]

In the garden of Hoppea Hall there was a magnificent old cedar tree which had a long branch extending over the lawn. This appealed to John Benn as providing a natural stage and during the summer he produced and acted in the first of the dramatic presentations that over the succeeding years became ever more spectacular. The play selected was *A Midsummer Night's Dream*, and all the family and many local people were marshalled into performing and making the costumes and scenery. Wedgwood was less enthusiastic than most, especially as he was chosen to be Puck, but he overcame his reluctance to play with the fairies by constructing, with a wire hidden amongst the branches of the cedar tree, a device which enabled him to make a sudden, dramatic entrance onto the stage.

The summer holidays over, the two eldest boys returned to Cable Street from where they walked each day to school through Spitalfield Market. A few months later, Ernest sat for the London Matriculation, but failed three of the five subjects. So, at Christmas 1891, he left school and started work in his father's firm as a junior office boy at five shillings a week. Although only sixteen, he also became his father's assistant political agent.

The election campaign was a family affair. John Benn was helped by his wife, who spoke at many meetings, by Wedgwood, Ernest, his brothers, and some of the employees at Benn Brothers. But an even greater asset was his family's long association with the area. In *Joys of Adversity*, John Benn records:

'Because of the work my father had done, there was a friend in every alley, and a welcome in every court. "This young man", said my opponents, "has no supporters among the respectable people in the leading thoroughfares." My reply was, "I aspire to the honour of being the member for the back streets," and the back streets stuck to me like wax. My address to the electors really grew out of the foregoing experience. I could not forget how my father's vote was lost through moving from one parish to another, and so I went in strongly for registration reform, three months' qualification, and "one man, one vote". I had seen sufficient of overcrowding and house-farming in the district of Cable Street to lead me to favour improved sanitary laws and better homes for the working-classes. My knowledge of common lodging-houses, and personal experience therein, led me to plead for the erection of poor men's hostels by the County Council. An acquaintance with the ins and outs of a business in which sweating is not, alas, unknown, prompted me strenuously to favour the cause of trade unions.'[8]

Although the Conservatives were confident that they would retain the seat, as the campaign neared its conclusion John Benn became convinced that he would win. His experience as the Chief Whip of the Progressive Party on the LCC encouraged him to keep meticulous canvassing returns and to ensure that he knew his supporters.

A few weeks before the election, on 11 May 1892, all the family were overjoyed when Florence Rutherford gave birth to a daughter, who was named Margaret. Many years later, as Margaret Rutherford, she became a famous and much loved star of both screen and stage.

The election was held in July, and John Benn defeated the President of the Local Government Board by a majority of 398. It was an impressive and decisive victory in a constituency that had little more than 4000 electors.

At that time Members of Parliament were not paid, and so John Benn was well aware that the honour and pleasure he felt at his success would have been impossible without the support of his brothers at work and of his family at home. But on being elected he knew that the continued and growing prosperity of his journal would permit him to become a full-time politician, working in both the LCC and the Houses of Parliament for the people of the East End whom he represented. The long recesses meant that he could spend more time with his family than he had been able to do when they were young. So the holidays became important family occasions, of which the centre-piece in the summer and at Christmas was John Benn's dramatic presentation.

So as to be near the Houses of Parliament, John Benn took a flat in the Westminster Palace Hotel. Ernest moved in there with his parents and, during week-days when at school, Wedgwood lived for over a year at Gladstone House alone, apart from the caretaker. This freedom he was permitted during the formative years when he was sixteen and seventeen allowed him to organize his days as he wished:

'The nights in the East End of London were extremely noisy at that time and so I conceived the notion of coming back from school about half past four, having a meal, going straight to bed and sleeping through the noise, and then starting work about midnight, so that I had the quiet and the cool for my task. (I might also say I made some experiments in the cost of living and bought a hundredweight of oatmeal which was turned into porridge and was supposed to be the staple and really only costly article in my diet. This experiment was stopped by mother and was not a success.)'[9]

Despite this failure, working to a demanding timetable and within tight financial constraints proved so successful and satisfying that Wedgwood continued to do so throughout his life.

During the stay at Gladstone House he learned a great deal, not only at school where he blossomed into an outstanding student, but during the periods of leisure he allotted to himself. Some of this time he spent at the music hall, an entertainment he most enjoyed and recalled with delight in old age.

There were other experiences acquired and valuable lessons learnt while he was living in the heart of London's East End. It was a period of change for St George's in the East and Wapping. The members of the closely knit community of small merchants and traders serving the docks were moving out to the suburban avenues that were spreading through London's outskirts. The spacious properties they had occupied in some style were turned into lodginghouses or multiple-occupied dwellings that rapidly became appalling slums like the many hovels that already existed. Most of these had long been occupied by migrant Irish labourers to whose plight and causes Wedgwood, like his father, became extremely sympathetic. But in the 1890s there arrived in the area vast numbers of Jewish refugees from the oppression suffered in Russia, Poland and Germany. At Fenchurch Station and at the docks, Wedgwood saw many little bands of forlorn new arrivals, nursing their pitifully few belongings in battered bundles, and he was moved by their tearful relief at having at last reached their chosen haven. He was impressed by their self-sufficiency and organization, for they immediately established Jewish charities, courts and Boards of Guardians that supported their community. He was even more impressed by their ability to work so hard for such long hours. From his bedroom in Cable Street he could see, in the house opposite, a Jewish tailor sitting on a table stitching by the light of a blue gas lamp. Whenever Wedgwood looked, at whatever time of day or night, the man was working. Living as he did among this expanding refugee community, Wedgwood observed, admired, and felt an affinity to the close protectiveness of the typical Jewish family, which was in many ways so similar to his own.

The Jewish community and all the other inhabitants of St George's in the East were represented by Wedgwood's father with enthusiasm and dedication both on the LCC and in Westminster. In the autumn of 1894 he was invited to accompany John Burns on a visit to America. This he readily agreed to do, for, having become the chief protagonist of the municipal control of the London tramways, he was anxious to investigate how tramways were operated in the American cities. The two friends set off for the United States just before Christmas, and spent six weeks lecturing and studying conditions in cities from New York to the Rocky Mountains.

While his father was away, Ernest Benn moved back into Gladstone House and concentrated on his work as registration agent in the constituency, for not only did a General Election seem a possibility but the Conservatives had selected as their candidate Harry Marks, the proprietor of the *Financial News* and a man with an uncertain past and an unsavoury reputation. In such a small constituency, Marks and his agents were able to indulge in many forms of dubious electioneering. He attacked John Benn for living in a flat in what he claimed was a luxurious hotel. He alleged that in the 1892 election John Benn had manufactured votes, but three charges relating to this matter he brought to the courts were dismissed. This did not deter Marks, for he was determined to unseat John Benn who, though his parliamentary career had been unremarkable, had been a most conscientious constituency representative.

The first few weeks of 1895 were exceptionally cold. Wedgwood Benn later wrote, 'I shall never forget the morning walk through Commercial Road and Great Eastern Street to the school at Cowper Street. In every corner of shelter were miserable, shivering, starving workmen.'[10] This was the period when John Benn was in America and Marks, taking advantage of the absence, founded a so-called 'Relief Fund' that distributed in the tiny constituency 11,000 tickets for free soup. On each ticket the name of Harry Marks appeared in large, bold letters.

Wedgwood did what he could to help his brother and father, but it was a busy time for him, because he was preparing for the London Matriculation which he triumphantly passed. He would have liked to have gone to Cambridge, but the family's shortage of money made this impossible. Fortunately Wedgwood secured a Rothschild scholarship which paid all his tuition fees at University College, London.

When the General Election was called for July 1895, John Benn clearly had an uphill struggle to retain the seat, even though he was helped by all his family. Both Ernest and Wedgwood worked desperately hard to secure support for their father from the cosmopolitan and often illiterate electorate. As the election day drew nearer and it became obvious that either side could be victorious, violence broke out. On 11 July supporters of the two candidates canvassing Watney Street began to fight and the police had to intervene. Special constables were called to the constituency and on 16 July they had to break up another fight between rival supporters.

When the votes were counted, 1583 had been cast for Marks and 1579 for Benn, who thus lost by four votes. Remarkably, 94 per cent of the electors on the register had voted, including some who were subsequently proved to have died several months earlier.

Incensed by the corruption of which he believed his opponent was guilty, John Benn determined to fight the result in the courts. On 8 August he presented a petition for a recount. After several hearings before Mr Justice Day, a revised result was issued on 14 November. Marks obtained 1581 votes and Benn 1570, thus increasing the majority to eleven.

John Benn then decided to embark on an inevitably hazardous election petition under the Corrupt and Illegal Practice Act of 1883, claiming that Marks 'before, during, and after the said election' had been 'guilty of bribery, treating, undue influence, and of aiding, abetting, counselling and procuring the offence of personation'. The petition came before Mr Baron

Pollock and Mr Justice Bruce on 13 February 1896. For seventeen days the court heard charges and counter-charges. Wedgwood and his mother went along each day, buying a bunch of violets on the way from sheer joy because they were certain that they would win the case; so was Ernest, who was busily engaged with the witnesses and solicitors.

Eventually the case against Marks was dismissed, but Benn was convicted of two malpractices. The first was that portraits of him stuck on sticks and carried by boys were classified as banners, the use of which was illegal. The other was that an annex of Gladstone House had been used as a political club, but no charge for this had been made in the election expenses. As a result, John Benn was forbidden to stand as a candidate in the St George's in the East constituency for the following seven years. Not only did this absurd judgment appear to end his parliamentary career, but it meant that he was faced with paying legal costs of £6000. When the news of the verdict was given to him, John Benn was presenting a slide-lecture to supporters in Gladstone House. He turned to Wedgwood, who was standing beside him, and said, 'I feel like throwing on the screen "Praise God from whom all blessings flow."' He then continued with his lecture.

Despite his courageous acceptance of the unexpected decision, his enforced separation from the constituency he knew so well was a deeply felt blow – and another was soon to strike the family. The Rutherfords, having spent a short time with their infant daughter in India, had returned to England to live with Florence's sister, Bessie, at 4 Berkeley Place, Ridgeway, Wimbledon. There, in May, Florence died, according to the death certificate, of 'Nervous Exhaustion – 4 years. Weak Heart.' John and Lily Benn decided that they would look after the three-year-old Margaret, but her Aunt Bessie was adamant that she would bring up the child. And so she did, passing on to her niece her own love of and enthusiasm for the theatre. William Rutherford, deeply upset by his wife's death, decided to return to India, where he was again employed as a silk and drapery merchant. It seemed the most sensible solution to Rutherford's sad situation, and the Benns provided what financial and moral support they could.

Having his own financial problems with which to deal, John Benn adopted a course much favoured by the impecunious Victorian middle class. He gave up Hoppea Hall, his property in Upminster, and moved temporarily to the Continent with all his family, including Wedgwood, who had just completed his first year at university. Together they travelled on the deck of a ship from Newhaven to Ouistreham and from there by train to Cabourg, where they hired a nurseryman's cottage among the dunes. Wedgwood's knowledge of French was enormously useful to the family, who spent three months in Normandy sun-bathing and bicycling. Somewhat to her family's surprise, Mrs Benn decided to wear bicycling bloomers which, although just becoming fashionable, were still considered rather risqué. So successful and pleasurable was the holiday that it was repeated annually for several years.

On returning to London, the whole family moved into the flat in Westminster Palace Hotel, for the Benns had no other home. Although his income from *The Cabinet Maker* was satisfactory, John Benn still had his substantial legal costs to pay.

Despite these worries, John Benn had not given up his own parliamentary ambitions, but his main concern was to ensure that, as he had been debarred, one of his sons would stand as the next Liberal candidate for St George's in the East. It might have seemed as though Ernest, the eldest, was the obvious choice. His work in the constituency meant that he knew almost every elector and his organizational ability was considerable. Yet he had already, like his uncles who ran *The Cabinet Maker*, shown himself more interested in the business than in public service. It was Wedgwood who was best fitted to follow in his father's political footsteps. Although still only a teenager, he was naturally sympathetic, extremely hard-working, and already an accomplished public speaker. His interest lay in politics rather than business, and he was, like his father, witty, amusing and charming, so that he easily won people's affection and support. John Benn had no hesitation in deciding that as soon as Wedgwood was old enough he would be presented to the Liberal and Radical Association of St George's in the East as the most suitable person to contest the constituency.

This Wedgwood gladly accepted, and politics increasingly began to dominate his life. At University College he became the President of the Union Debating Society and, as throughout the South African War he uncompromisingly stood for Boer independence, he introduced a pro-Boer resolution. A group of medical students carrying jingoist banners broke up the debate and threw Wedgwood out of the ground-floor window. He managed to return and conclude the proceedings by signing the minutes. The incident resulted not from a wild student adventure, but from Wedgwood's determination to stand by his convictions, no matter how unpopular they were. Like his father, who was his mentor, he inherited a distrust of established authority, a passion for freedom of conscience, and a determination to work for improvements in the condition of those whose circumstances were less fortunate than his own. (He always expressed approval of the man who insisted that his charitable donations should be given to the '*un*deserving poor'.) Yet his was not a grim-faced mission, for the adolescent Wedgwood loved life, enjoying the pleasures of the music hall and the company of his friends whom he often took home at the weekends. Although small of stature and, like his father, always appearing to be much younger than his years, he looked forward with enthusiasm to his future political battles.

Meanwhile his father faced political battles of his own. In the summer of 1897, Charles Darling, the member for Deptford, was appointed a Judge of the High Court by the Tory Government and resigned his seat. This caused something of a furore in the Liberal press, it being claimed that Darling had been appointed only because he sat for a safe seat which would not fall to the Liberals, who had won several by-elections in the previous months. When John Benn was selected as the Liberal candidate for Deptford, he received a postcard from Gladstone, who was then eighty-eight years old, saying: 'May I be allowed to wish you success in your fight for a seat *somewhat strangely vacated.*'[11]

The campaign fought at Deptford was again a very bitter one, for Harry Marks, not content with his victory at St George's in the East, was determined to see his rival defeated again. Having acquired an evening newspaper called the *Sun* (which in 1902 he sold to the even more notorious political opportunist, Horatio Bottomley), he daily used its columns to carry out his vendetta. When the result was declared on 15 November, John Benn, despite considerably reducing the Conservative majority, was defeated by 324 votes. After the poll, John Burns told the crowd: 'This election has been won by a newspaper, owned by blackguards, edited by scoundrels, and with the marks of the beast on every line of it.'

Following this defeat, which made John Benn even more determined to fight against the vicious electoral tactics of the Conservatives, Wedgwood continued with his university studies. He left in the summer of 1898 with a first class honours degree in French and a special prize. Immediately he entered the family firm as an office junior. Six days a week he spent twelve hours a day in the office at Finsbury Square, and often in the evenings he went to Gladstone House in Cable Street.

Before the selection meeting for St George's in the East was held, Wedgwood's father became the candidate for Bermondsey, which the Conservatives had held in 1895 with a majority of just under 400. To pre-empt the criticism likely to be made by Marks, he and his family moved out of the flat in Westminster Palace Hotel, where they had lived for seven years, to a house in Thorburn Square in Bermondsey.

Shortly afterwards, when Wedgwood was twenty-two, the Selection Committee of the Liberals in St George's in the East met at Gladstone House. That evening, Wedgwood was taken by his father to Shadwell Station and left in the waiting-room. John Benn went on alone to the meeting, returning two hours later with the bitter news that Wedgwood had not been selected as the candidate, mainly because he had limited financial resources and looked no more than eighteen years old. This was, however, to be only a temporary setback.

Ernest Benn was having more success in his chosen business career. In

March 1900, he brought out the first issue of *The Hardware Trade Journal*, which began the expansion of Benn Brothers into a most profitable publishing company. John Benn's slowly improving fortunes enabled him to look for a new family house. He selected the Old Knoll at Blackheath, an ugly mansion with large reception rooms and small, inadequate bedrooms. He also purchased at Stansgate in Essex a field facing the Blackwater and next to a farm in which were the ruins of the old Cluniac Priory of Stansgate. There he built a cottage which Boulton and Paul's of Ipswich sailed in sections up the river. It was black and white, half-timbered and thatched. The nearest station was seven miles away, and there was no electricity. But it made a pleasant, if simple, home for the Benns to use at weekends and in the holidays. All of them loved Stansgate and Wedgwood was especially happy there. So different from London, where for most of his life he had lived and worked, this rural retreat, with its flat fields fronting onto the broad expanse of the Blackwater Estuary, provided a place where he was always to feel happy and relaxed.

After the holidays, while the rest of the family went to the Old Knoll at Blackheath, Wedgwood and Ernest returned to Bermondsey with their father to prepare for the General Election which was to be held on 6 October. This was the Khaki Election, fought in an atmosphere of jingoism that led inevitably to a heavy defeat of the Liberal Party. John Benn's own chances of victory were further lessened by a pamphlet issued by the opposition at the last minute which claimed to give an account of his political career. It contained many untruths, including the statement, 'Mr Benn, appreciating the serious consequences of his conviction, asked for relief in order that he might be capable of sitting in Parliament, and the Court refused it.' After his defeat by 300 votes, John Benn took an action against the printers of the pamphlet, which he won, being awarded £300 damages and costs.

In the Khaki Election, the Liberal candidate at St George's in the East was also defeated. As he decided not to stand again, the Selection Committee of the Liberal and Radical Party in the constituency in March 1901 – just after the funeral of Queen Victoria – chose Wedgwood Benn as the prospective candidate for St George's in the East and Wapping. It was a popular choice, for Wedgwood, although only twenty-four, not only was a member of a family with a long tradition of service in the community, but was himself well-known and much liked. The Liberal press applauded his selection to fight against the sitting Conservative member, Sir T.R. Dewar, who had replaced the disgraced Harry Marks at the Khaki Election. The *East London Observer* stated: 'After the meeting of the teetotal stripling and the whiskey giant developments are possible!'

Wedgwood continued to work long hours in the family firm, but he spent all his spare time in the district, maintaining and expanding the political activities begun by his father. Concerned about exorbitant rents, in August he led a deputation to the House of Commons to protest against key money and rent rises. He was appointed a Governor of Raine's School and a Trustee of the Henderson Charity, which gave small pensions to aged local residents.

All his activities in the constituency were discussed with his parents, to whom he remained very close and with whom he lived at Blackheath. To his regret, his father in 1902 decided to sell the cottage at Stansgate, because the migraine attacks from which he had suffered since first being elected to the LCC occurred more frequently there, perhaps because of the brightness of the sunlight reflected from the water. As a replacement holiday home, his father bought two small cottages at Crowborough and, as usual, carried out many internal improvements.

By the beginning of 1903, Wedgwood, Ernest, and their father were all extremely busy with their separate but associated activities. John Benn's campaign to introduce municipal electric trams to London had almost reached fruition; Ernest Benn's expansion of the family's publishing firm continued apace; and Wedgwood Benn worked as hard in his constituency as if he had already been elected its Member of Parliament. On 23 February, he organized at the Town Hall a variety concert which raised a substantial sum for the East End Distress Fund.

A few days later, he suffered from a personal setback that was unexpected and shattering. Unknown to him, his father had during the winter received a letter from Rutherford in India saying that he had met an English girl there whom he intended to marry. As the guarantor of his younger brother's conduct, John Benn was dismayed by the news. After much heart-searching, he decided that he had no alternative but to inform the girl's parents that their prospective son-in-law had murdered his father in a fit of madness. The engagement was called off, and, greatly agitated, Rutherford returned to England to berate his eldest brother. John Benn, feeling that he could not in good conscience continue to be responsible for his brother, consulted doctors who immediately recommitted Rutherford to a lunatic asylum.

A witness to all the events following Rutherford's return to London, Wedgwood, for the first time, was told the full story of his grandfather's murder and understood the distress it had caused his family. His parents, ever solicitous and affectionate, decided that he should take a sea cruise to the Canary Islands. The prospect of travelling abroad again so obviously excited Wedgwood that Ernest actually bought him a return ticket all the way to Durban.

On 14 March, Wedgwood set sail from Southampton in the *Roslyn Castle* with twenty-five golden sovereigns stitched into his vest. Years later he said:

'I was so much a novice on the outward journey that I was a willing and even grateful victim for all the devices for entertaining the passengers. I was proud to be put on the Social Committee and joined in all the organised efforts to pass the time. But I learnt my lesson: joint travel is no travel at all. You just carry about with you the very thing you are travelling to escape.'[12]

Just after arriving in Durban his bag was stolen and, because he was short of money, he stayed in a cheap lodging house where he slept in a dormitory with five other men. Having visited sites made famous in the South African War, such as Ladysmith, Spion Kop and Maritzburg, he decided to extend his travels. He cashed in the return half of his ticket and cabled Ernest to send him enough money to return to England via East Africa.

During the return journey, he refused to participate in any of the social activities. Indeed he pretended that he was not English, and spoke nothing but French. The ship called at many ports along the African coast, and in his notebook Wedgwood kept a detailed record of what he saw. His greatest thrill was visiting Egypt, for while the ship sailed slowly through the Suez Canal, he went to Cairo. The next port of call for the ship was Naples, where to Wedgwood's relief a medical inspection proved that he was not suffering, as he feared, from cholera. Having spent several days there, the ship sailed for Southampton, calling briefly at Lisbon on the way.

It was early in July when Wedgwood arrived back in England. His journey around Africa had been long and adventurous – he had seen exciting places and met interesting people; his notebooks contained a detailed record of his kaleidoscopic memories. But there had been many hours of enforced inactivity spent among pleasure-seeking passengers with whom he felt ill at ease. He could not wait to throw himself even more enthusiastically than before into the hurly-burly of political activity in St George's in the East.

The whole experience changed Wedgwood and his attitudes. From then on he believed that holidays taken for their own sake were a waste of time; everything must have a purpose. Work, as useful and as intense as possible, was the best way of preventing depression. Unable to understand why Rutherford should have either behaved as he did or be treated as he was, Wedgwood was determined to seize the opportunity provided by his family's circumstances to work for the benefit of others. Although he was never to surrender his wit or his sparkle, he was to pursue this mission with zest and thoroughness throughout his life. He determined to achieve his aim through politics, in which he had long been interested, rather than through the religious faith which was such a dominant influence on his parents. He never rejected it, but there were things in Victorian nonconformity with which he did not sympathize, especially the puritanism that forbad innocent things. Later he was to make fun of an uncle who had called the children in the house with the remark, 'Come in now. You've had enough pleasure for today!'

So, in the first six months of 1903, Wedgwood Benn acquired the resolve and independence which, though never separating him from his family, allowed him to chart his own course, rather than one perhaps mapped out for him by his father. On his return from Africa, he threw himself into his constituency work with a clear and burning ambition of his own.

I I 1903-1914

While Wedgwood Benn was travelling around Africa, his father, already one of the best-known men in London, achieved new fame by being responsible, as the Chairman of the Highways Committee, for the inauguration of London County Council's first electric tramway. As part of the opening ceremonies on 15 May 1903, he collected the halfpenny fares of the Prince of Wales and his family as they travelled on the first tram.

John Benn's long, but successful, struggle to provide London with a cheap, efficient and integrated municipal transport system brought innumerable benefits, especially to working-class people. Because of it, they were able to move out of the inner London slums into the low-cost suburban housing and still travel back daily to work in the East End.

Wedgwood Benn was one of the few people to suffer from this migration, for it included many of his voters from St George's in the East. In 1903 all the officers of his constituency's Liberal and Radical Association left the area, and the total number on the electoral roll shrank to just over 3000. About a sixth of these were Irish, and a few hundred were Jews who had been naturalized after their arrival from Eastern Europe.

Following the system used by his father, Wedgwood Benn ensured that he knew all his varied voters by preparing for each a printed card, listing name, marital state, place of work, and whether transport was required to reach the poll. Political leanings were also noted, not only from the regular canvasses he conducted, but from other signs–including willingness to sign petitions, participate in political activities, and display election posters.

With increasing frequency he addressed public and association meetings in the constituency. On 12 July 1903, immediately after his return from Africa, he spoke to a crowded gathering which had met at Gladstone House to welcome him home. The following day, the *Morning Leader* reported:

'Mr Benn, on rising to speak, was loudly cheered ... The most telling part of his speech was the discussion of the wage question, which was fully appreciated by the working men present.'

His concern for the welfare of the inhabitants of the area was not prompted solely by hopes of achieving political success. He was genuinely concerned by, and determined to help alleviate, the distress that was then all too common: he helped to organize a benefit for George Marsh, a cabman disabled by an accident; he spoke on behalf of the Municipal Employees' Union; and he assisted in raising funds for the St George's and Wapping Relief Committee. Obviously not a rich man, having no money other than his income from Benn Brothers, he won the respect and affection of the working people. In September 1903, the Borough of Stepney Labour Council unanimously agreed to support his parliamentary candidature.

Yet his successes were only local ones, and he was very aware that outside the constituency he was all but unknown, even in the Liberal Party, other than perhaps as John Benn's son. Determined to stand on his own feet, but lacking the money to make any extravagant gestures, he wrote to every Liberal Member of Parliament offering his services for a nominal fee. These letters, on which he had spent many hours, produced replies from only Oswald Partington, Charles Hobhouse and Reginald McKenna, a fellow Congregationalist. Wedgwood Benn heard nothing more from Partington. He had an interview with Hobhouse, but it was obvious that his grasp of matters was uncertain, for he then wrote a letter to Benn beginning 'Dear Mr Dyer'. The reply from McKenna was slightly more encouraging. Dated 11 December 1903, it stated:

'... I have only just received your letter on my return from meetings in S. Wales & Gloucester and tomorrow morning I start for the Riviera. I am so sorry to be prevented from meeting you. But if I can do anything by correspondence please write to me at the Hotel Prince de Galles, Monte Carlo. I shall be away for five weeks.'[1]

Wedgwood Benn did write again, the two men met, and they became lifetime friends. It was an association that was to bring Wedgwood Benn important parliamentary promotion and at least one personal disappointment.

By the beginning of 1904 Wedgwood Benn was feeling confident that he would be able to win the seat once occupied by his father. The Tory Government, elected with such a large majority at the Khaki Election, was faltering: resentment had been aroused in the country, especially among nonconformists, by their Education and Licensing Bills; the adoption of Chinese labour in South Africa had created great indignation; and Joseph

Chamberlain's conversion to the Protectionist cause was disrupting the Conservative Party. It seemed apparent that the next General Election would produce a Liberal victory.

An indication of this was provided in the spring of 1904 when the Progressives spectacularly increased their majority on the London County Council. Following this, Wedgwood Benn's father was elected the Chairman of the Council, and a meeting to congratulate him, held at Gladstone House, was attended by the largest crowd ever assembled there.

But John Benn's close connection with his son's work in St George's was shortly afterwards suddenly ended. A by-election was called at the dockyard town of Devonport. The prospective Liberal candidate tendered his resignation and the local Liberal Party asked John Benn to stand. Despite his heavy involvement in the work of the London County Council, he readily agreed, even though all his previous elections had been fought as a Londoner with a proud record of service to the capital and its community. Because of this, the *Daily Telegraph* dismissed him as 'an adventurous cockney carpet-bagger'. This could have been extremely damaging, because John Benn's Conservative opponent was Sir John Jackson, a local man and a large employer of labour, but in the event neither this nor an attempt to reopen the controversy of the St George's election petition could stem the anti-Government tide which swept John Benn to victory by 1040 votes, a majority so convincing that it caused something of a sensation when news of it was passed around the House of Commons. Liberal Members of Parliament shouted for the resignation of the Conservative and Unionist Prime Minister. In an interview that appeared in the *Daily News* on 21 June, the day after the poll, Asquith described the result of the Devonport by-election as 'a notice to quit given to the Government'.

But it was to be another eighteen months before a General Election took place. During this period Wedgwood Benn benefited from his father's return to the House of Commons in several ways. While still receiving his father's valuable guidance, he was able to establish himself as a candidate of merit rather than as merely a stand-in for his father. He also obtained increased access to the political world and its leading figures. Some of these he invited to meetings in his constituency. Reginald McKenna and Colonel Seely (later Lord Mottistone) addressed large, enthusiastic gatherings. With all the other Liberal candidates from the East End he went to a luncheon at the Edinburgh Castle in Tower Hamlets where Sir Henry Campbell-Bannerman, the main speaker, predicting a mammoth Liberal victory, announced:

'We will make England the pleasure ground of the poor rather than the treasure ground of the rich.'

Faced with Wedgwood Benn's obvious popularity, Sir T.R. Dewar, the sitting member for St George's who was only forty years old, announced that he did not intend to stand at the next election. The Conservatives selected as their prospective candidate Hallifax Wells, whom even Liberals conceded was an agreeable gentleman. His connections with the music hall enabled him to bring Miss Marie Lloyd to the constituency for a day's canvass. Unfortunately the party entertained themselves so lavishly at lunch-time that the visit was abruptly halted in the early afternoon.

The selection of Wells came too late for him to make an impact on the area to rival that of Wedgwood Benn, who had been actively involved in its affairs for over twelve years. A leaflet distributed throughout the constituency in the autumn of 1905, entitled 'Mr Wedgwood Benn and St George's & Wapping', listed the contributions he had made, concluding:

'He is not a rich man, but many of his less fortunate neighbours have to thank him for practical help rendered them in various ways. In short, one may say that he can and will number among his friends not only those who have always supported the Liberal Party, but many old residents who believe in a good man, and, above all, one who belongs to the district, and sympathizes with its needs.'[2]

At last, in December 1905, after the Conservative Party had been weakened by the defection both of Chamberlain's supporters and of Lord George Hamilton's Free Traders, Balfour resigned and, for the first time for twenty years, a Liberal Government was formed, led by Sir Henry Campbell-Bannerman. Immediately a General Election was called, to take place over several weeks in January 1906.

Because his father was standing again in Devonport, Wedgwood Benn conducted his own campaign, assisted by his own friends and his younger sister, Irene, who canvassed daily, helped organize meetings, and at Gladstone House in Cable Street – Wedgwood Benn's official residence – did all she could to look after her brother, on whom she doted.

On 13 January, John Benn was re-elected as one of the two Members for Devonport. Four days later, after the polls had closed in St George's in the East, the result of that constituency's election was announced from the steps of Stepney Town Hall:

Wedgwood Benn	(Liberal)	1685
Hallifax Wells	(Unionist)	1064

Despite the drop in the number of electors, Wedgwood Benn's majority of 621 was the largest ever recorded in the constituency. Aged only twenty-eight, he had been triumphantly elected to join his father in Westminster.

After the election, many reporters interviewed him, for he was the youngest person returned to the new Parliament. Under the headline, 'The Boy MP', the *Evening News* reported:

'He is slim and boyish looking, with clean-shaven, clear-cut features, light hair, and eyes sparkling with enthusiasm. He does not look a day more than twenty-two, but confesses to being "just a little older".

Although young in years, Mr Benn is by no means young politically, for, as the son of Mr J. Williams Benn, MP, LCC, he has been born and brought up amid parliamentary surroundings. From his cradle he has been able to devote himself entirely to his one hobby – politics.

For the last five years, whilst most young men of his age have been less usefully employed, Mr Wedgwood Benn has been carefully "nursing" his constituency.

When not engaged in politics, Mr Wedgwood Benn, who is associated with his father in trade journalism, devotes himself to *The Cabinet Maker* (surely a happy omen, politically, for the future).'

Although the youngest MP, Wedgwood Benn had much in common with his fellow Liberals whose spectacular landslide victory had given the Party a clear over-all majority. In the Parliament, the Liberals had 401 seats, the Labour Party 29, the Irish Nationalists 83, and the Unionists, who had been humiliatingly defeated, only 157. Like Wedgwood Benn, 180 of the Liberal Members were nonconformists, 220 were new to Westminster, and two-thirds had not been to public school. The Earl of Birkenhead, in *Contemporary Personalities*, somewhat testily recalls: 'The swollen Liberal majority of 1906 contained, as I suppose, a larger number of wordy men wholly ignorant of international politics, and of the affairs of the world, than any House of Commons within living memory.' The members elected in 1906 formed the first really middle-class Parliament, for the majority worked for their living as lawyers, teachers, journalists or businessmen. Because at the time MPs were unpaid, most of them had to continue in employment after their election.

This applied to Wedgwood Benn, who, it was decided, would continue, while a Member of Parliament, to receive from the family publishing firm his full salary, which was then £207 a year. It was naturally assumed that as a backbencher in a Government with the largest anti-Conservative majority for over eighty years he would have plenty of time to continue his work as a publisher. In his own mind, however, he was determined to become a successful Parliamentarian.

Resplendent in a frock-coat and a black silk hat, Wedgwood Benn was taken to the Palace of Westminster by his proud father, who introduced him to acquaintances including the officers and staff of the House of Commons.

It was not his father's acquaintances, however, but his own that brought Wedgwood Benn his first parliamentary position. Reginald McKenna, the First Secretary to the Treasury, appointed him as his unpaid Parliamentary Private Secretary. It was an insignificant post, but it seemed likely to lead to better things, for McKenna, a rich bachelor, aged only forty-two, was both able and ambitious. It was certain that he would in time achieve high office.

Wedgwood Benn's maiden speech was delivered on 28 March. Fulfilling a promise to his constituents, he spoke about the need to reform the Port of London. The speech was extremely well received. *Tribune* stated:

'Mr Wedgwood Benn delivered a remarkable maiden speech. The topic did not invite rhetoric, but by sheer mastery of his subject and a perfect delivery, Mr Wedgwood Benn held the close attention of the House, and when he sat down there was quite a demonstration. His father, who was on one of the cross benches, held a levee for the next ten minutes, members of all parties congratulating him upon his son's promise of becoming one of the debaters of the House.'

But it was to be some time before Wedgwood Benn did become one of the outstanding parliamentary debaters. In the next two years he delivered only two major speeches in the Commons, both on the Port of London Bill. Yet during that period he was one of the most regular attenders, learning much about both parliamentary procedure and, because of his work with McKenna, the administrative processes of government. An opportunity of becoming even more involved in parliamentary affairs came in January 1907, when McKenna, whose Parliamentary Private Secretary Wedgwood Benn remained, entered the Cabinet as the President of the Board of Education.

It was not long before McKenna was again promoted. Campbell-Bannerman, whose health had rapidly deteriorated after his wife's death, resigned on 5 April 1908, and Asquith became Prime Minister. Immediately he strengthened the Cabinet. In place of the inept and senile Lord Tweedmouth, who was moved to the Presidency of the Council, McKenna was made the First Lord of the Admiralty, then considered to be a post only a little less important than that of Chancellor of the Exchequer, to which Asquith had appointed David Lloyd George. Unfortunately these two new chief Ministers distrusted each other intensely. Shortly before their new appointments McKenna had told Balfour: 'If George ever should become Chancellor he would be a very unsound one. Of course, *you* disagree with us, but you *can* understand our principles. Lloyd George doesn't understand them and we can't make him!'[3]

His spectacular promotion occurred at a most opportune time for

McKenna. A few weeks before he had become engaged to Pamela, the younger daughter of Sir Herbert Jekyll, an official at the Board of Trade. A beautiful teenager, twenty-six years younger than McKenna, Pamela Jekyll was about to marry a man with a considerable fortune of his own, whose new position provided him with an imposing official residence at Admiralty House and the use of the Admiralty yacht *Enchantress*.

Continuing to be McKenna's Parliamentary Private Secretary, Wedgwood Benn was allocated a private office in Admiralty House, where his task was to look after the First Lord's constituency affairs. Not only did his work with McKenna bring him, at least momentarily, to the attention of his political leaders, but it allowed him to share in the First Lord's sumptuous social life. Naturally he was a guest at the wedding of Pamela Jekyll and Reginald McKenna which took place at St Margaret's Church, Westminster, on 4 June 1908. It was an impressive occasion. The bride's maid was her elder sister, Barbara, who was as great a beauty as Pamela.

The new Mrs McKenna and Wedgwood Benn rapidly became close friends and he was frequently welcomed as a guest at the lavish dinner parties held at Admiralty House and on cruises aboard the *Enchantress*. Wedgwood Benn, who had considerable charm and wit, was extremely popular, and Pamela McKenna decided that he would make a perfect husband for her sister.

There were obvious difficulties. Wedgwood Benn was not a wealthy man and his only income was the relatively meagre one he received from his father's firm. Although a successful political career seemed possible, it was by no means certain. So he had neither the security nor the means that Lady Jekyll expected any suitor of her daughters to possess. These expectations had been most adequately realized by McKenna, who had already arranged to have built as his family home a mansion designed by Edwin Lutyens in Smith Square.

Yet, encouraged by Pamela McKenna, Wedgwood Benn contemplated asking Barbara to marry him. There was no suggestion that his suit would be rejected, even when he spent a weekend with the McKennas at Sir Herbert and Lady Jekyll's home at Munstead in Surrey. He was not to know that Lady Jekyll had already informed Barbara that he would not make an acceptable husband because he had insufficient wealth.

So, unprepared for what was to happen, Wedgwood Benn happily accepted an invitation to cruise around the Mediterranean on the *Enchantress* with the McKennas, Barbara Jekyll, George Lambert (the Civil Lord at the Admiralty), Dr Macnamara (McKenna's Financial Secretary), and some other guests. The party travelled by train to Villefranche, where they joined the Admiralty yacht on 5 January 1909. Cosseted in great luxury, the passengers enjoyed a spectacular winter cruise: off Sardinia they watched HMS *Indomitable* at battle practice; at Messina, which had been almost destroyed by a recent earthquake, stores were landed to assist British survivors; in Malta they inspected the Naval establishment and were entertained by Their Royal Highnesses the Duke and Duchess of Connaught; at Tunis they were the guests of the French Naval Authorities; and then they steamed back towards Villefranche.

Throughout the cruise, Wedgwood Benn had been able to see a good deal of Barbara, and after dinner on Wednesday, 20 January, he asked her to marry him. She did not reply, but, having listened to him for a while, she burst into tears and ran away. At the time he had no reason to suspect Lady Jekyll's attitude to him, and so he was naturally bemused and upset. When Pamela McKenna heard what had happened, she wept. Ernest McKenna, trying to console Wedgwood Benn, said, 'You've no idea what it would be like to marry one of these girls, my dear boy. There's absolutely nothing useful they can do. They can sing and speak French, but they've really been brought up just to look wistful.' But Wedgwood Benn, who had fallen in love with Pamela's sister, was deeply bruised.

It was a salutary experience. Like a moth attracted by the brightness of a light in which it will inevitably be immolated, Wedgwood Benn had momentarily sought to enter a dazzlingly luxurious world for which he was conspicuously ill equipped. As it was, Lady Jekyll's attitude and her elder daughter's acceptance of it meant that he would not in future be forced to concern himself largely with amassing a personal fortune. This, of course, he did not think about at the time. With determination, he worked so that he could forget her.

Already he knew that the new parliamentary session would bring at least one excitement to compensate for his personal disappointment. He was given the honour of seconding the motion proposing the Loyal Address to the King after the State Opening of Parliament. This he did on 16 February 1909, wearing full Court dress, as was then the custom. As he had been provided with only a few opportunities to speak during his three years in the Commons, it was a considerable ordeal, but it provided proof that the leaders of his Party regarded him as one likely to merit promotion.

He spoke of the problems about which he had learned so much from his experiences and consistent work in his East End constituency – voting anomalies in London, Irish problems, unemployment, and poverty. While praising the benefits that had resulted from the Government's introduction of old age pensions, he pleaded for far more social reforms, especially those demanded by the Report of the Poor Law Commission. He concluded:

'If we accept the dictum of a famous Member of this House that "a nation lives in its cottages", new Members like me may feel some pride to have sat in a Parliament which has attempted so much for the national welfare. Much of the coming Session is to be devoted to kindred endeavours, and though I recognize the complexity of the problem, the elusiveness, yet persistency of the evils, I for one have not lost confidence either in the sympathy of this House or in its power to find adequate remedies. I must apologize if I seem to have dwelt too long on the references to social reform. I can only say that these questions continually confront those who represent, as I do, the very poor.'

By urging the Liberal Party to re-establish as its priority a determination to improve the social conditions of the poor, Wedgwood Benn was making a bold stand, for he was very aware of how difficult that was. In the previous three sessions, the smallest Conservative Opposition returned to the Commons for decades had, by unashamedly using its inbuilt and overwhelming majority in the House of Lords, effectively prevented the introduction of any measure, other than a money Bill, of which its leaders did not approve. It was not to be long, however, before the House of Lords was to be used by the Opposition to oppose the most important annual money Bill of all. On 28 November, the Lords rejected Lloyd George's Budget, but that could not be the end of the matter. 'If the Budget has been buried,' the Chancellor declared, 'it is in the sure and certain hope of a glorious resurrection.' On 2 December, the Prime Minister moved in the Commons 'that the action of the House of Lords in refusing to pass into law the financial provision made by this House for the service of the year is a breach of the Constitution and a usurpation of the rights of the Commons'. During his speech he announced that 'at the earliest possible moment we shall ask the constituencies of the country to declare that the organ and voice of the free people of this country is to be found in the elected representatives of the nation'. So Parliament was dissolved and a General Election called to take place over a fortnight beginning on 15 January 1910.

Although the Budget attracted much public interest throughout most of the country, the electorate of St George's in the East and Wapping was far more concerned about local issues. The widespread support Wedgwood Benn received made his re-election seem certain. He was, however, greatly distressed when, three days before the election in his constituency, he heard that his father had failed by 141 votes to be re-elected at Devonport, which like the other dockyard seats of Portsmouth and Chatham had been captured by the Conservatives. No such upset occurred at St George's in the East and shortly after the polls had closed on 18 January 1910, it was announced that Wedgwood Benn was returned to Westminster with a majority of 434.

The final results of the General Election produced a stalemate. The Liberals won 275 seats, the Tories 273, the Irish Nationalists 82, and the Labour Party 40. Gone was the Liberals' massive overall majority and the Government could continue in office only with the help of the Irish Nationalists and the Labour Party. Although this obviously meant that concessions would have to be made to both groups, the Liberal leaders were determined to continue their battle with the House of Lords and ensure the passage of Lloyd George's Budget. To strengthen the Chancellor's parliamentary team, Asquith in late February appointed three new Junior Lords of the Treasury. One of these was Wedgwood Benn, who was also made a Junior Government Whip.

His first Government appointment meant that he would receive an annual salary of £1000 and, to his delight, would be working with Lloyd George. It also meant that, as was then the legal requirement, he would have to submit himself to his constituents at a by-election. The procedure was usually a formality, for only in exceptional circumstances was a newly appointed Minister opposed. But when this did happen, there was always the possibility of defeat. In 1908, for example, Winston Churchill, after being made President of the Board of Trade, lost the by-election in his North-West Manchester constituency, and had to stand again in Dundee, after the sitting Liberal Member had been persuaded to accept a peerage.

Wedgwood Benn did not expect any such difficulties. But the local Executive Committee of the Conservative Party, knowing that by winning the by-election the Tories would have as many seats in the Commons as the Liberals, decided to oppose him and again adopted Percy C. Simmons as the Tariff Reform candidate. The short contest was extremely bitter and bad-tempered.

To help him in his fight, Wedgwood Benn was able, because of his new Government salary, to appoint a full-time agent. His brother, Ernest Benn, took charge of the canvassing and, as the *Westminster Gazette* reported on 22 February, he was greatly aided by 'an earnest and loyal band of workers, all of whom are proud of their young leader's success in the House of Commons'.

With his father's assistance, Wedgwood Benn drafted a circular listing some of the measures Simmons had either supported or opposed on the LCC In his election address, Simmons stated:

'You can form your own conclusions as to what reliance is to be placed upon statements such as that I helped to turn 3000 men out of work and that I voted to sell the steamboats to the foreigners. I have taken legal proceedings against Mr Wedgwood Benn, the *Daily Chronicle* and the *St*

George's and Wapping Progressive Champion, and shall take similar action against anyone else I find repeating these falsehoods.'[4]

Undeterred, Wedgwood Benn issued a circular giving full details of Simmons' voting record to show that his opponent's denials were incorrect.

Much amusement locally was then caused when, after Simmons had announced that he would pay £100 if one of the original charges that he had voted against the feeding of children was proved, Wedgwood Benn issued another circular headed 'Facts About Feeding Children' which gave in full two motions Simmons had voted against. One was:

'It was moved that it be referred to the Education Committee to consider and report as to putting into immediate operation the powers of the Education Committee (Provision of Meals) Act, 1906, for providing meals for necessitous children out of rates.'[5]

Several people then claimed, but were not paid, the £100.

For Wedgwood Benn, a more important concern was the attitude of the Irish in the constituency. As the Government required the support of the Irish Nationalists in Parliament, John Redmond, the leader of the United Irish League, advised his supporters not to vote for Wedgwood Benn unless Asquith promised a Home Rule Bill. Local branches voted to ignore this request, but the matter was not resolved until, on the eve of the poll, E.G. Hemmerde drove from Parliament to a crowded meeting in the constituency and announced, 'We in the House of Commons have just got into fighting order. We discussed how we should proceed and just before I left we found everybody united – Irish, Labour and Liberal. I believe that we can now go forward to certain victory.'

The following day, 1 March, Wedgwood Benn defeated his opponent by 509 votes, an increase of seventy-five over the previous majority. The vast crowd assembled outside the Town Hall received the result with jubilant enthusiasm and as soon as Wedgwood Benn appeared on the steps people pushed forward, knocking the police out of the way, and the successful candidate was raised shoulder-high and carried off to Gladstone House. St George's went wild with excitement. Rockets were set off, bonfires were lit, and, carrying flowers and bedecked in party colours, the extremely popular re-elected Member addressed a large number of his delirious constituents from a window-sill of the house.

Unfortunately Wedgwood Benn was not able for long to celebrate his victory. Shortly afterwards he was served with a writ for libel because of the statements he had made about Simmons voting against 'the feeding of children'. Protracted negotiations with lawyers followed, but all were convinced that, if the case went to court, Wedgwood Benn would lose, because by voting against the provision of meals out of the rates 'for necessitous children' Simmons could not be shown to have opposed 'the feeding of children'. So Wedgwood Benn was advised to settle out of court. The lawyers from both sides agreed on the sum of £5000, which he was assured was considerably less than the total bill he would have to pay if he proceeded with the case.

Having no money of his own, he assumed that he would be dragged through the Bankruptcy Court and would then automatically have to leave the House of Commons. But his father, who had just lost his own parliamentary seat, determined that the libel action would not wreck his son's career and so, even though his own wealth was limited, he undertook to pay the sum demanded.

Moved by his father's act of generosity and love, Wedgwood Benn became even more determined to make a success of his work. At first, in his enthusiasm, he made some mistakes. Hilaire Belloc, the writer and Liberal Member of Parliament, sent him this curt letter, dated 20 April 1910:

'Dear Sir,

I am in receipt of an undated communication from you, with no name nor even indication of my sex. It addresses me as "Dear", and proceeds to tell me that you have booked me for the Hatcham Liberal Club, on Wednesday the 27th. It further asks me to "pencil" this date in my "diary".

I have never received such a communication before in my life, and you will easily understand that I shall *not* appear at the Hatcham Liberal Club (whatever that may be) upon the date you see fit to mention. When you desire the unpaid or, for the matter of that, the paid services of another person, you cannot expect to obtain them without a little courtesy and consultation.

I am,
Your obedient Servant,
H. BELLOC.'[6]

But Wedgwood Benn learned quickly and was soon thoroughly enjoying his work.

Throughout the eventful parliamentary session of 1910, much of his time was spent not with Lloyd George but with Alexander Murray, the Master of Elibank, who had been made the Liberal Chief Whip after the General Election. This remarkable and efficient man insisted that Wedgwood Benn should memorize the faces and names of every Member of the Commons. Armed with this knowledge, he was able to fulfil his responsibility of ensuring that there were always enough Liberals and their allies in the House to win each division of the debates that began with the reintroduction of the Budget and then moved on to a Bill designed to limit the powers of the House of Lords. The inevitable rejection of this Bill by the Lords would create a constitutional crisis involving King Edward VII. What was not expected was that on 6 May 1910, the King would suddenly die and be succeeded by the less politically experienced King George V.

There followed much political intrigue, about which Wedgwood Benn, as a Junior Whip, was able to learn a great deal. Early in June, the Liberal and Unionist leaders began a series of confidential, constitutional meetings. But in November the talks on both the coalition and the constitutional crisis broke down and it was apparent that Asquith must call another General Election so that with the people's backing he could request the new King to create, if necessary, sufficient peers to ensure the passage through the House of Lords of the Bill limiting its powers.

But before the election was called, the Benn family suffered from a severe and unexpected setback. The manufacturers of a tramways system that had been tried but rejected by the LCC entered an action for libel against Wedgwood Benn's father because of his published criticism of their equipment. The case began in mid-November and on 1 December the jury found John Benn guilty and the Judge, Mr Justice Ridley, awarding the plaintiffs £12,000, ordered that £5000 must be received within fourteen days.

It was yet another blow from the legal system. Not only was John Benn unable to pay the huge damages, coming as they did so soon after he had settled his son's libel action, but he believed that the verdict was unjust. He therefore immediately appealed. To secure the £5000, a bailiff moved into a small furnished room at the Benns' home in Blackheath, where he made an inventory of all the household goods. Anticipating his arrival, Wedgwood Benn's mother had marked all her possessions with labels stating, 'This is the property of Mrs Benn.'

While the bailiff was still in the Benns' house, the second General Election of 1910 took place. Despite his personal worries, John Benn stood in the safe Conservative constituency of Clapham, while his son contested St George's in the East for the third time within a year.

The election campaign was rather dull. The public was not excited by the issue of whether the Lords should be able to veto Bills passed by the Commons. The candidates, however, did their best to interest their electors. In his constituency Wedgwood Benn distributed hundreds of coloured posters and leaflets denouncing the House of Lords. He was, however, somewhat chastened when his bill-poster said, 'Look here. These bills won't do. This *vetto* – what is it? The fellows don't know what it is. Now if you give me bills with a real argument on 'em like "Vote for Benn", I'm sure they would do a great deal more good.'

In the election Wedgwood Benn easily retained his seat, and his father was again defeated. Nationally, the results produced only the smallest of changes. The Liberals lost three seats and the Conservatives one; the Irish Nationalists and the Labour Party gained two each. So Asquith had, with his allies, won a sufficient majority to demonstrate that the people supported the Liberals' plan to curtail the powers of the House of Lords. It was but a question of time before the Conservative Party and the House of Lords were forced to capitulate.

Parliament was opened on 6 February 1911, and a few weeks later John Benn's application was heard in the Court of Appeal before Mr Justice Fletcher Moulton and Lord Justice Buckley. Finding that Mr Justice Ridley had misdirected the jury in the original case, the judges allowed John Benn's appeal and awarded him costs. It was both a triumph and a relief, but many commentators felt that John Benn had been sued originally for his political views rather than for what he had written. From all over the country John Benn received congratulatory messages, for it was widely acknowledged that his victorious appeal had helped to establish the right of free criticism of public affairs.

The successful conclusion of the case, which freed the family from financial worries, came at a most opportune time for Wedgwood Benn, who was involved in a measure which was to take up much of his energy and time throughout 1911. Aware of his ardent desire for social reform and delighted by his enthusiasm, Lloyd George had secured Wedgwood Benn's continuation as a Junior Lord of the Treasury so that he could become a member of the small team that would work on the introduction of a health and unemployment measure. The main Parliamentarians involved were Rufus Isaacs (the Attorney General), McKenna, and Charles Masterman. They were assisted by extremely able Treasury civil servants, including, most notably, W.J. Braithwaite.

Lloyd George's National Insurance Bill was approved by the Cabinet in April and introduced in the House of Commons on 4 May. It proposed compulsory insurance for manual workers and all others with an income of less than £160 a year. The wide-ranging benefits included sick pay, medical and maternity benefits, disability allowances and the right to treatment for tuberculosis in a sanatorium.

Not surprisingly, the measure, which more than any other was to establish the Welfare State, was bitterly opposed by many vested interest groups, including doctors, who feared that lucrative private practices would be ended, trade unions, whose own insurance schemes attracted new members to the unions, and employers of servants, who resented being asked to pay 3d. a week for each of their staff.

Faced with a considerable work load, all those involved had to play a full part. In *Lloyd George's Ambulance Waggon*, Braithwaite describes how queries raised at Question Time were answered:

'L.G. of course was very good indeed in answering questions, and very great interest was taken every day in his answers ... Masterman, McKenna, MacKinnon Wood and Wedgwood Benn all took a hand at various times in answering Questions.'[7]

So Wedgwood Benn, after only five years in the Commons, found himself answering questions directed to the Chancellor of the Exchequer on one of the most important pieces of legislation introduced this century. Rightly accepting it as a great opportunity, he kept detailed records and files on each aspect of the Insurance Bill. These were the beginnings of the complex reference system he maintained for the rest of his life.

Throughout 1911 Wedgwood Benn worked a good deal with Lloyd George, whom he greatly admired. He later described these days:

'On Saturday mornings I used from time to time to go round to No. 11 Downing Street in the hope of being asked to do a few jobs. In this way I got to know Lloyd George and his household better. I remember with great affection his wife, Margaret, dispensing bacon and eggs from the fender in the dining-room.

Sometimes the Chancellor was a little forgetful. Once I had been bidden to go for a "quiet chat", but when I arrived I was told by the Messenger, Mr Newman, that I was to be the fellow guest with twenty-two Baptist ministers, whom the Chancellor had forgotten to mention to me. Needless to say, I fled.

On another Saturday morning the Chancellor himself threw open the front door and welcomed me with open arms. This I thought was deserved, though unexpected, and then I realized that he had come to meet his dainty little daughter who returned home from school at about that time every Saturday morning.'[8]

In the new parliamentary session which began in January 1912, Wedgwood Benn concentrated on his duties as a Whip. His work brought him into contact with all Liberal Members. One of the newest was Daniel Turner Holmes, who had been elected as Liberal MP for Govan in a by-election the previous year. Wedgwood Benn and Holmes, a scholarly ex-teacher, got on well together, for they shared an enthusiasm for French literature.

Margaret Holmes, the MP's young daughter, took a special interest in Wedgwood Benn when she saw him for the first time. Seventy years later, she described the event:

'I first saw him on 3 April 1912. I was sitting in the Ladies' Gallery with my mother. At five minutes to three, the door opened and he came in.

He was very alert and lively, with very fair hair. He was looking round and counting people. I said to my mother, "Who is that?" And she said, "That's Mr Wedgwood Benn. He's a Liberal Whip, and he's counting to see if there are enough supporters of the Government in case there's a Division."

I thought he looked very nice. I was fourteen and he was thirty-four! I first met him at a wedding six or seven months later. To my great surprise he greeted me with a friendly smile and remarked, "Oh, I believe you come to the House of Commons sometimes!" I did not know that earlier another MP had told him in my father's presence that he had an admirer in the Ladies' Gallery. My father need have said nothing, but his spontaneous reaction was to protest, "Tut! Tut! She's only a child!"'

Wedgwood Benn, greatly touched, never forgot the incident and, although it was to be some time before he met Margaret Holmes again, he was to remind her of her father's words when he proposed to her almost eight years later. 'So it might appear', Lady Stansgate said to me recently, 'that our life's happiness hung on the frail thread of an idle word, but we thought otherwise.' In 1912, however, Wedgwood Benn was seriously contemplating marrying the sister of a parliamentary colleague.

He was now an established and successful young man in the Commons, and, being increasingly active in public affairs, was attracting much attention. In Parliament, he continued to answer questions from the Front Bench, not just for the Chancellor of the Exchequer, but also for other members of the Cabinet, who, after six enormously busy years, seemed to be becoming weary with office.

Yet there were disappointments to temper his successes. The second woman he had wanted to marry had first encouraged and then rejected him. More serious in its long-term effects on him was the Marconi scandal, which greatly increased the troubles of the Government throughout most of 1912 and 1913, and which revealed to Wedgwood Benn that at least some of his political leaders, the Olympians he had at first so much admired, were not the men of integrity he had assumed them to be.

The scandal arose because of the involvement of four Ministers – Lloyd George, Rufus Isaacs, the Master of Elibank, and Herbert Samuel, the Postmaster-General – in the purchase of shares in Marconi, a company that was then given an improperly favourable contract by the Government. An impartial inquiry would almost certainly have ended the political careers of both Isaacs and Lloyd George, but as it was the House of Commons cleared all those involved. Isaacs was immediately made Lord Chief Justice; the Master of Elibank was created Baron Murray; and Samuel remained in office. Lloyd George was able to turn the scandal to his own advantage and increase his public popularity. But there were members of the Liberal Party, including Wedgwood Benn, who doubted both his judgment and his honesty.

During this period, Wedgwood Benn worked with Percy Illingworth, who succeeded the Master of Elibank as the Chief Whip. Determined to prevent a repetition of the Government's unexpected defeat in a snap division on 11 November 1912, Wedgwood Benn experimented with and then had installed in the Whips' Room several important innovations, including a counting machine, telephones and a pneumatic tube that carried messages to and from the front bench. As he was prevented by his duties from making major speeches in the Commons, he readily accepted every opportunity of being involved in any other way. Because Lord Beauchamp, the Chief Commissioner of Works, sat in the Lords, Wedgwood Benn dealt in the Commons with all matters concerning the Office of Works. He presented the estimates for replacing the beetle-infected roof of Westminster Hall, steered through the Commons the first Ancient Monuments Bill, and spent much time considering what improvements could be made to the structure of the Houses of Parliament. As a result of his efforts, cellars along the Terrace were turned into tea rooms and two staircases were built from the Lobby to the Terrace. The defeat of Charles Masterman in a bitter by-election caused by his promotion to the Cabinet left Wedgwood Benn one of the few men in the Commons, apart from the Chancellor of the Exchequer, capable of dealing with questions on the National Insurance Commission. Because of this, in the spring of 1913, he was more active at Question Time than anybody else in the Government.

By the beginning of 1914, Wedgwood Benn had as much knowledge as anyone of the structure, Members and procedure of the House of Commons. In his eight years in Parliament he had proved useful to the leaders of his Party, was well liked by almost all Members, and disliked by none. By keeping in close contact with his constituents, he also knew well the difficulties and aspirations of the ordinary people. Moreover, his organizational ability had been fully developed both as a Whip and as an undefeated parliamentary candidate. His future seemed bright.

There was perhaps only one thing that he lacked – like his Party, he put parliamentary procedure before political ideas. Much later he stated:

'I don't think for the first eight years in the Commons I learned a single thing about the real theories of government. My position was a simple one – Vote for Benn.'[9]

So uninterested in policies was his Party that between 1908 and 1914 the Liberal Parliamentary Party held only two official meetings, at one of which the Budget League was formed. Nationally, the organization of the Party,

despite having won three successive General Elections, was most unsatisfactory. Sir George Riddell recorded in his diary on 24 May 1914:

'L.G. said the Liberal Party organization is very bad. Illingworth has too
much to do. The Party should appoint a whole-time assistant. I suggested
Wedgwood Benn. L.G. said he thought he was the best man available.'[10]

Some discussion took place and, on 5 June, Lloyd George wrote to the
Prime Minister:

'I had a long talk with Elibank ... He thought that Percy [Illingworth]
would be more likely to accept tranquilly the appointment of an outsider
rather than one of his own subordinates like Wedgwood Benn. He was
of the opinion that the proposed rearrangement of functions should be
put in such a way to Percy as not to offend his susceptibilities.'[11]

But before anything could be done to reform and revitalize the Liberal
Party, the long, idyllic summer days of 1914 were disrupted by the sudden
threat of a war that was soon to maim and kill millions. In some way or
other, almost all involved in it were to be scarred or changed. Wedgwood
Benn was one of them.

III 1914–1918

Even in the days of uncertainty before war was declared Wedgwood Benn's
parliamentary duties were substantially changed. 'The task of organizing
conflicting Parties in Parliament', he later wrote, 'seemed ridiculous and
distasteful. I looked for something else to do.'

He soon found something important in which to become fully involved.
On Friday, 31 July, he was discussing with A.P. Nicholson, a journalist on
the *Daily News*, the inevitable social and industrial distress that would
immediately follow the declaration of war. Nicholson, having reminded
Wedgwood Benn of his success in raising money during the 1912 London
Dock Strike, said, 'Why not raise a National Relief Fund for the coming
need?'

Accepting the suggestion, Wedgwood Benn immediately sought the
assistance of the leading newspapers. Within hours he had been given the
support of several proprietors including Henry Lawson of the *Daily Telegraph*. His visit to *The Times* was less successful, for Lord Northcliffe
insisted that any fund with which he was associated had to be run exclu-
sively by his newspaper. Somewhat dismayed, Wedgwood Benn went on to

see Lord Burnham, who suggested that the scheme would obtain national acceptance if the Prince of Wales could be persuaded to become the fund's President. This suggestion Wedgwood Benn then put to Asquith.

On Wednesday, 5 August – the first day of the war – Asquith informed Wedgwood Benn that the Prince of Wales had agreed to be the President. That evening, as a vast crowd jammed the Mall, Wedgwood Benn went to Buckingham Palace and he and the Prince drew up the plans for the fund's launch: the wording of the appeal was agreed; the stables at Buckingham Palace were to be used as a Post Office; and York House was selected as the fund's headquarters. The following day, a major item in most national newspapers was the launch of the National Appeal Fund, which included on its committee six Cabinet Ministers and Ramsay MacDonald.

Money flowed rapidly into the fund: George Coats gave £50,000, Lord Ashton £25,000, the 1st Life Guards £18,000, the Duke of Westminster £15,000, and Messrs N.M. Rothschild £10,000. At the first meeting held at York House on 7 August there was a huge pile of cheques on the table. According to Sir George Riddell, Wedgwood Benn said to the King, 'In future there will be no need for a tax-gatherer. Your Majesty will be able to dispense with the Chancellor of the Exchequer. To provide public funds it will only be necessary to make an appeal such as the Prince made yesterday. In two days we have got £400,000, which is more than a good many taxes produce in a year!' The King laughed and said, 'More than some taxes I have heard of have produced!'[1]

The same day, Friday, the banks opened for the first time in a week, and this further increased the flow into the fund. The rapid re-establishment of normal banking arrangements, unaccompanied by any panic, was the result of Lloyd George's sound and courageous policies. By preventing a financial crisis, his personal credit leapt. By being decisive when his Cabinet colleagues seemed shell-shocked even before the first shot had been fired, Lloyd George instantly became the political hero the people on the brink of war so desperately needed.

By 15 August, the National Appeal had surpassed £1,000,000 and the Prudential Assurance had arranged for its 20,000 agents to make door-to-door collections for the fund. Wedgwood Benn, with a large team of helpers, worked up to eighteen hours a day dealing with the donations that were eventually to exceed £5,000,000.

It soon became obvious, however, that it was far easier to raise money that to distribute it. The local committees set up to handle claims proved to be inadequate and incompetent; the scale of the war and the artificial prosperity it produced had been underestimated; but some necessary benefits were provided, especially for the dependants suddenly separated from the thousands of newly volunteered soldiers.

By October, Wedgwood Benn's work with the National Appeal had become for him an unsatisfying, irksome routine. Although as a Member of Parliament he was not expected to volunteer for military service, he desperately wanted a greater involvement in the war. He found it difficult, as a fit bachelor, to see joining the armed forces men far less healthy than he was and with far more family commitments. In his own constituency, which had an electorate of only 3000, the names of 3300 soldiers were listed in 'The St George's Roll of Honour' which was published by the local Liberal Party. His younger brother, Oliver, whose health was poor, had joined a service battalion of the Somerset Light Infantry in September.

Not having a military background, Wedgwood Benn consulted Mrs Asquith, and through her received an invitation from Sir Matthew 'Scatters' Wilson, her relative and a Tory MP, to join the Middlesex Yeomanry. Immediately, he resigned from the National Relief Fund. He also sent a letter of resignation from the Government, but this Percy Illingworth refused to accept, saying that the position would be held open until the end of the war, for as the winter of 1914 approached it was still widely assumed that hostilities would cease within a few months.

Wedgwood Benn's decision to volunteer for military service received the full support of his father. The family had a deep hatred of war, but held the common view that force had to be used to prevent German militarism destroying the traditional liberties enjoyed by Britain and the rest of Europe. When Wedgwood Benn left them early in November, his parents, although proud, were naturally anxious, for he was the last of their children to move away from home. Throughout all his parliamentary career he had daily discussed his activities with both his mother and father. They had always been, and would remain, very close to each other.

Joining a mounted regiment was for Wedgwood Benn a great adventure. Freddie Guest, a fellow Liberal MP and Churchill's cousin, had given him a polo pony accompanied by a groom. As instructed, he had bought almost all the kit required, including the uniform which was expensive and occasionally bizarre because he was joining what, until the outbreak of the war, had been a Territorial regiment with rich part-time officers. The jodhpurs, for example, had to have a slight touch of pink and could be purchased only from a certain shop in Savile Row. Unfortunately the correct caps were unobtainable and so, when Wedgwood Benn reported to the camp at Moulsford in Berkshire, he was wearing a homburg hat with his new officers' uniform!

Wedgwood Benn was delighted to find that the second-in-command of the regiment was Harry Brodie, who from 1906 to 1910 had been a Liberal MP; but despite having two old parliamentary colleagues as his senior officers Wedgwood Benn immediately encountered difficulties that, because of his enthusiasm and ignorance of military organization, he could hardly have expected. At thirty-seven, he was at least ten years older than the average age of his fellow officers, most of whom had been elevated by the war into what they considered to be important positions. In their eyes, only military rank was important, and Wedgwood Benn was the most junior officer. Also, as he later wrote: 'To be an MP was a positive handicap (not to say disgrace) among these young persons who felt that they had been suddenly called upon to assume unaided the full burden of Empire.'

Undeterred, he threw all his energies into becoming an accomplished soldier. According to Brodie:

'He was intensely keen and being 37 years old was more worn and exhausted by the work he did than he himself at all realized. He was constantly at work endeavouring to master the rather petty details of regimental life – easy enough to fall in with at 20 to 25 – but irksome and almost incomprehensible to a Junior Lord of the Treasury aged 37.'[2]

A major problem Wedgwood Benn had to overcome was that he could not ride. His pony proved to be difficult to manage, but he refused to find a quieter mount. Shortly after the regiment had moved in November to Mundesley in Norfolk, he had a nasty accident when his pony ran away with him into some barbed wire. He was fortunately not seriously hurt, and continued his efforts to master his mount.

Not even the offer of parliamentary promotion could deviate him from his avowed intent to be a soldier. When Percy Illingworth, the Chief Whip, died in January 1915, Wedgwood Benn was one of the men thought likely to take his place. On 17 January, Asquith wrote to Miss Stanley:

'To go back to the Whipship, about wh. I talked to the Assyrian [Edwin Montagu] – he suggested Maclean, quite an impossible person – I am not sure that I shall not have to fall back upon Gulland (for the House) and Benn (for organization & the country).'

But Wedgwood Benn refused Asquith's offer to be the Joint Chief Whip. Having become a soldier, he had no intention of resigning until the war was won.

In April the Middlesex Yeomanry set off for Avonmouth prior to sailing. Wedgwood Benn felt exhilarated, not just because he would soon be in action, but also because he felt convinced that his decision to leave the Commons was correct. From his friends he heard the rumours of plots to overthrow Asquith and counterplots to discredit Lloyd George. In the press he saw demands that the Prime Minister should, in the words of *John Bull*, 'openly invite Opposition leaders to his Councils and share with them the responsibilities of the hour'.

The *Nile*, the ship on which the Middlesex Yeomanry embarked at Avonmouth, did not sail, as had been rumoured, to the Dardanelles, but landed the soldiers at Alexandria, from where they moved to a camp at Moascar, near Ismailia on the Suez Canal.

It was announced shortly afterwards that Asquith, faced with the severe decline in his Government's fortunes, had agreed to form a coalition. The new Cabinet, which was created on 25 May, contained thirteen Liberals, eight Unionists, and one Labour member. The Chancellor of the Exchequer was McKenna, Lloyd George became Minister of Munitions, and Balfour went to the Admiralty. The formation of the new Government meant that Wedgwood Benn had lost his position as Junior Lord of the Treasury.

Although naturally interested in the political developments, Wedgwood Benn was far more concerned by the promise of early action, but it soon became apparent that this was not to be realized and for week after week there was little to do in the insufferable heat but water the horses and practise cavalry exercises in the early morning. Impatience gave way to ill-feeling, which, as Brodie relates, some of his officers directed towards Wedgwood Benn:

'After we got to Egypt there was a gradual change of feeling in the Mess towards Wedgwood. Several fellows who had positively fawned upon him – I suppose thinking that he might some day help them through his political influence – began to murmur against him behind his back. There was, as far as I could see, absolutely no reason for this change of feeling. He himself was full of good feeling towards these others – he was constantly telling me what fine fellows they were and certainly did not realize that his ability and intelligence were regarded with suspicion and dislike ...

Wedgwood was not and never could be what our General called a "regular", and yet he had more brains than most of the regulars including the General and his Brigade Major – the former a very stupid, dull man, the latter a very ill informed and illiterate but competent soldier, extremely alive to his own interests.'

Certainly some of the officers were upset because Wedgwood Benn, being an MP, was treated differently by the civil administrators. He was invited to visit the High Commissioner, Sir Henry MacMahon, in Cairo, where Sir Ronald Storrs showed him around. In Port Said he flew, for the first time, in a seaplane that belonged to the French Navy.

On his return from Port Said, he received a cable saying that his younger brother, Oliver Benn, was missing after an attack at Achi Baba in the Dardanelles on 4 June. He was never heard of again. Knowing well the grief from which his mother was suffering, Wedgwood Benn determined to write to her every day it was possible. He did so throughout the war.

Some weeks later it was announced that the Middlesex Yeomanry were to be converted from a mounted regiment into an infantry brigade. Having been shipped out to Egypt, all the horses and their equipment were to be left behind with some soldiers while the others and their new equipment left for the Dardanelles. Unworried by the wastage and their lack of suitable training, the troops were taken to Alexandria from where they sailed on 13 August. After trans-shipping at Lemnos, they travelled on the *Doris*, which was so crowded that there was only standing-room, and arrived at Suvla Bay on 18 August, ten days after the first landing. Digging themselves into holes in the cliff above the beach, the soldiers, for the first time, came under fire as shells and machine-gun fire continuously hammered their make-shift positions.

On 21 August, the 2nd Mounted Division of the Middlesex Yeomanry received the order to advance, in the middle of the afternoon, across the Salt Lake towards Chocolate Hill as the first line of reserve for the attack that had started earlier in the day. With 'Scatters' Wilson in command and Wedgwood Benn as the adjutant, the soldiers of the Middlesex Yeomanry marched for the first time into battle to the sound of a mouth-organ played by one of the troopers. In his book, *In the Side Shows*, Wedgwood Benn describes what happened:

'After about half-an-hour's progress we reached the enemy's shrapnel, through which, of course, we were bound to pass if we were to attain Chocolate Hill. As each line of the division advanced into the beaten zone, the shells did their part, being timed to burst just ahead of our march. Casualties began, but our orders were strict, and forbade us to stop for anyone. When men fell they had to be left for the stretcher parties which were following. As adjutant I was to and fro with Colonel "Scatters", who, though slightly injured in the foot, was marching in front of the line. Suddenly I saw with horror my troop hit by a shell and eight men go down. The rest were splendid. They simply continued to advance in the proper formation at a walk, and awaited the order, which did not come for another quarter-of-an-hour, before breaking into the double. Some men exhibited extraordinary calm. One NCO, observing a man drop his rations, bent and gathered them up for him, an act which just brought him in reach of a splinter which wounded him. Everyone was intensely excited, but all were bravely self-controlled.'[3]

That night, the 2nd Mounted Division were ordered to retreat and the following night they advanced again to re-capture the positions they had left twenty-four hours before. By that time, a third of the soldiers had been killed.

There were no further advances, and the survivors settled down as best they could to the discomfort of life in the trenches which Wedgwood Benn described:

'Dysentery was becoming common, and hundreds were being evacuated every day from the beach at Lala Baba. Jaundice too had appeared, due, no doubt, to intense fatigue and the complete breakdown, in consequence, of digestion. When we arrived on the Peninsula in August it was generally remarked that we were free at least from one of the plagues of Egypt, the flies; but by the end of September the pest had become so great that food could be eaten only with one hand. The other was required for defence. Myriads of beautiful large bronze-green creatures settled on everything, and it is hardly an exaggeration to say that if a piece of meat was uncovered to be cut there was scarcely room for the knife edge, so many were the flies that instantly settled on it.'[4]

A few weeks later, because he was suffering from jaundice, Wedgwood Benn, who refused to be evacuated, was relieved from his duties in the trenches and sent for a couple of days to the island of Imbros, nominally to obtain a cock and some hens so that the soldiers could have fresh eggs. While he waited for the boat, he wrote to his mother:

'I like soldiering, especially when there is plenty to do. You feel you are wanted, but for a long time now there has been inactivity, of which, of course, we get very tired. I couldn't do with soldiering for always – most of my fellow officers are so under-educated and narrow, and side by side with it they are so particular about absurd little things that don't really matter, the "rise, my lad" sort of spirit carried greatly to excess. They know nothing of books or music or pictures, nor have they any of the breadth of sympathies which constitute real education.'[5]

When he returned from Imbros, it was obvious that his jaundice had worsened, and so he was ordered by a doctor to leave on the hospital ship *Valdivia*, which was lying off the beach at Suvla. On board he had, for the first time in nearly three months, a hot bath and food that did not contain sand. But to his great disappointment the *Valdivia* did not sail for Egypt, as he had hoped, but for Malta on the way back to Britain. 'I saw myself suffering the humiliation', Wedgwood Benn later wrote, 'of being given the temporary rank of Major and appointed OC of a laundry at Putney!' So he cajoled and pleaded with the doctors until they agreed to allow him to land at Malta where he was sent to a convalescent camp. His ceaseless struggle to leave the island triumphed when, with an Australian padre, he obtained a passage in a West Indian fruit ship sailing to Port Said.

After he had arrived, he called on Major Fletcher, an old friend who was part of an Anglo-French flying mission and with whom Wedgwood Benn had flown while visiting Port Said the previous June. The major proposed that Wedgwood Benn should accompany him on a three-day trip on a seaplane carrier along the Palestine coast. Although there was nothing else for Wedgwood Benn to do, permission was refused and he was ordered to report to the Divisional Headquarters of his brigade which was temporarily based in a hotel under the shadow of the Great Pyramid at Mena, near Cairo. There he heard news of the successful evacuation of the Gallipoli Peninsula, and was informed that there was no immediate possibility of his regiment, which had lost two-thirds of its soldiers, being involved in further active service.

So he planned his escape. As he had been invited by Major Fletcher to join the seaplane squadron at Port Said, he applied to his Brigade Major for a transfer, but his request was received most unenthusiastically.

While he waited for a reply, he had plenty of spare time in which to explore Egypt and write letters home, including requests to friends in London that they should help secure his transfer to the air service which was then in its infancy and regarded by many, especially Naval officers, as having little wartime use.

In mid-April, he called on his general at El Shatt, opposite Suez, to inquire if there was news of his transfer. Hardly able to conceal his satisfaction, the general announced that the request would not be granted because Wedgwood Benn was too old and had already been trained as a Yeoman. Wedgwood Benn, however, was not dismayed. From out of his pocket he triumphantly produced a signal he had received from London that day ordering him to report for duty at Port Said without delay.

The next morning he arrived at the East India and Egypt Seaplane Station, which was little more than a ramshackle collection of sheds on an island in Port Said harbour. The seaplane carrier was the *Ben-my-Chree*, an Isle of Man passenger steamer on which had been built a hangar capable of housing four Short and two Sopwith seaplanes. Only the Shorts could carry passengers. There were also two cargo steamers, the *Anne* and *Raven II*, both of which had been captured from the Germans.

The atmosphere of the station suited Wedgwood Benn. Unlike the regiment he had just left, petty regulations were not made apparently for their own sake. The experimental nature of the work meant that initiative was required and encouraged. The dangers faced and the expertise required by all produced a welcome *esprit de corps*, even though the men came from different services, for the ships were manned by the Navy, the pilots were from the Royal Naval Air Service, and most of the observers, like Wedgwood Benn, came from the Army.

In May, shortly after Wedgwood Benn was posted there, Colonel Charles Samson took command of the station. The two men soon became close companions. In his war memoir, *Flights and Fights*, Samson states:

'I soon realized that in Benn I had found gold. He had a very keen brain, and a distinct flair for the organization of our intelligence into a quick and accurate system, whereby you could at a glance see the situation in Palestine, Syria, and the Red Sea, which of course altered from day to day. In addition, he shortly devised a service of intelligence boxes which could be got up to date within half an hour, and when any ship went to sea the box arrived on board complete, not only with the latest state of affairs, but replete with all the charts, documents, etc. required.'[6]

Samson's seaplanes undertook three types of mission in the Eastern Mediterranean: surveillance of the railway line from Aleppo to Beersheba, on which the Turks depended for their communications; aerial spotting to produce accurate shelling; and aerial reconnaissance of the Red Sea. Between May and December 1916, Wedgwood Benn's Flying Log Book records that he flew on forty-one different missions with Samson.

His correspondents at home continued to keep him well-informed about the constantly changing political situation. In June, the letters he received described the succession struggle that took place after the tragic death at sea of Earl Kitchener, the War Minister.

The appointment of Lloyd George as War Minister on 6 July resulted in a small reshuffle of Asquith's beleaguered Coalition Government. As Munitions Minister Lloyd George had been assisted by two Parliamentary Secretaries: Christopher Addison and Arthur Lee (later Viscount Lee of Fareham), whose official title was Parliamentary (Military) Secretary to the Munitions Department. When Edwin Montagu was made Munitions Minister in place of Lloyd George, Lee resigned. Early in September, Montagu contacted Wedgwood Benn to ask if he would return home to become Lee's replacement. Without hesitation, he declined the offer, for he was happy with his work and convinced that it was more valuable than anything he could do in Parliament.

On 6 October, Christopher Addison wrote to Wedgwood Benn, sympathizing with his decision. He said:

'I am afraid this place absorbs one's energies and thoughts so much that there is little time to keep in touch with "current politics", if there are any such things these days ... One's impression is that so far as constructive capacity and powers are concerned the House has worn a little threadbare during the last eighteen months.'[7]

In his lengthy reply, dated 10 November, Wedgwood Benn first criticized the absurdity of 'keeping huge armies idle for more or less purely defensive work', and stated that 'there is not enough ability at the head of these organizations to make use of the material under command'. He then went on to describe in detail the valuable work of both attack and reconnaissance undertaken by the seaplane squadron and how he had organized the intelligence work. 'The fundamental problem of flying has been solved,' he wrote, 'but now comes the whole question of the use of flying for military purposes.' He concluded by saying that, if the Ministry of Munitions could manufacture tanks, it should be able to undertake the more desirable task of building many, substantial aircraft.

Addison was obviously impressed by the letter, for on 24 November he sent a copy of it to Lloyd George stating that it was 'very useful and instructive'.[8]

When Wedgwood Benn's letter arrived, Lloyd George was preoccupied with his plan of engineering Asquith's political downfall. Addison, whom A.J.P. Taylor has called 'the real maker of the Lloyd George Government', had acted as an intermediary between Lloyd George and Bonar Law, both of whom on 20 November had met Edward Carson to discuss the idea that the three of them should form a committee to run the war. The proposal was put by Max Aitken (Lord Beaverbrook) into a memorandum that five days later Lloyd George presented to Asquith.

Wedgwood Benn soon heard that there were rumours of change. On 29 November his father wrote to him:

'I was waiting on Montagu to-day at the Ministry of Munitions on LCC business, and there was of course a reference to you. He said something about "something else turning up soon". I did not pursue the point. I merely report this to prepare you for some other wire on the same lines. You will know how to deal with it. I have every confidence in your judgment, but be careful not to hold your good self too cheaply.'[9]

On 1 December, Lloyd George threatened to resign if the proposal for a War Committee was not accepted. Asquith, as had become his wont, delayed making a decision, and four days later both Lloyd George and Bonar Law tendered their resignations. Knowing that he was no longer supported by a majority in the Commons, Asquith had no alternative but to resign himself. The following day, Lloyd George was asked to form a new Coalition Government.

Among the first appointments the new Prime Minister decided upon was

to make Wedgwood Benn the Government Whip in partnership with Lord
Edward Talbot, who had been the Conservatives' Chief Whip since 1912.
On 8 December, Wedgwood Benn received a telegram from Lloyd George
offering him the post. Not being sure of what was happening, he tele-
graphed his father and McKenna asking for their advice. McKenna replied:
'ASQUITH AND ALL HIS LATE LIBERAL COLLEAGUES ARE
ABSENT FROM NEW GOVERNMENT.'[10] His father wrote:

'Some thirty of our Liberals (?) have gathered round L.G. As you will
see not the pick of the bunch. Up to the present he has not captured any
Liberals of first rank. Naturally Dr Addison is his Munitions Minister,
and some of his Welsh pals are included.'[11]

Wedgwood Benn also received a telegram from the National Liberal Fed-
eration on 10 December: 'PARTY MEETING HELD TODAY UNAN-
IMOUSLY   CHOSE   ASQUITH   AS   PARTY   LEADER.
MCKENNA RUNCIMAN AND ALL OTHER EXMINISTERS
PRESENT.'
Wedgwood Benn was left with no doubts as to what he should do. On
10 December he telegraphed Lloyd George: 'DEEPLY GRATEFUL BUT
PREFER REMAIN HERE. GODSPEED NEW GOVERNMENT.' It was
a step that he was never to regret, and which Lloyd George was never to
forgive.
In a letter sent to his mother the next day, Wedgwood Benn gave the
reasons for his decision:

'Of course it was very exciting getting L.G.'s offer of Chief Whip. I didn't
suspect all that had happened, but I saw something about trying to
"oust" McKenna so I wired to ask him how he stood. The truth is I am
very happy here, and not at present greatly dazzled even by the things
that would have pleased me most a few years ago. I know I am doing
useful work & taking my share - at rare intervals - of war & I am not at
all sure that at home I should be doing any of these things. I feel so sorry
to see the persistent attacks on the House of Commons & so sorry to see
under war pressure so many things going under that I sympathize with.
    I have always hated the idea of being a civilian in khaki & have wanted
to do the job well alongside of anyone. Gradually in the air job I am
doing this & feel glad about it.'[12]

Wedgwood Benn was right in assuming that by not returning home he
would see far more action. On 7 January 1917, the *Ben-my-Chree* was
ordered to rendezvous with Admiral de Spitz, the French commander, at
Castelorizo, a small island lying between Rhodes and the Turkish coast

(only some thousand yards away) which offered protection to the inner harbour. The island was occupied and administered by French Naval Forces, but the local population of over 10,000 were Greeks, who by avoiding paying Turkish taxes or dues had become a prosperous trading community.

Arriving at Castelorizo on 9 January during a gale, the *Ben-my-Chree* was guided through the narrow channel into the harbour opposite the Turkish coast by a French pilot. Samson and Wedgwood Benn were invited to dine with the island's Governor at 4 p.m., but it was an appointment they did not keep. At 2.30 p.m., while he was resting in his cabin, Wedgwood Benn heard a loud explosion and saw a column of water shoot up some fifteen yards from the ship. He assumed it was an aeroplane attack, but then two further explosions followed and it was obvious that the ship was being shelled by a Turkish coastal battery. Rushing from his cabin, he found Samson giving orders to his men to return the fire. Just as Wedgwood Benn reached his commander, a shell hit the hangar which caught fire and soon huge scarlet flames and clouds of black smoke were shooting into the sky. The fire was instantly too intense to be brought under control. The Turks, having found the exact range, hit the ship with further shells, one of which ignited the petrol store.

The fire, heat and fumes made it impossible to stay in the engine-room and Samson ordered the crew to shelter on the port side amidships while the injured were evacuated. Seven or eight 6-inch shells continued to hit the ship every minute. As Samson and Wedgwood Benn were standing on the upper deck a shell hit the whaler directly over their heads, leaving only a plank dangling from one davit. Meanwhile all the other ships in the harbour, including the Admiral's yacht, rushed out to sea, dodging the explosions.

At 2.45 p.m. the order was given to abandon ship. As the men either swam to the shore or were taken in the motor boats to the quay, Wedgwood Benn searched the engine-room to ensure that nobody had been left behind. Within an hour, despite the continuous bombardment, the evacuation was complete. A count of the crew on shore revealed that one of the pilots was missing. With a couple of volunteers, Wedgwood Benn went in a motor boat to search for him, both on the fiercely burning ship, where the bombs in store were constantly exploding, and in the harbour, which was being heavily shelled by the Turks. Having found no trace of the missing pilot, he took the boat back to the quay where he was told that the man for whom he had searched had swum ashore further up the coast.

It was later estimated that over a thousand shells were fired by the Turks. As an invasion of the island seemed imminent, the inhabitants fled to the hills. While Samson took the majority of the crew to an inland monastery, Wedgwood Benn was ordered to take a small party of men to help defend the town. Shortly afterwards, the Governor, Monsieur de Saint Salvy, invited him also to take command of the French troops, which he then set off to gather together, armed with the order:

'Pour toutes les dispositions de combat et de resistance vous êtes placés sous les ordres de l'officier Anglais.'

In the pouring rain, the force of seventeen from the *Ben-my-Chree* and forty-six French sailors gathered in a tiny whitewashed church. From there Wedgwood Benn organized a roster of sentries and then set off on a tour of inspection.

For eleven days, he was 'Commandant le Détachement Franco-Britannique du Cimetière Turc, Castelorizo'. He and his troops were in sole control of the town and its defences. Despite the constant bombardment, he thoroughly enjoyed his task, insisting that the British sailors, in addition to their sentry duties, attended the daily French lessons he gave. Because of this and the obvious ability he had to command in an emergency the men got on well with each other and appeared to enjoy the experience as much as he did. When at length he held his last parade, before marching the British sailors over the mountains to be evacuated on the other side of the island, the French troops and the Governor embraced him in a noisy, tearful farewell.

For his bravery after the *Ben-my-Chree* had been attacked, Wedgwood Benn was awarded several honours. He was mentioned in both an Admiralty Dispatch ('He went away in a boat to search for men who were missing and was exposed to very heavy shell fire.') and a French Admiralty Dispatch ('Having landed from the *Ben-my-Chree*, which was in flames, he contributed with great vigour to the defence of the island.'). Later he was awarded the Distinguished Service Order and, by the French Government, the Croix de Guerre and the Légion d'honneur.

Back in Port Said, it appeared certain that the seaplane squadron would not be reformed, and so, as he had been overseas for nearly two years, Wedgwood Benn applied for and was granted home leave. With many other crew members from the *Ben-my-Chree*, he arrived back in Britain in mid-February.

His reunion with his parents was joyous, although he was saddened to observe that his father, who had always looked much younger than his years, had clearly been weakened by a prolonged illness. His visits to the House of Commons confirmed his conviction that his war service was more useful than being a Member of Parliament. So, when he was asked by Lloyd George if he were willing to join the Government, he again declined. Afterwards he wrote:

'My dear Prime Minister,

I hope you will not be angry with me & I need not tell you how much I thank you. But when the war broke out I resigned my office because at my age & with my health it was unendurable not to be in the fighting line. Then there were 5 Benns of my generation & now only 2 remain. I know that reason won't appeal in vain to you.

You have shown that there is but one thing worth doing & in my little corner I shall strive unceasingly for you & every minute wish you victory.'[13]

It was the development of air power, rather than party politics, that had become Wedgwood Benn's wartime obsession. He wrote to Lord Curzon, who was the Chairman of the Air Board, asking for an interview. When he visited Curzon at his home in Carlton House Terrace he was surprised and gratified to discover that Curzon, although apparently understanding little about aeroplanes, seemed to know all about Wedgwood Benn's work in Parliament. Years later the man who had been Curzon's private secretary told Wedgwood Benn that when his letter had been received Curzon had asked, 'Who the devil is this fellow Benn?' and had then been briefed by his secretary. More successfully, Wedgwood Benn spent several weeks visiting aerodromes and aeroplane factories, learning all he could about the manufacture and use of aircraft.

Among the people he met was Commodore Murray Sueter, who was gathering a staff to form the Adriatic Barrage, an air defence against submarines. Wedgwood Benn was persuaded to join, but he insisted that first he should qualify as a pilot. This Sueter accepted, providing the coveted 'wings' were obtained by the end of July. So, aged almost forty, Wedgwood Benn tried to obtain permission to begin his training. After a considerable amount of correspondence, he went to see Major General Sir Godfrey Paine at the Air Ministry, who immediately gave his consent and arranged for Wedgwood Benn to be posted to Calshot Air Station.

Wedgwood Benn was not the best of trainees, unfortunately damaging no less than five machines. But by mid-July he had flown 129 flights lasting in all 59 hours 25 minutes, of which 20 hours were flown solo. On 15 July he was awarded his flying brevet and, after a short leave, set sail from Southampton to join Commodore Sueter in Italy.

So well liked had Wedgwood Benn been by his instructors and fellow trainees at Calshot that they arranged a spectacular send-off for him in the Solent. When his ship sailed by, they sent up showers of Verey lights and from a picket boat bellowed farewells through a megaphone – much to Wedgwood Benn's embarrassment and his fellow passengers' amusement.

He arrived at Taranto in Southern Italy on 9 August and began his anti-submarine flying duties. As usual he worked hard at learning the local language. Unfortunately his Italian studies and his flying were soon interrupted, because in September he caught malaria, which was then endemic in the area. He was sent on leave to Rome, but there became worse and was taken to the Calvary Hospital at Monte Celio where under the kindly care of the Blue Nuns he began to recover. But when he returned to his squadron it was clear that he was still unwell and so he was sent back to England.

At home he heard that it had been proposed that his constituency of St George's in the East was to be joined to Whitechapel. The seat that both he and his father had held for so long would cease to exist, and as Whitechapel already had a Liberal Member there was every chance that at the next election he would not be returned. There was, however, nothing he could do for, following the news of the Italian retreat at Caporetto, he was posted as an observer with the new air force wing then being formed to work with other British troops in support of the Italians against the Austrian invasion.

Although extremely anxious about his parliamentary future, Wedgwood Benn happily returned to Italy, determined to keep on fighting. To Ernest, his brother, he wrote:

'I have definitely taken on this war job. The end of it is not in sight. I have made a definite interest of it & am trying to cover the ground thoroughly. It has a small political & also commercial value, i.e. to know the air. The real reason I want to stay till the end is I hate leaving a job half done & chiefly I am most unhappy at home with a war going on.'[14]

For the next ten months he was to remain in Northern Italy, serving as an observer and intelligence officer. His enjoyment of the demanding, exciting routine of front-line air-service was marred only by nagging doubts about whether he would be able to return to Parliament after the war. His father and brother had promised to look after his interests, but on 17 February 1918, after visiting the House of Commons to discuss with various people how his son would be affected by the amalgamation of the two constituencies, John Benn caught pneumonia and for a time it was feared that he might die. Fortunately he recovered, but as his health was permanently undermined he had to resign from the leadership of the Progressive Party on the LCC. There is no doubt that John Benn was deeply troubled that the son he loved so deeply seemed likely, despite his heroic war service, to lose his parliamentary seat.

Distressed as he was by the news, there was little that Wedgwood Benn could do about it, stationed as he was in Italy. Once his father had recovered, there was no point in returning home, as he wrote on 8 March to his brother:

'Of course I could apply instantly for leave for reasons of father's health or family danger. But for political reasons it comes to this. One fortnight in London is of little value unless there is a special objective. *Yes* to meet an executive or do a campaign arrangement beforehand. But to come home sketchily for 2 weeks isn't any use and moreover can't be done till it is my turn. That is quite serious. It can't be done.'[15]

Although he did not return home, Wedgwood Benn did, as part of his duties, travel through much of Italy. After the Royal Air Force had been created on 1 April 1918, he was given the task of co-ordinating in Italy the work of the Royal Naval Air Service and the Royal Flying Corps. So he was able, to his delight, to visit most of the main towns throughout the country for which he felt a great affinity. Escaping the restricting supervision of military transport officers at railway stations, he explored the churches, castles and buildings in every place he visited.

Wedgwood Benn's most exciting mission took place in the summer of 1918 after nearly two months' preparation. With the Italian Army he organized the first successful parachute drop of a spy behind enemy lines. As his pilot he selected Colonel Barker, the Canadian air-ace who was soon after awarded the Victoria Cross to add to his Distinguished Service Order and his three Military Crosses. Together they chose the plane, a twin engine SP4 with three seats, one behind another. After much experiment, they devised an apparatus for holding the parachute under the plane and a hinged trap-door through which the parachutist could be released. So novel was the idea that the parachute had to be brought from England by an instructor who taught Wedgwood Benn and Barker how it was folded. Wedgwood Benn had also to find a way of navigating in complete darkness, and after several trials perfected a system of using fixed searchlights on the ground that he directed by wireless from the aircraft.

On the night of 9 August, just before a storm began, he and Barker set off with their passenger, Lieutenant Alessandro Tandura, with his knapsack containing his civilian clothes. As they flew through the lightning, Wedgwood Benn's navigational system worked perfectly, and eventually they reached Vittorio, which was Tandura's home town and the agreed dropping place. In his book, *In the Side Shows*, Wedgwood Benn describes what happened:

'The searchlights have begun to look for us and they could hardly have failed to know we were there, for we might have awakened the dead with the terrible rumble of those two engines. Barker is to make a signal to me with his foot when he is ready. I sit down on the two bombs, with my hand on the thick ash handle which by means of a long wire controls the bolt under Tandura's seat. Barker slightly stalls the machine, the foot

69

presses, I pull, and wait. No jerk, no apparent result. The bolts have stuck! I pull again. The wire slacks with a rush, the machine shivers and resumes its course. I peep hurriedly through the floor, and imagine I catch a glimpse of a small black sphere flying past us, but that is all. That is the consummation of two months of hard work. For good or ill, Tandura is gone.'[16]

Afterwards the plane turned for home where it landed safely.

When the war was over, Wedgwood Benn heard that Tandura had survived his parachute jump and, despite twice being captured by the Austrians, was able to send by carrier pigeon much valuable information to his commanders. Later he married his childhood sweetheart and their first son was named Wedgwood Benn Tandura.

For organizing the parachute drop of Tandura, Wedgwood Benn was awarded the Distinguished Flying Cross, the citation referring to him as 'a gallant observer of exceptional ability who at all times set a splendid example of courage'. He was also decorated by the Italian Government which, in awarding him the Bronze Medal for Military Valour, called him 'an aviator of the greatest skill and courage'.

Throughout the two months of preparation for the Tandura mission, he had been receiving messages from home pleading with him to return so that he could find a parliamentary constituency to contest, for with the end of the war in sight an early General Election seemed possible. His father, for example, had written:

'My own view is that we may have an election before the end of the year. It is sad to find that the same old feeling of bitterness remains among your - our - old friends as to L.G. They are annoyed that he should have lasted so long and that all their prophecies are wrong. They still fancy that cheers in the House for Asquith - and he does remarkably well - represent the echo of the voice of the country. It is not so. If they stick to their present vendetta the bulk of them won't come back.'[17]

It was to prove the most accurate of prophecies.

After Tandura had been landed, Wedgwood Benn, deciding to heed his friends' advice, applied for leave, which was readily granted, and in early September returned home.

Captain Wedgwood Benn, DSO, DFC, MP, was welcomed by his family, friends, and the press as a hero. His war service had been exemplary, proving considerable personal courage and tenacity. His organizational ability, his decisiveness, and his perception had been widely recognized and applauded. He took home with him masses of notes on places and people he had visited throughout Italy and the Middle East, which would later prove to be invaluable. His expertise as a pioneer aviator and his knowledge of air warfare were considerable.

There were for him other, less obvious, but permanent results of the war. The malaria he had caught in Italy would recur throughout his life. The hideousness of the flies that had swarmed everywhere in the Gallipoli trenches would for ever haunt him, so that years later a fly landing on his food would instantly make him nauseated.

More importantly, the war had made him question many of his attitudes. No longer could he accept that the political figures he had so much admired in his youth were above reproach and could do no wrong. Even though he had witnessed incredible acts of individual heroism, he could not accept that war was glorious. In his memoirs, *In the Side Shows*, he states:

'Soldiers know from bitter experience what militarism really means; its stupidity, its brutality, its waste. They are chivalrous because they have learned the one good thing that war teaches, namely, that peril shared knits hearts together – yes, even between enemies. They have mingled with strangers. They know that common folk the world over love peace and in the main desire good will.'[18]

Having observed the pettiness and incompetence of officers who too often strove to accomplish nothing more than the destruction of their soldiers' individuality, he did not accept that there was an inherent right of members from one social class to rule over all others. So, after returning home, he wrote:

'The belief that one stock is born to command, another to obey is the real secret of the struggle to preserve commissions in all forces for the upper classes. The fort is not held by any open means; there are no regulations to say that none but the privileged class is permitted to enter; the existence of social barriers is denied; but those who have been on the inside know perfectly well that the gate is strictly kept and that the inner ward is the insurmountable inertia against which the unfavoured candidate throws himself in vain.'[19]

His knowledge of the unfairness inflicted upon society by the class system, and his disillusionment with the political figures who had once been his heroes meant that Wedgwood Benn was not content to be no more than a loyal and hard-working member of the disarranged and discredited Liberal Party. So, he put principles before expediency, and beliefs before promotion. Such a radical approach meant that, even though his military war was over, many fierce political battles inevitably lay ahead.

IV 1918-1922

When Wedgwood Benn returned home in 1918, he found much had changed. His father, who had been created a Baronet in 1914, though still most astute and politically aware, had deteriorated physically. The house at Blackheath had been sold and his parents had moved to Limpsfield. His brother, Ernest, despite having worked voluntarily at the Ministry of Munitions, had, as managing director, built up Benn Brothers into a very profitable and expanding publishing company. As a result, Wedgwood Benn's shares in the family firm were producing very satisfactory and welcome dividends.

Politically, the Coalition Government had produced an uncertainty about party identification that contrasted greatly with the clear-cut divisions that had existed between the Liberals and the Unionists when Wedgwood Benn was first elected to Parliament in 1906. Because of the war, MPs could find themselves more in agreement with their former political enemies than with members of the same party. Some Liberals continued to support Asquith rather than Lloyd George. The Labour Party was split between pacifists and those who supported the Coalition. For the Conservatives, the major difference was between those who wanted to use Lloyd George and those who wanted to reject him. The party political situation was made worse both by the virtual collapse during the war of the organization of all three parties and by the extent of the powers assumed by the Prime Minister.

Having built a secure base on the interrelated groups that had most benefited from the war – bankers, press-lords, self-made industrialists and his own close political allies – Lloyd George was determined as the end of the war approached that his premiership would continue. With no political organization of his own, he had to rely on the considerable electoral advantages of being the victorious leader and of having the Conservatives' support. Growing increasingly autocratic, he determined that in the next election those who had opposed him would be defeated. It mattered not whether they were fellow Liberals; indeed, such was the animosity he felt towards Asquith's supporters that they were regarded as his chief opponents. For Lloyd George, the test of an MP's loyalty to him became largely based on whether he had supported or opposed Asquith's motion on 9 May 1918 that there should be an inquiry into a claim made by Sir Frederick Maurice that the Prime Minister had misled the House about the strength of the Army.

Wedgwood Benn was, of course, abroad when the Maurice debate took place, but his refusal to join the Coalition Government had made him suspect in Lloyd George's eyes. So when the Prime Minister entered into secret negotiations with Bonar Law, the leader of the Conservatives, about fighting the next election as a coalition, Wedgwood Benn's name was not included in the lists of either 114 definite or forty-four possible supporters that Freddie Guest drew up on 20 July. Quite a number of these would have to be found new constituencies, for, as with Wedgwood Benn, the ones they represented would cease to exist at the next election, following the passing of the Parliamentary Reform Act in June 1918, which in addition to the boundary changes extended the vote to include some women and increased the national electorate from 8,250,000 to 21,000,000.

When Wedgwood Benn arrived in Britain, neither the General Election nor the arrangements for the Coalition had been announced and he had considerable hopes that he would be able to obtain the local Liberal Party association's nomination for the constituency of Whitechapel, with which St George's was to be combined. The sitting member there, James Kiley, had a year previously sent a letter to the Whitechapel Liberal Association saying that he would stand down at the next election and support Wedgwood Benn's candidature. So, with some confidence, Wedgwood Benn called a joint meeting of the selection committee of the two old constituencies at St George's Town Hall, Cable Street, on 18 September 1918. Although Kiley's name was not put forward as an alternative, the committee by a small majority rejected the motion that Wedgwood Benn should be accepted as the Liberal candidate.

Wedgwood Benn, who had gone to the meeting with Ernest, was naturally shocked by a decision he found to be unexpected and incomprehensible. Full of enthusiasm and proud of his war service, he had miscalculated the mood of the committee members, most of whom had been elected during his absence and had seen far less of him than they had of Kiley. Having not taken the time to woo them, Wedgwood Benn was summarily rejected. Disconsolately the two brothers left the meeting and walked along Cable Street, Commercial Street and Old Street to the family firm's offices in Finsbury Square where, dispirited, they spent a disturbed night on the floor.

The following morning, Wedgwood Benn decided that he would not leave the matter in the hands of the joint committee, but would appeal directly to the electors. He prepared a short address, stating that he wanted to continue representing the area, and sent a copy with a stamped self-addressed postcard to every elector. The replies he received were encouraging and so, in order to live in the constituency (for Gladstone House had been surrendered as an economy during the war), he obtained a room at Toynbee Hall, the centre for East End working men.

Then, on 7 November, Kiley wrote to him:

'Last week I was waited on by a Deputation who asked that I should allow my name to be submitted as the prospective Liberal Candidate, and I asked for time to consider the matter. At a Meeting held last night I agreed to my name being submitted and after the discussion, with only one objecting, I was invited to contest the Division, which invitation I accepted.

Should you also decide to stand for the Constituency, as I understand you may do, I assure you that as far as I am concerned I will endeavour to keep personalities out of the Election, and hope you will see your way to do the same.'[1]

As Kiley was, like him, a Liberal, a supporter of Asquith and a Free Trader, Wedgwood Benn knew that it was impossible to stand against him.

That evening he went to a dinner party at the home in Smith Square of the McKennas. Understandably able to think only of his situation, he discussed it with several of his fellow guests. One of them, Augustine Birrell, who between 1908 and 1915 had been Chief Secretary for Ireland, listened carefully and then said, 'Well, my advice is: Do the high sublime!'

Wedgwood Benn thought about the advice and the next day wrote to Kiley:

'We are both fighting for the same cause, we both want to win, we both face great difficulties, and we will both be fighting against Lloyd George's Coalition. What I propose to do is to hand over to you, if you will take them as a gift, my organization, my committee rooms, my canvass cards, and, if he is willing, the services of my agent. I wish you luck and will give you any help I can.'[2]

It was a noble, selfless act that ended, after nearly seventy years, the Benn family's active involvement in the life and problems of St George's in the East.

It was not, however, the end of Wedgwood Benn's political ambitions, and so he went to see Freddie Guest, the Coalition Chief Whip with whom before the war he had been on the friendliest of terms. Guest spelt out the arrangements that would be made for each candidate approved by Lloyd George to be given a coupon of endorsement. All that was required was a general assurance that the Prime Minister would be supported and no difficulties created. It was then pointed out that if Wedgwood Benn accepted the coupon, he could contest Whitechapel for the Coalition and would almost certainly be elected. But the whole idea of a nominated Parliament was unacceptable to him, and so he determined to fight against it, the Coalition, and Lloyd George. In doing so, he knew he would be supporting what he saw as the real tenets of Liberalism and the leaders he respected, including Asquith and McKenna.

Though he had a cause to fight, when on 14 November Bonar Law, as the Leader of the House, announced that Polling Day would take place in a month's time, Wedgwood Benn still did not have a seat to contest. Nor did it seem likely that he would obtain one, for the Asquithian Liberals, being opposed to the Coalition, were thrown into disarray by the election. With a severely weakened organization, that was as divided as the Party in Parliament, local Liberal associations had to decide whether to support the Coalition candidate, who might be a Conservative, or nominate an independent Liberal to contest the election. The latter option would mean in some seats that there would be two Liberal candidates, one supporting and the other opposing the Coalition.

As the election campaign gathered momentum, the prevailing theme became one of strident nationalism. Even Lloyd George, who at first endeavoured to remain aloof, proclaimed that the Germans would be made to pay for the war to the last farthing and that 'we shall search their pockets for it'.

Yet, although such demands attracted much approval, the war-weary electorate was far from unanimous in its support of the Coalition. On 25 November, Cecil Harmsworth wrote to Lloyd George:

'I was down in my constituency on Saturday and I found an intensely bitter feeling about the ousting of Liberal Members, like H.J. Craig of Tynemouth and Wedgwood Benn, in favour of Conservative candidates. I have been through five contests and I have never had before so difficult a time with my own political friends. The belief seems to be that the Conservative wirepullers have had very much the best of the deal. I am afraid that the resentment that has been excited will recoil on you, especially as the conviction is that you could smooth over some of these difficulties by arrangement with the leaders of the Conservative Party.'[3]

On 28 November, the British Weekly stated:

'Men in whom we have the fullest confidence have been put into difficulties about their seats. These may possibly be corrected, and we hope they will. The feeling is strong that a preference should be given to men like Captain Wedgwood Benn who have gallantly fought their country's battle.'[4]

By the time that edition of the British Weekly was published, Wedgwood Benn had accepted the invitation of the Leith Liberal Party Executive to contest the constituency which had been held since 1914 by G.W. Currie, the first Conservative ever to be returned by the burgh. Currie had been given Lloyd George's coupon, but, as his majority had been only sixteen, it seemed possible that Leith could be won by an Independent Liberal.

The news that Wedgwood Benn was to stand as an anti-Coalition candidate was widely acclaimed. On 29 November, the *Edinburgh Evening News* reported:

'Captain Wedgwood Benn will be a most acceptable candidate ... He will secure in Leith great political honours, just as he has won worthy military honours against the common enemy. In short, Liberalism is going to return to its own in Leith, and the party will win "hands down". Mr Currie and his friends can order their political funeral cards ... Captain Benn ... is standing as an out-and-out Radical.'[5]

He felt very much at home in Leith, which with its docks and working-class housing was not too unlike his beloved St George's. Fortunately he found in Leith an efficient local party organization that responded readily to his enthusiasm and determination. Even more importantly, the inhabitants of the ancient Scottish burgh, then threatened with amalgamation with Edinburgh, loved independence and were thus attracted both to Wedgwood Benn and his anti-Coalition stand.

When the polls closed on 14 December, Wedgwood Benn and his supporters knew that they had fought as well as they could to win the seat, but they could not be confident of victory. The declaration of the results was delayed in all constituencies to enable the votes of servicemen away from home to be included. During this waiting period, Wedgwood Benn could not help but feel concerned, for as the national campaign had reached its climax it had been obvious that, despite much public apathy, it was the Coalition that had attracted the greatest support.

On 24 December, it was announced that Asquith had been defeated by 2002 votes in East Fife, the constituency he had represented for thirty-two years. Among the many other Liberals rejected by the electorate were Herbert Samuel, McKinnon Wood, and Runciman.

Both Wedgwood Benn in Leith and his parents in Torquay heard the long list of Liberal defeats, until they received the result for which they had waited:

W.W. Benn (Liberal)	10,338
G.W. Currie (Coalition Tory)	7613
S. Burgess (Labour)	4251

It was a spectacular, resounding victory that obviously went against the national tide of support that had so convincingly swept Lloyd George back into power.

In the lowest percentage poll over recorded at a General Election (58.9 per cent), the Coalition obtained a massive majority, winning 478 seats (335

Tories, 133 Liberals and 10 Labour) out of 707. With sixty-three Members, the Labour Party, despite the defeats of MacDonald and Snowden, became the official Opposition and for the first time could be seen as an alternative Government. The Irish Nationalist Party, having won only seven seats, was destroyed as a political force, for seventy-three of the Irish seats had been won by Sinn Fein, although its Members, including Countess Marciewicz, the first woman elected to Parliament, refused to attend the House of Commons.

The independent Liberal Party had been all but annihilated, with every one of its leaders being defeated. It has been variously estimated that between twenty-six and thirty-three non-Coalition Liberals were elected, but several of these either were or soon became supporters of Lloyd George. *The Times* reckoned that only fourteen MPs were loyal to Asquith. Of these, only Francis Acland, George Lambert, and Wedgwood Benn had obtained any Ministerial experience. Little wonder then that John Benn wrote to his son on 29 December:

'The disastrous figures came rolling in, and we had all given up hope of your winning when your delightful wire arrived! It was just "heaven" to both of us. And you deserve all the credit. You took the straight and narrow road of your own free will ... I've been looking this morning at the Asquithian survivors, and, as far as I can see, the front bench will be you, Maclean, and G. Lambert. Out of these a leader must be selected – why not you? ... Please – *no more whipping for your Party*. Take the place for which you are so well equipped – Leader or watch dog on the front bench ... Don't be pushed out of your heritage. It is with God's blessing – the Chance of your life ...

You have a fine standing with Labour and Irish MPs. You will "go" for the Tories without losing their admiration or their respect. What impertinence of your proud old father to advise such a pastmaster in politics!'[6]

Three days later, on 1 January 1919, Wedgwood Benn's father wrote again in a similar vein:

'What occurs to me for the moment is – You must return to London at the earliest moment. You must be the central figure in the organization or future of the "Liberal Wee Frees" (a title of mine own invention!). There is an attempt on the part of the Coalie Libs to pretend they still belong to the N[ational] L[iberal] Party and they want control of the funds etc. etc. Organization in Leith can wait for a bit, but your seizure of your present party advantages will not wait. Further there ought to be an early meeting of the Free Libs. – they are looking for guidance and a Leader. You must appoint your whips & not be one yourself.'[7]

'Wee Frees', the name Sir John Benn selected for the independent Liberals, was an appropriate one, for it had earlier been given to a small group of Free Church of Scotland members who, refusing to accept the union of their church with the United Presbyterian Church, under the name of the United Free Church of Scotland, had claimed the church funds and the right to remain independent.

As his father had advised, Wedgwood Benn returned immediately to London, but once there he was left in no doubt as to how difficult it would be to preserve an independent Liberal Party in the House of Commons. In a letter Freddie Guest sent to Lloyd George on 30 December 1918, only four MPs apart from Wedgwood Benn were listed as being definitely hostile to Lloyd George. They were Glanville, Arnold, Hogge, and Maclean. Of the defeated independent Liberal candidates, some had already decided to move either to the Tory or the Labour Party, while others, including McKenna, would shortly leave politics altogether.

The major decision the Wee Frees and their remaining supporters had to make was who should lead the Party in Parliament, following Asquith's defeat. McKenna was convinced that Asquith should resign, but conceded in a letter to Runciman on 4 January 1919, 'The old man is stoical to the point of indifference, but he hasn't the slightest intention to resign.'[8] Yet, despite his apparent apathy, Asquith, fearing that he might unceremoniously be dethroned, acted quickly, appointing Sir Donald Maclean as 'sessional chairman' until he was re-elected. As Asquith's return to Parliament at an early by-election seemed certain, Maclean's position was endorsed by the twenty-three Liberal MPs who met for the first meeting of the Wee Frees on 3 February. But when Asquith nominated George Thorne as Chief Whip, the Wee Frees refused to accept. Wedgwood Benn declined the post, and so his colleagues insisted that Thorne should hold it jointly with Hogge, whom Asquith thought was unsuitable. Thus the Wee Frees served notice on their absent leader that his decisions were not automatically going to be accepted.

As the group's organizer, Wedgwood Benn arranged that its members would have weekly meetings, for he was well aware that, although they were bound by a common distrust of Lloyd George, they did not all share his radical views and for them to be effective in the Commons they needed to speak with a common voice.

Lloyd George's impressive electoral endorsement meant that there would be a continuation of the almost presidential status he had assumed during the latter part of he war, so that there would be far less political activity in Parliament than before 1914. What opposition there was to the Government came from the fledgling Labour Party and the Wee Frees. Wedgwood Benn rapidly established himself as the effective spokesman of this opposition.

On 12 February, for example, he proposed a motion of no confidence in the air policy of Churchill, who had been given the joint appointment of Secretary of State for both Air and War. Wedgwood Benn was also the spokesman of those opposing the unification of the Liberal Party under Lloyd George. In a private memo to the Prime Minister, dated 13 March, Freddie Guest referred to 'the evident fact that the Independent Liberals (inspired by Hogge and Benn) would not accept *any* terms of reunion'.

The confidence and status of the Wee Frees were greatly increased in the spring of 1919 by three by-election victories at the expense of the Coalition Unionists. In one of these, J.M. Kenworthy won Hull Central with a swing of 22.9 per cent.

Feeling that these victories presaged a revival of Liberalism, Wedgwood Benn seized every opportunity to attack the Government. As one of the most frequent attenders and most regular speakers in the House of Commons, he became one of the best-known MPs, universally respected not only for his war record but for his acumen, sincerity and wit. He revelled in having opportunities to present his views and oppose the Government's errors. Yet he was not willing to use his fame for personal advancement, even though the lack of leadership in the Liberal Party precented an opening. But by keeping the independent Liberal opposition to Lloyd George alive he was largely instrumental in preventing the Prime Minister either assuming or being given the leadership of the Liberal Party. This would ultimately contribute greatly to Lloyd George's downfall, for deprived of his own political base he had to rely on the Tories' self-interested political support.

As his political and parliamentary reputation grew, Wedgwood Benn determined to increase his efficiency and efficacy by fully organizing both his papers and his time. Since first entering Parliament in 1906 he had kept a job-book in which he had entered his general objectives for the year; but having read a book by Arnold Bennett entitled *How to Live on 24 Hours a Day* he decided, from the beginning of 1920, to keep a daily record of how each of the twenty-four hours had been spent, whether in work or rest. He also decided to reorganize the considerable number of files he had amassed on all topics that interested him. To solve the problem of quick retrieval, he devised his own system of classification. Using this, he was able to file all his papers and the newspaper cuttings he pasted daily onto uniform sheets of paper that had more often than not been already used, for his early experience had made him most reluctant to waste money. He also filed any quotation he thought might be useful in a speech. All this organizational work was to be continued throughout his life, ensuring that he was always a most knowledgeable politician.

In addition to his desire to make the best possible use of his time, he had a very good reason for arranging his files. Early in 1920, Sir John McCallum, the independent Liberal MP for Paisley, died. Although the majority in the 1918 election had been only 106, Paisley was obviously a good seat for Asquith to contest. Faced with an ultimatum from the Wee Frees that if he did not stand he would be repudiated as the Leader of the Liberal Party, Asquith agreed to be nominated and on 21 January the Paisley Liberal Association selected him as their candidate. The National Liberal Federation, excited by the news, made preparations for the imminent return to Parliament of the Party's leader. Wedgwood Benn, as organizer of the Wee Frees, was given an office and a secretarial staff at 102 Parliament Street. Throughout the previous year he had prepared background papers for the Wee Frees, but he now undertook to produce daily for all the independent Liberal MPs an abstract of newspaper articles and official papers. In doing this, he made much use of his own files, which were kept in his office at Parliament Street, and on which his secretarial staff worked. One of these was a young radical ex-teacher and writer, called Victor Gollancz, who a year later would, with Wedgwood Benn's introduction, be given a job by Ernest with Benn Brothers and would thus be launched on his publishing career.

Not having a home of his own, Wedgwood Benn spent most of his time either at his office or in the Commons. When Parliament was sitting he stayed at the National Liberal Club, returning most weekends to his parents' home at Limpsfield. His life revolved around his political activities and his chosen task of ensuring the continuation of the Liberal Party's radical tradition.

On 27 January, Asquith with his wife, his daughter Violet, and Vivian Phillipps, his secretary, arrived in Glasgow where they installed themselves in the Central Station Hotel and began an election campaign that naturally attracted much attention in the press. A few days later, the two politicians Asquith had invited to help him joined the family. They were Lord Buckmaster, the Lord Chancellor in Asquith's wartime Coalition Government, and Wedgwood Benn.

On 26 February it was announced that Asquith had been elected with a majority of 2834 over the Labour candidate. The Coalition Unionist was humiliatingly defeated and forfeited his deposit. Wedgwood Benn and his fellow independent Liberals were naturally delighted by their leader's return to Parliament, which they saw as the dawn of a new political era. Asquith's victory was extremely popular and on the day he took his seat a great crowd gathered and cheered him enthusiastically. Inside the House, however, his small band of followers could do little to take the chill off the reception he was given by the massed ranks of the Coalition.

With Asquith back in Parliament, Wedgwood Benn with even greater determination worked in the Commons and on the organization of his fellow independent Liberals. With the regular attendance of Asquith, the Wee Frees' weekly meetings that Wedgwood Benn arranged became important political occasions attended by sympathizers and guests, as well as MPS.

In the Commons, Wedgwood Benn was in the forefront of the attacks made jointly by the Labour Party and the independent Liberals on Lloyd George's proposed solution to the growing unrest in Ireland. Determined to establish a province of Ulster and thus impose its own solution on the Irish people, the British Government recruited from the unemployed ex-servicemen a military division of the Royal Irish Constabulary which, because of the uniforms worn, became known as the Black and Tans. Their ruthless brutality, which the Irish Republican Army reciprocated, was meant to affirm the Government's determination to quash any rebellion. Early in February, Wedgwood Benn made an impassioned attack on the extension of the Defence of the Realm Act to Ireland for a year after the conclusion of peace. On 16 February he said:

'Step by step with this repressive administration in Ireland there have been outrages or crimes. Every step which the Government, as represented by the Irish Administration, has taken to put down liberties in Ireland has been followed by further outbreaks of crime in that country, and those who deplore and condemn, as we do, outrages in Ireland desire to see the Administration of Ireland altered in order that the outrages may come to an end.'

Unbowed by inevitable accusations of supporting terrorism, he sustained throughout the parliamentary session his outspoken criticism of the Government's Irish policy. With a fervent faith in his cause and unquenchable energy, he stood his ground and proclaimed his view so authoritatively that he became the real spokesman of the independent Liberals and a figure as much in the public eye as fifty years later his son, Tony Benn, was to become.

Despite the pressures created by his parliamentary work, Wedgwood Benn frequently visited his constituency, for he knew well how necessary it was not to be an absentee Member. As a Scottish MP he also did what he could to help any independent Liberal candidate fighting a by-election in Scotland. So in April, he worked in the North Edinburgh constituency, helping his old friend, Daniel Turner Holmes, who having refused to accept Lloyd George's coupon had been defeated at Govan in the 1918 election. Naturally Wedgwood Benn met again Holmes' daughter, Margaret, who in the years since he last had seen her had grown from the girl with flaxen pigtails into a most personable, intelligent and sparkling young woman. Aged twenty-three, she shared her parents' commitment to radicalism and was naturally delighted to meet the popular hero of independent Liberalism, whom she had so much admired when first she had seen him eight years earlier. Wedgwood Benn, always a romantic at heart, was equally pleased by the reunion and was instantly much attracted to Margaret, who so obviously shared his interests and concerns. Although never spending any time alone together, the two saw a good deal of each other during the campaign.

After his defeat at the by-election, Holmes with his wife and daughters went to live at Seaford, a seaside resort on the south coast near Brighton. Shortly afterwards he received a letter from Wedgwood Benn saying that he would be visiting the area while on a bicycling tour with his nephew and asking if it would be convenient for him to call. Delighted at the opportunity of seeing again an old friend, Holmes readily agreed. It was, however, Margaret whom Wedgwood Benn really wanted to see, and she has described what happened:

'So it was arranged and he came with his nephew. Then he asked us to tea at the House of Commons and we went. After that there were just one or two engagements that he made for us and we met, but always with my family. Then one day he was very brave and asked me to go to the theatre with him. This was a great surprise to my father. However, I was allowed to go with him. On the way home, as we walked by Hyde Park Corner, he said, "Well we could live near the House in Westminster and you could have a chop at the House every night." (I hate chops.) And so that was his proposal. My reply was, "And what shall I call you, Captain Benn?" For I'd always called him Captain Benn, and he'd called me Miss Holmes.

I remember there was a seat at Hyde Park Corner and sitting on it was a poor, broken-down tramp. So he said, "Oh, I'm so happy. I must give him something." And he gave him half-a-crown, which the tramp put in his pocket, but the pocket had a hole in it and so the coin fell on the ground. Then we went home and said we were engaged. My father couldn't believe it. He thought that all the visits had been to see him. He was quite sure of that!'

In his excitement, Wedgwood Benn's organizational ability for once momentarily deserted him. He sent a circular to his close friends announcing that he was going to be married, but he forget to mention the name of his bride!

All too aware of the twenty-year difference in age, he was concerned as to whether his young wife-to-be fully realized the problems of being married to a prominent politician. But he had no need to worry on that score. The 'very frail hazard' had served him well, for he could not have found a more able wife, who while being ever supportive developed her own considerable abilities and interests. She might have found it difficult to deal with his parents, who had throughout his political career been his confidants, friends, and constant support. Yet Margaret, displaying an admirable mixture of tact and independence, proved she was able to cope even with Wedgwood Benn's formidable mother:

'I didn't know a single member of his family – not one. I met them all for the first time and my mother-in-law very much took me in hand. Fortunately I was young enough for her to see me as a grand-daughter. She thought she'd teach me how to be a good MP's wife. This amused me no end and I used to listen to her by the hour.'

The only request that Wedgwood Benn had to make was that Margaret should become, like his family, a teetotaller.

'Give me a reason,' she asked.

'If we have any children, I'd like them to be brought up as teetotallers,' he replied and Margaret agreed to his request.

The wedding at St Margaret's, Westminster, on 17 November 1920, was an impressive social occasion. As he walked to the church from the National Liberal Club, Wedgwood Benn passed through cheering crowds kept in order by mounted police. Along the route were placards announcing that the wedding would be covered in the following day's newspapers. The church was crowded and among the guests were Asquith, Lord Crewe, T.P. O'Connor, the Irish Nationalist (all of whom signed the marriage certificate with the fathers of the bride and groom), Lady Bonham-Carter, the McKennas, General Seely and Lord Hankey. To this gathering of prominent Liberals, Lloyd George was not invited, although he did send as a wedding present a book of Macaulay's Essays.

The wedding cake, which was over four feet high and surmounted by a large model aeroplane, had been made by J.K. Smith, a master baker and the Chairman of Leith's Liberal Association, who accompanied his spectacular creation in the guard's van of a train all the way from Leith to London.

At the reception, Wedgwood Benn said to his wife, 'Let's forget about all these people for a while. We'll go abroad and get away from them all.'

'That's lovely,' she replied. 'Where shall we go?'

'Well,' he said, 'we'll forget all about politics for a couple of months.'

'All right. But where shall we go?'

'I thought we might go', he replied, his eyes twinkling, 'to the first meeting of the League of Nations!'

And so they did. In the Salle de la Réformation in Geneva, they attended the inaugural meeting of the Assembly of the League of Nations. They then travelled to Italy where unfortunately he suffered from a malaria attack. Suddenly he went stiff and his face turned yellow. Margaret, fortunately a most capable woman, nursed him during his slow recovery, as she was to do many times throughout his life.

On their return to London, the couple took a furnished flat in Westminster Mansions, and Wedgwood Benn, fully recovered, eagerly resumed his work with the Wee Frees, whose main concern at the beginning of the 1921 session of Parliament was still Ireland, where in January martial law had been declared.

Although debates on the Irish crisis continued into the summer, for Wedgwood Benn there was another excitement. To their delight, he and his wife learnt that she was expecting a baby. On 5 September, Margaret gave birth in a Brighton nursing home to a son, whom they named Michael. As they had no home of their own, the Benns and their baby went to live temporarily with Wedgwood Benn's parents, a less than satisfactory arrangement for both were old and unwell. But Michael proved to be a delight to all four grandparents, especially Wedgwood Benn's father, who after his grandson's first visit to Limpsfield wrote to his son:

'My dear old Daddy-Boy.

Michael's "entry" has been such a success. He has captured every one here, particularly his doting old Grandpa ... He is doing so well ... And what about the brave little Mother! I declare – as an expert – she is just prettier than ever, and as for pluck? We have awarded her the National Medal for valour – *first class*.'[9]

By this time, Wedgwood Benn had found a suitable small house to rent in Cowley Street, Westminster, which, after some alterations, provided a comfortable home.

Although having increased responsibilities as a husband and father, Wedgwood Benn continued as devotedly as ever with his political life. He staved off all moves to unite the Liberal Party under Lloyd George, and by the end of 1921 the two groups were as far apart as they had ever been. Believing that a General Election would shortly be called, the Wee Frees acted with determination when they discovered that Lloyd George and his National Liberal Council planned to hold a rally at Westminster Hall on 20 January 1922. The next day the Wee Frees held their counter-rally in the same hall and Asquith launched what he called 'the election campaign against Lloyd George'. But there was not to be an early election. The primary reason for this was that the Irish Settlement, which created the Irish Free State, enraged the Conservatives and made it impossible to fight an election in coalition with them.

During the following months, Wedgwood Benn became increasingly concerned about his father's obviously declining state of health. So it was with some hesitation that he set off on 22 March to visit Budapest and Prague where he was to meet Schober, the Austrian Prime Minister, and members of his Cabinet. When he arrived back at Victoria Station ten days later, he received the news that his father had been taken seriously ill. Sir John Benn lingered on until the morning of Monday, 10 April, when he died in the presence of his family, who had spent the night by his bedside.

Among the many tributes received was a letter sent by Asquith:

'My dear Wedgwood,

One word of deep-felt sympathy for you and all your family, in this most lamentable loss. I have still a vivid memory of your father in the early County Council days, when we have often stood on the same platform and fought for the same causes. That is a long time ago – measured by the mechanics of the calendar; but he never seemed to grow older, and was among all the public men I have known the one whom I should select as the incarnation of perennial youth. It is a splendid and rare gift to live and fight, and work and die, with an undiminished faith in great ideals; and that gift was his.'[10]

Many other tributes were made to a man who seemed so obviously to have fulfilled the Victorian ideal of a truly self-made, successful man. Yet Sir John Benn had far more facets to his personality than merely the ability to strive consistently for success. True, he worked long hours throughout his life and, far more than his father, was resilient in the face of the many misfortunes that afflicted him. But, for example, he was a capitalist who had a complete disregard for money. The financing of his business was left first to his brother, Julius, and then to Ernest, his eldest son. He never had a personal bank account and seemed either incapable of or unwilling to plan for even basic monetary needs. When the family lived at the Westminster Palace Hotel, his wife used to have a weekly settlement with the hall porter from whom Sir John continually borrowed the money he needed to pay the cab on returning home. When he took his family out for lunch, it would be a matter of speculation as to who would be expected to pay the bill. As a politician he was far more interested in causes than in party, and so, although through his untiring efforts much was accomplished on the LCC, he was not in the wider sense a successful politician, especially in Parliament. He continued to be a Progressive on the County Council long after that radical alliance had been deserted both by the Labour Party and the bulk of the electorate. As late as March 1922, even though then extremely ill, he was returned to the LCC for the tenth successive time as one of the few surviving Progressive members.

His greatest interest, despite his many achievements, was in his family, and his major struggle throughout his life had been to provide for it and keep its members bonded together. In this he succeeded admirably, although by the time he died he was virtually the sole survivor of his generation. Almost all his brothers had died: Robert at the early age of thirty-seven in 1907; Julius, who was the real businessman in the family, in 1919; and poor William Rutherford in 1921. It was the progress of his two surviving sons that gave Sir John Benn his greatest pleasure in the latter years of his life. Although very different in personality, they remained close to each other and integrated within the family. Separately they pursued Sir John Benn's dual interest in publishing and public service with even greater successes. Ernest Benn, who inherited his father's title, already ran the business and was widely respected for his acumen and innovative ideas. Wedgwood Benn was one of the best-known politicians of the age. It seemed certain that both would achieve pre-eminence in their chosen careers. Yet, although it could scarcely have been predicted, the political upheavals of the twenties and thirties were to cause the two brothers, after their father's death, to adopt totally opposing views that sometimes strained their friendship.

Partially responsible for this was that, in addition to following but one of the two careers their father had combined, the brothers inherited different qualities from their parents. Wedgwood Benn was much like his father – wiry, ebullient, witty and affectionate. Ernest Benn was more like his mother, who came from a business background and was less tender, with an inflexible sense of duty and an immense determination of purpose. Not surprisingly, when they were children, Ernest was known as 'Mother's right hand'.

An insight into Lady Benn's character is provided by Wedgwood Benn's description of his mother at the time of his father's death:

> 'Mother had been sitting by him for days without changing her clothes. The morning that he died she appeared at the breakfast table and presided, without flinching, over the whole family there gathered and, more remarkable still, a few days later stood heroically at the open grave throughout the burial service.'[11]

Afterwards, Lady Benn said to Margaret, Wedgwood's wife, 'When my husband died I wondered what my purpose in life should be. Now I know. It is to look after Wedgwood.'

Margaret Benn said nothing, but, despite her youth, she was also a very determined woman and knew that, without causing her mother-in-law offence, it was she who would be responsible for the welfare of her husband and their family. A new Benn dynasty had been founded.

3
WEDGWOOD BENN

1922–1925

Just over a month after John Benn's funeral, the surving members of the family, with guests including Asquith and McKenna, gathered on a happier occasion for the christening of Wedgwood and Margaret Benn's son Michael in the crypt of the House of Commons. Wedgwood Benn jestingly commented in a letter to his mother that Margaret 'had, in addition to pledging the infant to the Church as by law established, pledged him as an Asquithian'.[1]

In the months that followed, Wedgwood Benn did all that he could to hasten the inevitable collapse of the Coalition Government. The ever-growing scandal of Lloyd George's profitable exploitation of the honours system led to a debate on 17 July about whether a Select Committee of both Houses should be established to investigate the matter. During the debate Wedgwood Benn proposed an amendment, which the Deputy Speaker, Sir E. Cornwall, ruled out of order, that the committee should also consider 'the desirability of abolishing hereditary titles'. If it had been accepted, the amendment might have led to moves that would subsequently have saved the Benns much heartache.

But by the beginning of September a far more serious problem than inquiries into abuses of the honours system had arisen for Lloyd George – four years after peace had been declared it seemed possible that Britain might again be at war. The Turks, in a fight to regain territory lost to the Allies in 1918, attacked the Greeks at Smyrna. The British Cabinet was divided about how to react, but Lloyd George, feeling he had lost both Egypt and Ireland, determined to stand firm. In the resulting Chanak Crisis, Britain lost the support of the Allies and Lloyd George's actions led to a split between him and Curzon, the Foreign Secretary. Curzon's decision to resign precipitated a crisis, and on 19 October the Conservatives met at the Carlton Club to consider the state of the Coalition. After Balfour and Bonar Law had both claimed that if they did not stop supporting Lloyd George the Conservative Party would inevitably be destroyed, it was decided by a vote of 187 to eighty-seven to withdraw from the Coalition. That afternoon Lloyd George resigned as Prime Minister, to be replaced by Bonar Law. Shortly afterwards it was announced that there would be a General Election on 15 November.

There were few people who believed that Lloyd George would not be Prime Minister again some day. But it was not to be. Despite all his manipulations and political expertise, he faced the coming election not as the head of a Coalition whose endorsement, as in 1918, could virtually ensure a nominated Parliament. He led only a non-Party of his own design, called the National Liberals, botched together from the remnants of his Coalition Liberal supporters. The Liberal Party itself had retained its independence, and for that, more than any other man, Wedgwood Benn had been responsible. Throughout the four years of post-war Coalition Government, he had used his mastery of parliamentary procedure and party organization to prevent Lloyd George from either reuniting the Liberal Party or being accepted as its leader. When others had grown tired of Asquith's inadequacies and seen no future in the Party, Wedgwood Benn had kept up the fight, often with little help, urging and encouraging the small band of Wee Frees to be a force for the radicalism that in the years immediately before the war Lloyd George had claimed as his own, but which, by the time he became Prime Minister, he had uncaringly rejected. Wedgwood Benn did not cause Lloyd George to fall from power, but the stand he took throughout the post-war Parliament and would continue to take after the election was a vital reason why Lloyd George never again returned to power. Almost certainly Lloyd George underestimated, perhaps at first did not even notice, his tenacious opponent, but Wedgwood Benn, a man of principle, committed himself to ensuring that the man he regarded as being without principle should not triumph.

Although the Tories, fighting on their own, had last won a General Election in 1901, Bonar Law could reasonably assume that his Party would be victorious in 1922, even though a dozen ex-Ministers, including Balfour and Chamberlain, had repudiated the Carlton Club decision. Generally considered to be the most uncertain question in the election was how the two Liberal factions would fare in what *The Times* referred to as 'the confused state of Party politics resulting from the break-up of the Coalition'. Lloyd George's National Liberals fielded 162 candidates, of whom five opposed independent Liberals who had been MPs; there were 328 Asquithian Liberal candidates, of whom twenty-four were standing against Coalition Liberals returned in the previous Parliament. The rivalry between the two factions was considerable, even though the two leaders studiously avoided attacking each other in public.

Polling Day on 15 November gave the Conservative Party an even greater victory than had been anticipated. With 345 seats, the new Government had a majority of seventy-seven over all the other parties, the largest of which with 142 MPs was the Labour Party, led by Ramsay MacDonald, who had been returned to the Commons after an absence of four years. As only fifty-four National Liberals were elected, Lloyd George's supporters were considerably depleted, with Churchill and Guest among the casualties. The independent Liberals fared better, winning sixty-two seats. But the Liberal Party had clearly suffered greatly from its disunity, for, although the two factions together achieved almost as many votes as the Labour Party, they had in total twenty-eight seats less.

In Leith, Wedgwood Benn, against both Labour and Unionist opposition, won easily with a majority greatly increased to 6599. Although naturally delighted by his victory, Wedgwood Benn was dismayed to hear the talk of reuniting the Liberal Party that began immediately after the election. And reunion was unnecessary, for, despite Maclean's defeat at the election, the augmented independent Liberals were a potent political power in the new Parliament, as Vivian Phillipps, who was made the Liberal Chief Whip, has stated:

'The independent Liberals under Asquith's leadership numbered, it is true, some sixty only, but this was more than double their representation in the previous Parliament, and in quality and debating power, they were as formidable a team as any in the House. On the front bench Asquith had with him Sir John Simon, Wedgwood Benn, Godfrey Collins, Charles Roberts, and George Lambert ... Few parties in the House can ever have worked together with a more unselfish team spirit, or in an atmosphere of happier personal relations.'[2]

Clearly likely to be more ardent in opposition than Lloyd George's dispirited followers, the independent Liberals still had to compete in the Commons with the Labour Party for seats on the Opposition front bench. When the House reassembled, MacDonald surreptitiously pushed Asquith to one side, as Josiah Wedgwood, the newly elected Deputy Leader of the Labour Party, tried to do to Wedgwood Benn and Simon. This good-natured rivalry between the two main Opposition groups brought Wedgwood Benn into close, daily contact with the leaders of the Labour Party, some of whom, including Wedgwood, were ex-Liberal MPs. Wedgwood Benn found it very easy to work with them.

He was still convinced, however, that the Liberal Party had a future, even though Asquith, who was over seventy, had little taste for the political fight. But Wedgwood Benn was convinced that Liberalism would die if it had to rely on the leadership of Lloyd George, whose reputation was further besmirched in the early months of 1923 by the scandal surrounding Lord

Farquhar, the treasurer of the Coalition Tory Party, who refused to hand over the funds to the Conservative Party on the grounds that it was not part of a coalition. When he died a few months later it was discovered that the Party Fund had disappeared. Not surprisingly, there were many Liberals who feared that the money contributed to Lloyd George's Coalition Fund might have been similarly misappropriated. Independent Liberals began to insist that if Lloyd George was to rejoin them, he must first hand over his fund.

In the Commons, where the different opposition strands were able to give the Government a difficult time, Wedgwood Benn was in his element. There were, however, more serious matters which the Government had to face. France marched into the Ruhr and the crisis was to prove the end of the fragile post-war dream of a pacified Europe. At home, Bonar Law again became ill and on 20 May he resigned. Much to Curzon's chagrin, King George V summoned Stanley Baldwin to offer him the post of Prime Minister.

Baldwin's Government continued uneasily throughout the summer. Faced with rising unemployment, the Conservative Party increasingly looked towards protectionism as a solution. As general tariffs were certain to be unpopular in the country, attention concentrated on establishing some form of preference for the Empire's trade. The defence of free trade was the one cause likely to unite the Liberal Party. Before the end of the summer recess, the major Liberal spokesmen were prepared and eager to fight their cause. But there was not to be a battle in Parliament, for on 25 October, Baldwin announced that he favoured protection as a means of curbing unemployment, thus making an early General Election inevitable.

By his announcement, Baldwin achieved that which previously had appeared impossible and against which Wedgwood Benn had striven so long – the reuniting of the Liberal Party, including Lloyd George. On 13 November, Asquith and Maclean met Lloyd George and Sir Alfred Mond and drafted a proclamation announcing that 'all candidates will be adopted and described as Liberals, and will be supported by the whole strength of the Party without regard to any past differences'. A Free Trade manifesto was then jointly signed and Lloyd George undertook to contribute £100,000 from his political fund towards party expenses. With the promise of this dowry, the shot-gun marriage was completed.

Polling Day was on 6 December, and in a two-cornered fight at Leith Wedgwood Benn again increased his majority:

Wedgwood Benn (Liberal)	15,004
R.F. Wilson (Labour)	8267
Majority	6737

Throughout the country, the newly united Liberal Party also did well, winning 159 seats. But the major victor was the Labour Party, which increased its representation from 142 to 191. The Tories remained the largest Party, with 258 seats, a loss of eighty-seven.

As Protectionism had been the cause of the General Election, it was impossible for the Tories to form a coalition with the Liberals, and Asquith announced on 18 December, at a meeting of Liberal members at the National Liberal Club, that he would not keep the Conservatives in power. To the horror of the traditional establishment, it seemed certain that Ramsay MacDonald would soon form the first Labour Government.

Although there was some doubt that Ramsay MacDonald could keep the left wing of the Labour Party in check, the divisions in the other two parties were more obvious. The Tories, led by Baldwin to defeat in the election, were anything but unanimous in their support for him. The Liberals, unexpectedly united by the exigency of a surprise Protectionist election, could not easily contain both the radical element and the pro-Tories, even though the latter's most forceful spokesman, Winston Churchill, had been defeated once again in the General Election. The radicals, like Wedgwood Benn, infinitely preferred a Labour Government to the return of the Conservatives, a view obviously not shared by the pro-Tory Liberals who claimed that communism and socialism were identical. So the Liberal Parliamentary Party could not at first decide whether or not to support the Labour Party's bid to bring down Baldwin's Government by an amendment to the King's Speech moved by J. Clynes, who in 1923 had replaced Josiah Wedgwood as the Labour Party's Deputy Leader. When the Government was defeated on 21 January 1924, ten Liberals voted with the Tories, despite Asquith's denunciation of those who feared a Labour Government.

Although the Labour Party could stay in power only with the support of Liberal MPs, Ramsay MacDonald was apparently little interested in liaising with them. His main concerns were to stamp his unquestioned authority on the Party and, by pursuing obviously moderate policies, to show the fitness of Labour to rule. So he curbed the socialists, of whom the most prominent were the Clydesiders, and, determined to brook no claimants to his own position as Leader, he gave lowly posts to the Party's more prominent supporters, including Clynes, who was made Lord Privy Seal, and Adamson, the Secretary for Scotland. In his Cabinet, there were four peers, and three ex-Liberals with Ministerial experience – Viscount Haldane, C.P. Trevelyan, and Josiah Wedgwood. Only five of the twenty Cabinet members were trade unionists.

Ramsay MacDonald's moderation and its own internal divisions made the Liberal Party, the tacit upholder of the Labour Government, ineffective in opposition. Frequently Liberal members voted on both sides during parliamentary divisions. This further demoralized the Party. On 13 March, Wedgwood Benn recorded in his diary:

'Feeling in the House is becoming very bitter. In our Party there is discontent: Mr A. away ill; Lloyd George sulking and awaiting an opportunity; our Front Bench speaking with two voices; Simon seldom there.'[3]

When the new parliamentary session opened, the radical Liberals received some overtures from Labour members, who were all too aware that Snowden's Budget could pass through the House only with Liberal support. On 30 April, for example, the Chief Labour Whip, B.C. Spoor, approached Wedgwood Benn with the cordial hope that the radical Liberals would approve the Budget. In the event, the Budget debate was an unpleasant occasion, and Henderson was so incensed by an interjection made by Herbert Spencer that he invited the Liberals to get on with the task of voting against the Labour Government. But that was no easy task, for many of the measures were seen by the Liberals as having been their own policy.

So the uneasy truce between the Labour Party and the Liberals in Parliament continued. But the Liberals, without effective leadership and wracked by self-doubt, held frequent meetings to consider their position. Some, like Freddie Guest, wished to form a coalition with the Conservatives; others, like Wedgwood Benn, felt growing, if at times guarded, sympathy with the leadership of the Labour Party. Neither Asquith nor Lloyd George, both of whom attended the House only infrequently, seemed decided about the direction in which the Party should move.

The Labour Government might then have remained in office for some time, even though there were signs of unrest in the country. But during the summer, Ramsay MacDonald's fate was sealed by what at first seemed a relatively trivial incident.

On 25 July the *Workers' Weekly* published a letter telling servicemen not to take sides during industrial disputes. Campbell, the editor, was prosecuted by Sir Patrick Hastings, the Attorney General, but the move was much criticized by both radical Liberal and Labour MPs. In August the prosecution was withdrawn, apparently at the Prime Minister's instigation. This provoked hostile criticism from the Conservatives and the pro-Tory Liberals. By the time Parliament reassembled in October, the Conservative Party, united under Baldwin and with a much improved organizational system, was determined to bring down the Labour Government.

The Conservatives decided to move on 8 October a Vote of Censure on the Labour Government 'for having, on political grounds and on account of pressure exerted by back bench Labour members, dropped the prosecution of the Editor of the *Workers' Weekly* for seditious libel'. To this the

Liberals moved an amendment calling for a Select Committee of Enquiry, which at a meeting in the Queen's Hall on the eve of the debate MacDonald condemned as 'a vote of censure conceived in a spirit of medieval crooked-ness and torture'.

Proposed by Asquith as an act of conciliation, the amendment made the Liberals appear weak and indecisive. MacDonald insisted on regarding it as a vote of censure and towards the end of the debate Baldwin told the Conservatives to vote for it. The amendment was carried by 364 votes to 198. So what had been seen by Asquith as a way of preventing the fall of the Labour Government was used by the other parties as a way of bringing it about. That night in his diary Wedgwood Benn wrote:

'This is the story, as I see it, of the suicide of the Liberal Party. Perhaps it is better boldly to commit hara kiri than to await senile decay. The Elections will probably result in a considerable increase for Labour, and a larger increase for the Tories, both at the expense of the Liberal Party which cannot, I should say, exceed a hundred. How many will be ex-Coalies and how many real Liberals it is difficult to say, and upon this distribution depends the character of the next Government. Many people will ask, "Would you put Ramsay back?" The answer is, "Could you put Baldwin back?" '[4]

The following day, Ramsay MacDonald announced the Dissolution of Parliament. The General Election would take place on Wednesday, 29 October.

Both the Conservative and the Labour Parties were able immediately to enter upon the campaign with enthusiasm. They had a stance to take and a case to promulgate, even though it was based on little more than mutual dislike. But at least each Party was united and organized, and that certainly did not apply to the Liberal Party which was woefully short of both funds and the desire to fight.

Having spent much of the year arguing over, but failing to resolve, who should control Lloyd George's election fund, the Liberal Party had in-adequate financial resources to contest the third General Election within two years. As a result, only 340 Liberals stood, as opposed to 552 Conservative and 512 Labour candidates.

Nor was this the Liberal Party's only humiliation. Ranging from Conservative supporters to left-wingers, the Liberals did not have a common policy. Afraid that his Party would not attract the anti-Labour vote because it would be blamed for having permitted Ramsay MacDonald to form a Government, Asquith decreed that the manifesto should 'show why the Liberals put the Labour Government out rather than explain why they ever put it in'. As the campaign progressed, he took up what Beatrice Webb has described as 'the fatal battle cry of "Labour – the common foe of Liberalism as well as Conservatism"'.

This line was unacceptable to Wedgwood Benn, who had consistently maintained that the Labour Government was implementing many Liberal measures. If he had a complaint, it was that Ramsay MacDonald was not moving fast enough. In an article on 'Nine Months of Labour Government', published in *The Contemporary Review* in October, Wedgwood Benn stated:

> 'For three years in succession the Labour Opposition moved official declarations in favour of the complete abolition of the inquiry into the means of the old age pensioner, but when Mr Snowden had the change to make, he found himself unable to do more than raise the money limit of disqualification – no doubt a great help to the pensioner, but by no means a redemption of the pledge.'

Yet he concluded that Labour's radical reforms 'produced at least something tangible to attract the working-class voter who had been sickened of the Liberal Party during the period of Coalition, and was now to be seduced finally from his old love by the argument that here was at last the realization of his Radical dreams'. This led him to express the hope that there would be formed around the Labour Party 'a *Bloc des Gauches* which, representing the true majority of the electors, might give us a stable Government for some years'.

When the results were declared, the Labour candidate at Leith had increased his vote by just under 3000, but, although Wedgwood Benn's majority had been reduced by 1418, it was still substantial:

Wedgwood Benn (Liberal)	16,569
R.F. Wilson (Labour)	11,250
Majority	5319

It was, however, the first time Wedgwood Benn had stood for re-election and not increased his majority.

Elsewhere the results for the Liberal Party were disastrous. Only forty Members were elected, a loss of 119, and, as Beatrice Webb recorded in her diary, they were 'a group divided among themselves – at least half of them supported by the Tories and in effect adherents of the Baldwin Government; whilst the other score are mostly moderates with a few energetic and progressive persons – Kenworthy, Wedgwood Benn, Harris, etc. who will probably join the Labour Party in the course of this Parliament'. The most notable casualty was Asquith, who was defeated at Paisley, which the Labour candidate won with a majority of 2228.

Nor was the Labour Party as successful as had at first been assumed, even though over a million additional votes were received. There is no doubt that the reduction of seats from 191 to 151 owed much to the scare following the publication by the *Daily Mail* of a letter purporting to have been sent by Zinoviev, President of the Communist International, to British Communists, giving instructions for disruptive action. Conservative Central Office used this forgery to claim, quite erroneously, that the Labour Party was influenced by the Communists.

The Conservatives had a spectacular electoral success, winning 419 seats. In addition, they were supported by several others, including Liberals like Freddie Guest, and Winston Churchill, who was returned as a Constitutionalist, but immediately took the Tory Whip.

When Wedgwood Benn returned to London, he had much to occupy him. As his wife was expecting their second child and the house in Cowley Street was too small for a growing family, he decided to find a larger home. With the financial support of his brother Ernest, he negotiated the purchase of a twenty-five-year lease on 40 Grosvenor Road (later renamed Millbank).

At the same time, he watched with growing alarm the attempts being made, following Asquith's defeat, to make Lloyd George the Leader of the Liberal Party. This Wedgwood Benn was not prepared to accept, even though he knew there was little chance of his view prevailing in a Party that was in a state of post-election disarray made even worse by Asquith's announcement that he was going to Egypt for a seven-week holiday.

On 5 November about a dozen elder Liberal statesmen met and decided that Asquith should address all Liberal MPs at a Reform Club lunch and that afterwards Lord Beauchamp would give a private reception, again addressed by Asquith, for Liberal MPs, peers, and defeated candidates. Fearing that at these meetings Asquith intended to announce that he had nominated Lloyd George as his deputy in the House, Wedgwood Benn prepared for presentation at the Reform Club lunch a statement opposing such a move. This he read on Saturday, 8 November, to Frank Briant, one of the few Members he believed would agree with him. To Wedgwood Benn's surprise, Briant opposed any immediate action. Fearing that he might have to act alone, Wedgwood Benn spent the weekend drafting a letter which, when the time seemed appropriate, he intended to send to the *Daily News*. It read:

'... I desire to say plainly that I cannot accept in any way, direct or indirect, Mr Lloyd George as Leader of the Party in the House of Commons.

Is it any matter for surprise that hundreds of thousands of sincere reformers have deserted the Liberal Party, and that many more are today hesitating in their allegiance? There is only one possible course for Liberals to pursue, and that is to repudiate for the future, as for the past, every trace of these malign hesitations, manoeuvres and intrigues, and boldly to proclaim that the old spirit of Liberalism, unfettered and uncompromised is the true alternative to the transient triumph of stagnation and reaction.'[5]

The letter as yet unsent, Wedgwood Benn went on 10 November to the lunch at the Reform Club prepared to stand against Lloyd George, if necessary alone. But Asquith said not one word about Lloyd George and no discussion followed his glib, inadequate speech. It was not appropriate, therefore, for Wedgwood Benn to say anything. In his diary he wrote: 'I felt like an anarchist with a bomb in his hand who learns that the route of the Royal procession has been altered.'

That evening at Lord Beauchamp's reception, after Asquith had spoken, Lloyd George pleaded for party unity, claiming that dissensions would only be ridiculous. Wedgwood Benn felt sure that Lloyd George's accession had been agreed; it was only the coronation that had been cancelled. He was, however, delighted to hear whispers of discontent from, among others, Rea, Kenworthy and Dick Holt.

Although the news of possible supporters cheered Wedgwood Benn, he was so determined to act that he was prepared to do so alone. After speaking to several of his colleagues, including Wimbourne and Buckmaster, he went on 13 November to the offices of the *Daily News* and gave his letter to Hodgson, the editor, who said that it would be inserted on the leader page. Immediately afterwards Wedgwood Benn rang up Godfrey Collins, the Liberal Chief Whip, to inform him of the letter. Later that evening, Collins visited him and begged him not to publish the letter because it might appear as though he were persecuting Lloyd George. Wedgwood Benn refused to change his mind, explaining that he would have done nothing if it had not been for the obvious plot, revealed at the Reform Club luncheon, to slip Lloyd George in as leader of the Liberals without even an opportunity for debate.

There was then anything but widespread support for Wedgwood Benn's anti-Lloyd George stance. In the first few days after the publication of his letter he waited anxiously for support to gather, but the only Liberal MPs who were prepared openly to agree with him were Trevelyan Thomson, McKenzie Livingstone, George Thorne and Hopkin Morris. The newspaper comment on the letter was universally hostile.

When Wedgwood Benn heard the announcement that a Liberal Convention was to be held on 29 and 30 January 1925, he feared that Asquith might have been persuaded to send from Egypt a letter of support for Lloyd

George and so, on 22 November, he drafted a manifesto which he hoped he would be able to persuade other Liberal MPs to sign. It read:

'We, the undersigned, have devoted our political life unswervingly to the promotion of Liberalism ...

We are far from being actuated by any personal considerations. We desire to secure Liberal union on the only terms on which it is possible, namely, the Liberal faith. For these reasons, and acting solely in the interests of the cause we hold dear, we are forced to declare that Mr Lloyd George does not possess the qualifications required as leader of the Liberal Party, and we regret that we cannot accept him as such.'[6]

Morris and Livingstone signed the manifesto, but Wedgwood Benn failed to persuade Thomson and Thorne to do so. It was decided, therefore, not to publish it, as a further demonstration of inadequate support would be harmful. It was arranged, however, that Morris and Livingstone would cable Asquith in Egypt to represent the anti-Lloyd George view in the hope that this might persuade Asquith not to make any statement.

Wedgwood Benn did not give up his attempts to win wider support for his position from his fellow Liberal MPs. To this end, he arranged for a dinner to be attended by supporters and their wives on 1 December. The news that Wedgwood Benn's opposition to Lloyd George was continuing made Godfrey Collins call a meeting of both sides at his home in Smith Square on 26 November. There Wedgwood Benn, supported by Runciman, Simon and Thorne, pressed for the compromise solution that Collins, as Chief Whip, should preside at Party meetings and that the Liberals should have no official spokesman in the House. Naturally, Lloyd George rejected the proposal, claiming that it was a breach of the Armistice terms of 1923.

In organizing his dinner, which was to be held at the same time as one given elsewhere by Lloyd George, Wedgwood Benn experienced many ups and downs, and invitations were refused by all the uncommitted but possible supporters. Runciman and his wife were unable to attend because they were in Swansea, but the dinner was a great success. Those attending, who were thus prepared to announce their opposition to Lloyd George, were George Thorne, Thomson and his wife, Harris and his wife, Mrs Hopkin Morris (whose husband was called away at the last moment), McKenzie Livingstone and his wife, Kenworthy and his wife, Ernest Benn and his wife, and H.E. Crawford. Urged by Wedgwood Benn that it was necessary to give Liberals in the country some definite leadership in the House of Commons, the group prepared a declaration that a radical group within the Liberal Party was to be formed.

On the afternoon of 2 December, the Liberal MPs met in the House of Commons to elect a sessional Chairman. Livingstone, seconded by Runciman, moved the motion framed by Wedgwood Benn that this should be Collins, pending Asquith's return to the Commons. An amendment was then proposed that Lloyd George should be appointed Chairman. The amendment was carried and the motion was rejected by twenty-six votes to eight.

There was another Party meeting the next afternoon, called, somewhat bizarrely, to discuss a motion of Thomson's that the Liberals were definitely an opposition Party – a matter about which Wedgwood Benn felt there should be no doubt. The motion, however, was rejected. Immediately after the meeting he issued the declaration agreed at his dinner announcing the formation of a radical group. He was convinced that only by the existence of such a group within the Liberal Party could Lloyd George be prevented from formally linking the Liberals with the Conservatives, who were led by friends with whom he had worked in the Coalition Government.

Working from his office in Parliament Street, Wedgwood Benn immediately threw all his considerable enthusiasm and organizing ability into the work of the Radical Group, which, although in other ways similar to the Wee Frees, was not paid for by official Liberal Party funds. He wrote to known supporters:

'It is necessary to collect material from existing sources of information and to prepare it for immediate and effective use in debate. For this and kindred purposes, secretarial and incidental charges will be incurred. The Radical Group have, therefore, asked me to write to a few of those who may be in sympathy with our aims to ask whether they would assume responsibility for an assured income of £500 per annum so long as this Parliament lasts. If you see your way to help, I need not tell you how gratefully assistance would be received.'[7]

Donations and letters of support were sent to Wedgwood Benn, but he also received much adverse criticism from many sources, including people in his own constituency. Because of this, he wrote on 8 December to A. Munro, the President of Leith Liberal Association. In the letter, which was subsequently published by several newspapers in Scotland, he stated:

'As a member of the Liberal Parliamentary Party, I was invited to give my vote for Mr Lloyd George as my leader. I have no desire to recall the past: I am looking solely to the future. But I cannot honourably promise sincere allegiance to Mr Lloyd George. This does not mean that I will not work whole-heartedly with him or anyone else in the pursuit of Liberal aims. It merely means that I cannot commit my political conscience to his keeping.'

Determined to maintain both his anti-Lloyd George stance and his role as one of the most active members of the Parliamentary Liberal Party, Wedgwood Benn attended every Party meeting and every day's sitting of the House. On 17 December, after fifteen hours' preparation, he moved a Free Trade amendment to the Loyal Address. In his reply, Baldwin paid Wedgwood Benn a generous tribute in which his constancy was mischievously compared to that of Lloyd George:

'I should like to express if I may, at the beginning of my speech, the delight I feel, after so many years, at still finding my hon. and gallant Friend the Member for Leith in the forefront of this old battlefield. Many of us have missed with great regret the faces of those who sat on those benches for many years in the past and it was a great consolation to us, when we heard the results coming out on that historic night, to find that Leith had been true to him. I cannot imagine this House, I cannot imagine this perennial Debate, without him. The words came into my mind, when I saw him rise this afternoon – and I offer them to him as a greeting from the whole House –

"Come, rest in this bosom, my own stricken deer,
Though the herd hath fled from thee, thy home is still here."'

I hope that when he is laid to rest – long, I hope, after I have been – there may arise someone who will carve these classic words on his tomb:
"*Vitrix causa Diis placuit, sed victa Catoni*"
which, being interpreted, means that the hon. and gallant Member will long champion Free Trade after it has been deserted by the right hon. Gentleman next to him [Mr Lloyd George].'

During the Christmas recess, Wedgwood Benn threw all his energies into making it as widely known as possible not only that the Radical Group existed but that its membership, consisting of a quarter of the Liberal MPs, would not accept under any circumstances Lloyd George's leadership. By accomplishing this, Wedgwood Benn pre-empted any possibility of Asquith, on his return from Egypt, meekly handing over his position to Lloyd George, who was all too aware that it would be politically disastrous for him to be again seen causing a split in the Liberal Party. Yet clearly Asquith could not continue to be the Party's leader while remaining outside Parliament, and he was certainly no longer sufficiently determined or able to contest, and face defeat in, another by-election. So he chose his most sensible solution and the only generally acceptable compromise. After arriving back in England he wrote, on 20 January, to the King: 'If it should be your Majesty's pleasure, in accordance with precedent, to confer on me the dignity of an Earl, I should propose to take the title of Oxford.' In this wish, as in so many others, Asquith was thwarted and was eventually forced to accept the cumbersome title of Earl of Oxford and Asquith.

By his elevation to the House of Lords, Asquith could retain the leadership of the Liberals, whilst Lloyd George, deprived only of the title, could at least in the Commons perform all the duties. But Asquith's move satisfied few people, apart from his own family. Wedgwood Benn was convinced that it would have as disastrous an effect on the Liberal Party as Lloyd George's assumption of the leadership, which in reality it was.

It was hoped by the Liberal Party's organizers that the two-day Convention, which had been planned the previous November, would revise the Party's flagging spirits, inject a feeling of unity, and successfully launch an appeal to raise a million pounds through the constituency organizations. The Convention ended with a Mass Meeting of Unity at the Albert Hall on Friday, 30 January. Despite the eulogies and the fine gestures, Wedgwood Benn, sitting unmoved on the platform, was convinced that, rather than a celebration presaging future greatness, he was witnessing a fiasco for the Liberal Party. In his diary he recorded:

'The Albert Hall meeting was extremely well stage managed. The leaders of the two sections met in some ante-room, and then, with what may be called a cabaret touch, at the appropriate time entered the hall from the back and walked up in pairs, that is to say Mrs Asquith and Mr Lloyd George, Mr Asquith and Mrs Lloyd George, and so on. It was a strain to watch them. Mr A. received the tribute due to his character and performance; but the constant argument that we shall recover, drawn from the parallel of the days when there was no Labour Party, is very unconvincing. Further, Mr A. lives among the Foxes and the Pitts, and really said nothing that could touch the working man. Ll.G. corruscated. It was unconvincing to those who know him, but it completely captured the meeting . . .

A leaf has been turned in the history of the Liberal Party: the influence of the Old Man will now definitely diminish, for all the work must be done in the Commons, and the decisions be taken there. Exactly how far Ll.G. will be able to shape these is a matter of doubt.'[8]

For Wedgwood Benn the meeting effectively marked the end of his war, although he was to continue for a time to fight the battle. He no longer felt comfortable in the Liberal Party. Yet, having striven for six years to ensure that the Party he had served so faithfully all his adult life should retain its separate, radical identity rather than be absorbed willy-nilly by the Conservatives, he was still determined to prevent Lloyd George, the arch-master of expediency, from bartering the Party for his own political advantage.

But the task of keeping alive the radical spirit of the Liberal Party was exceptionally difficult. Not only was the Party being torn apart by conflicts that increasingly concentrated on personalities, but few of the leaders attracted popular support. Ernest Benn, who, like the Liberal MPs Sir Alfred Mond and Hilton Young, was adopting an increasingly right-wing position, wrote to his brother: 'Yours is the only name which is ever mentioned without an "if" or a "but": L.G. (crook); Simon (shifty); Runcie (cold); Masterman (booze) and so on.'[9]

Yet, despite the inadequacies of his colleagues, Wedgwood Benn in waging his campaign was not motivated by personal ambition. He neither wanted nor expected to be the Leader of the Liberal Party himself. He did not even wish to lead the Radical Group, and Runciman was made its Chairman. The desire for political position he had experienced in his youth had gone. His wartime experiences and his contact in his constituency with those trapped into poverty by unemployment had led him to believe in causes rather than in leaders. Increasingly he felt that to have one's eye on the main chance, to be concerned first with self-advancement, was to be prevented from achieving worthwhile results. So he had grown to despise, and rigorously oppose, the cult of personality engendered by Lloyd George and opportunist politicians of his ilk.

Selflessly he threw his remarkable administrative abilities and knowledge of parliamentary procedure into organizing the efforts of others. At first he worked from his office in Parliament Street, but as the Liberal Party was so short of funds that the rent could no longer be paid he was forced within weeks of commencing his campaign to move all his files and his helpers to his house in Grosvenor Road where the basement and much of the ground floor became used solely as offices. He did manage to obtain a room in the House of Commons for the special use of the Radical Group and each week he arranged a lunch for its supporters. As he had done for the Wee Frees, he also issued daily an abstract of news relevant to the business of the House and arranged a rota for the attendance and participation of the Group's members in the parliamentary debates. Wedgwood Benn's life was then spent, as he always wished it to be, at a hectic pace.

In addition to his political work, there was a personal matter of great interest to him. His wife was expecting their second child, and to the delight of both parents a brother for Michael was born on 3 April 1925. The doctor attending the delivery was, somewhat appropriately in view of future events, named Attlee. During the following weeks, the proud father wrote regularly to his mother reporting on the progress of his wife, whom he always called Peg, and the baby. The first of these letters was written on 8 April:

'As you have kidnapped my elder son, I shall have to start giving you a record of the younger one. Born at about ten minutes to three on Friday afternoon, 3 April, when you were most providentially in the house, he is a fine boy, and has given no trouble, except by yelling the house down. He and Peg are going on famously, and Attlee didn't come yesterday because he didn't think it worth while! The baby has made no remarks yet, but last night he slept through the night, I am told. Lady Astor sent a very sweet note to Peg, and has deluged the house with tulips.'[10]

Twelve days later, Wedgwood Benn wrote:

'No decision yet about the baby's name, but it is practically settled that Anthony will be one, and Wedgwood. So call him Anthony for the time being. I just record that today he produced his first smile which was genuinely not due to wind.'

Shortly afterwards it was agreed that the baby would be named Anthony Neil Wedgwood Benn.

When Parliament reassembled after the Easter recess, Wedgwood Benn continued his intense activity, which was far more directed towards retaining the Liberal Party's radical traditions than to harassing the Tory Government. As the Labour Party was the official opposition, Wedgwood Benn, in order to make his presence felt, frequently resorted to the procedural ploys of which he had for long been a master. On 5 May he questioned the propriety of embodying several taxes in one Resolution, forcing Winston Churchill,* the Chancellor of the Exchequer, to withdraw it. A fortnight later, he challenged a Division on the suspension of the 11 o'clock rule. In Committee he attacked Churchill's Budget clause by clause, even introducing a motion expressing regret at the Speaker's action in granting a closure on a Finance Bill.

His untiring, Herculean efforts and the apparent lack of interest of his colleagues in the fragmented Liberal Party often meant that Wedgwood Benn was the only active Liberal in the House. In his diary on 11 July he noted, 'I was the only Liberal on the benches for some time today. I spoke on the Unemployment Insurance Bill, the Scottish Education Bill, and on the Wireless Bill.'

Even during the vacation he could not limit his activities. Wishing to ensure that his constituents properly understood his position, he paid several lengthy visits to Leith, but when Parliament met again it was clear that the split in the Liberal Party was even deeper than before. Unable to claim the support of a united Party, Lloyd George was still refusing to hand over his funds and, as the campaign to raise a million pounds from Liberals had failed abysmally, the Party was virtually bankrupt.

*Churchill, having at the last election been elected as a Constitutional candidate, immediately took the Conservative Whip and was made Chancellor of the Exchequer.

Fearing that they would be likely to lose their seats at the next election, several members of the Radical Group were losing their enthusiasm for the increasingly bitter conflict. Still occupying daily his seat in the Commons, Wedgwood Benn found himself sharing opposition only with sympathetic members of the Labour Party. On 25 November he wrote in his diary, 'The relations in the House between ourselves and Labour have completely changed. In place of the pin pricks and suspicions of the last Parliament, there is a very warm feeling of friendship.'

Not surprisingly, both Wedgwood Benn and his wife were unofficially approached to see if there was any possibility of his actually joining the Labour Party. Margaret Benn knew Philip Snowden's wife and they often talked together in the Ladies' Gallery. 'You know,' Mrs Snowden would say, 'your husband's so much wanted in the Labour Party. Don't you think he could take just that small step and join?'

And it was something over which Wedgwood Benn agonized. All his roots were in the Liberal Party, which he had served in Parliament for twenty years. But he felt strongly that it was no longer the committed radical Party he had known. Moving after the wartime Coalition inexorably to the right, it no longer stood for the principles of social justice that both he and his father had so consistently expounded. Yet, very conscious that his was still the main support to the admittedly crumbling barricade that alone prevented Lloyd George taking the Liberal Party lock-stock-and-barrel, he did not want to leave his post. His doubts and worries, however, began seriously to threaten his health.

It was Sir Alfred Mond, however, not Wedgwood Benn, who was the first to leave the Liberal Party during the life of the Parliament. As had long been expected, on 26 January 1926, he joined the Conservative Party. Momentarily feeling that this might presage a move by the Liberals away from the political right, Wedgwood Benn at a Party meeting on 1 February opposed the motion that Lloyd George should be made Chairman. His unsuccessful stance was widely reported and he received many critical letters from Liberals accusing him of perpetuating an unnecessary vendetta.

These attacks and his internal conflict made him ill. Seeing what was happening and concerned that Wedgwood Benn might join the Labour Party, Ernest Benn spoke to his brother's wife. 'He must go on a holiday,' he said, 'or otherwise he'll make a decision he'll regret all his life. You must both go on a cruise in the Mediterranean.'

Knowing that her husband had no time for leisurely holidays, Margaret Benn said, 'What about the children? What shall we do about them?'

'Send them to us,' Ernest Benn replied 'We'll take care of them.'

So it was all arranged. The affairs of the constituency and the Radical Group were handed over to a secretary; and young Michael and Tony were safely ensconced with their uncle. On 19 February – two days after Lloyd George's land policy had been backed by Asquith at a conference held at Kingsway Hall – Wedgwood and Margaret Benn set off on their Mediterranean cruise with only two suitcases and a hat box. It was somewhat inadequate luggage for the journey they eventually undertook, for, prompted by Margaret Benn's desire to explore the Holy Land, they left the boat at Haifa and instead of being away from home for a few weeks they spent three months travelling through thirteen countries.

Apart from the sadness caused by their separation from the young children, the extensive trip was a great success. Away from the unceasing political struggle to which he had been committed without any substantial break since the end of the war, Wedgwood Benn was able again to broaden his horizons from the narrowing intrigues of Liberal Party politics. Having as an adolescent rejected her parents' agnosticism, Margaret Benn was a devout Anglican with a deep interest in theology and Biblical history. She was delighted, therefore, to be in the Holy Land.

Margaret Benn's religious studies and Wedgwood Benn's political investigations were not pursued separately, but together. So in Jerusalem they first visited the sacred places of the Christian faith and then went to discuss the Holy City's current problems with Sir Ronald Storrs, the British Governor. By being able to share their individual interests, they strengthened their already close relationship. And there were many experiences to share, and not a few dangers. In order to see the British mandate at work in Baghdad, they travelled through 700 miles of desert by the only transport available – an open car driven by a Scotsman named Nairn who had the contract to deliver the desert mail. While making this hazardous trip, Wedgwood Benn gazed across the vast expanse of the desert and was suddenly reminded of the flat barrenness of the Blackwater Estuary and the land on which his father had built his holiday cottage. 'This so reminds me of Stansgate,' he said, and his wife determined that on their return to England they would visit it together.

From Mesopotamia they travelled to Turkey, where they both decided that they would like to visit the Soviet Union which, only nine years after the Revolution, was little visited and greatly feared by many in the West. Having managed to obtain visas, they sailed across the Black Sea to Odessa. Not knowing what to expect, they were surprised to be met by an official delegation with an address of welcome. Travelling by train to Moscow they saw many signs of upheaval, including beggars at every station and hordes of homeless children, but they also observed the clear beginnings of the new economic order.

In Moscow, the couple's political and religious interests were most spectacularly combined in May Day, which was also Easter Eve. For five hours they watched the impressive, if at times seemingly interminable, march of workers and the Red Army through Red Square. Afterwards, in the evening, they joined the surprisingly large crowd that thronged St Saviour's Cathedral for the midnight Easter Mass.

A few days later, they received news of the General Strike in Great Britain. As there was no British embassy in Moscow at the time, it was very difficult to obtain accurate information and so Wedgwood and Margaret Benn were deeply concerned about the safety of their young children. (They had no need to fear. Ernest Benn, whose anti-Socialist position had been made clear the previous year with the publication of his *Confessions of a Capitalist*, closed up the Benns' London houses and moved with his family and his two young nephews to the country.) Their anxieties were not allayed either by the publication in *Pravda* of a cartoon showing George v sitting on a ledge of coal that was being hacked away from underneath by miners, or by a Russian acquaintance saying to them, 'Ah, Britain is on the verge of revolution. Stay here. This is the only safe place. The Communist revolution is going around the world.' As quickly as they could, Wedgwood and Margaret Benn returned home to be gratefully reunited with their two sons.

The aftermath of the General Strike had many consequences. The public disagreement between Lloyd George and Asquith over their different responses to it destroyed their uneasy coalition. For Wedgwood and Ernest Benn it marked the end of their very close relationship, for they had almost exactly opposite reactions. Ernest Benn, an early monetarist whose views were very similar to those much later adopted by Margaret Thatcher, founded the Individualist Movement which primarily attacked what he saw as being unnecessary state expenditure. Wedgwood Benn was almost convinced that only the Labour Party could provide satisfactory answers to the country's social and economic problems.

For a time, however, the activities of the Radical Group again fully occupied Wedgwood Benn's thoughts and energies. With his return, a flurry of motions were put down by the group and multitudinous questions were asked in the House. But there was a general awareness that his future as a Liberal was uncertain. On 7 June, after Wedgwood Benn's first speech in the Commons following his long absence, Churchill said:

'Perhaps I may say here what a satisfaction it is to us to see the hon. and gallant Member for Leith back in his place in time to take part in the stages of the Bill which yet remain to be dealt with, and to know that he will be able to spare sufficient time for these Debates in spite of his other preoccupations.'

Outside the House the various factions of the Liberal Party conspired against each other, despite Asquith having on 12 June suffered from a stroke that incapacitated him for nearly three months. In the Commons, Wedgwood Benn was frequently the only Liberal present. On 7 July he wrote in his diary, 'Nobody came to speak for the Liberal Party, so that I have the place entirely to myself and can speak just when I like.' The next day he made a similar entry, 'Today I repeated the experience of being for the greater part of the five hours absolutely alone on the Liberal benches.'

The summer recess brought a welcome break from political problems, and, as he had agreed, Wedgwood Benn took his wife to Stansgate. She shared his enthusiasm for the house and the area he remembered with such affection from his childhood. To their delight, the owner, Captain Gray, agreed that they could rent the house next door, so that the Benn family acquired once again a holiday home at Stansgate.

Back in Parliament, Wedgwood Benn throughout the autumn agonized over whether or not he should leave his Party, but events were finally to leave him with no alternative. On 15 October, Asquith resigned from the leadership of the Liberals. The Party was then prepared to accept Lloyd George and, perhaps more importantly, his money on almost any terms.

During what was to be his last visit to Leith as a Liberal MP, Wedgwood Benn on 11 November, just after the Edinburgh Tattoo, delivered a speech in which he movingly condemned militarism and the idiocy of war:

'Surely if you wish to show war, you should show it all. So tell the story of sacrifice and devotion and patriotism; but let us also have the rest. Show the ex-soldier puzzling over his pension paper and wondering why, if he was passed into the Army A1 he has no claim for his shattered health. Show the man who comes home from the war to find his little business ruined and himself and his family without means. Show the pitiable queue at the Employment Exchange. Show the hundreds of men struggling at the Albert Dock Gates for the few jobs the foreman has to offer. Parade the broken men. Let the army of the sightless feel their way past the saluting point. Show the asylums, and the heartbroken mother, unrecognized by the poor clouded brain of her son. If you want a tattoo, tell the truth, the whole truth, and nothing but the truth.'[11]

Returning to the Commons, Wedgwood Benn opposed, as he had done every year since the end of the war, the continuation of the Emergency Regulations. Yet again, he was the only active Liberal, a fact commented on during the Debate, on 29 November:

SIR H. SLESSER: The hon. and gallant member for Leith, who is the only Liberal who has taken any special part in these Debates . . .
SIR W. MITCHELL: He is the only Liberal here.

SIR H. SLESSER: He is not only the only one here, but is the only one in England.
CAPTAIN BENN: I sit for a Scottish constituency!

That was to be Wedgwood Benn's last contribution as a Liberal MP to a Debate in the Commons.

He and his family spent Christmas as usual at his brother's home. Political controversy was not allowed openly to spoil the festivities, for Wedgwood Benn had not made any announcement about his future. One last event had to take place before the Liberal Party totally surrendered to Lloyd George and Wedgwood Benn was forced to resign. This happened on 19 January 1927, when the terms by which Lloyd George's fund was to be acquired by the Liberal Party were finally agreed. These determined that Lloyd George would finance, and therefore effectively select, each Liberal parliamentary candidate.

To Mr Munro, the President of the Leith Liberal Association, Wedgwood Benn wrote a personal letter, which began:

'Now that effective control of the official Liberal Party has been handed over to Mr Lloyd George, I am compelled to make a decision which I have long considered. Apart from a political mistrust which, being based on experience, I cannot overcome, the special character of the arrangement concluded on 19 January forces me to sever my connection with an organization which is now perhaps more accurately described as a following than a party.'[12]

In the letter he requested that a special meeting of the Leith Liberal Association should be called. It took place on 4 February, and Wedgwood Benn accompanied by his wife formally announced his decision to leave the Liberal Party, resign his seat, and join the Labour Party. Although the experience had been deeply traumatic, for it separated him in middle life from old political comrades, he was never to regret his decision.

Ten days later, Wedgwood Benn, on his return to the House of Commons, strode deliberately to the Labour benches and sat down. Then, when the Labour cheers had subsided, he walked up to the Speaker, shook hands, and left the Chamber to tender his official resignation.

It was a step that was even more courageous than it appeared, for he was aware that the Leith Labour Party already had nominated a Labour candidate against whom he was not prepared to stand. So he knew that he was leaving Parliament without a seat to contest as a Labour candidate and with the possibility that, after more than twenty years, he would never again be a Member of Parliament.

It was not, however, his resignation but the stand that he had taken over the previous eight years which, although it did not seem certain at the time, ensured that Lloyd George would be unable either to lead a united Liberal Party or to establish a Conservative-Liberal coalition. In less than five years, the Liberals split into the National Liberal Party (which in 1932 further divided into Samuelite and Simonite Liberals), the official Liberals, and a small group of independent Liberals consisting of the again isolated Lloyd George and his family. These splits had, of course, nothing to do with Wedgwood Benn, for the Liberals had been a Party divided since 1916. It was the personal ambition of Lloyd George that primarily caused the break-up of the once great Party. By refusing to accept that a leader could dictate the Party's policy and alliances, it was Wedgwood Benn as much as anyone who ensured that the Liberal Party which did survive retained its radical beliefs and traditions.

4
WEDGWOOD AND TONY BENN

1927-1950

The upper-middle-class home in which Tony Benn grew up was somewhat unusual. There were no obvious displays of wealth: the house was a family workplace that included his father's extensive office. There were servants, including a cook; but there was never any lavish entertaining – politics and religion were the main interests of the household.

Margaret Benn was determined that her children would be provided with a peaceful and loving home environment in which religious education was important from the earliest days. Nightly she told Tony and his elder brother Bible stories illustrated by her own collection of religious pictures bought from the Medici Society and bookstalls. She ensured that each morning the boys prayed together and that each night they said their private prayers.

Not only did she have a considerable influence on her children, she also provided immense support for her husband. Partly because of the times in which she lived and partly because she was twenty years younger than he was, she believed that her prime task was to look after him. So she nursed him when he was ill, always encouraged him in his work, and consoled him when he was down.

And after his resignation in 1927, Wedgwood Benn had many worries, especially about money, for without his parliamentary salary he had only the Benn Brothers pension of £500 a year with which to support his home and family. It was at that time a substantial sum, but he was still very anxious. Despite the latter-day affluence of his parents, he was well aware of the misfortune and early poverty they had endured. This made him so determined not to waste money that people outside the family might well have thought of him as penny-pinching. Referring to himself jokingly as the Economical Patriarch, he ensured that all unnecessary lights were switched off, that his notes and files were kept on scrap paper, and that old envelopes were reused. Unprepared to borrow, he always lived strictly within his means.

Although he did write a few articles and give some lectures, Wedgwood Benn spent most of his time, as he had always done, on political activities. He entered as fully as he could into the often complex factional world of the Labour Party. He also pursued his already extensive study of international affairs, travelling in May 1927 to Albania where he discussed the country's perilous economic state with the beleaguered President, Ahmed Bey Zogu. These activities did not, however, occupy him as fully as he wished and so he threw himself into reorganizing his office and rearranging his files. In the basement he installed a staircase so that the room above could also be used for storing files.

The influence of his mother and of his father's political interests on the young Tony are revealed by his earliest memories. He told me:

'The first thing I can recall is being in my mother's arms. I must have been very young. She was ill and somebody came to the house. I remember being held in this person's arms. I must have been two at the time. It's a very strange, disconnected memory. Then in 1928, when I was three and a half, I was taken to tea with Sir Oswald Mosley, who was then a Labour MP, in the house now occupied by the CBI in Smith Square. I recall very vividly the house, especially what were called the fire dogs in the fireplace. One was a redcoat soldier and the other a bluecoat sailor. After the tea I stood up and made a short speech: "Thank you very much for inviting us to tea!" That I think was the first speech I made.'

Wedgwood Benn became increasingly involved in the social and political life of the Labour Party, attending in October 1927 his first Party Conference. In the *Daily Herald* he recorded his impressions:

'A great sense of responsibility seemed to overshadow the gathering. They were making decisions that in the near future would pass from being the resolutions of a party to becoming the policy of the British Government.'

(If the links between Conference resolutions and Labour Party policy had continued to be as clear as Wedgwood Benn saw them to be in 1927, many years later Tony Benn would not have experienced the difficulties he did in trying to affirm the right of the Labour Party Conference to control the Party's manifesto.)

Shortly after the Conference, Wedgwood Benn was selected to be the Labour candidate for West Renfrew at the next General Election. A month later, while he was in the constituency, an unexpected natural disaster brought temporarily to an end the Benns' ordered domestic routine. On the night of 6 January 1928, the Thames burst its banks. At one o'clock in the morning, Margaret Benn woke up as the cook suddenly threw herself across the bed shouting, 'The Thames is in the house!' The sound she then heard was like Niagara, as the filthy waters rushed through the ground-floor rooms. Naturally terrified and fearing for the safety of her children she ran with the cook upstairs. She arrived in the children's bedroom just as the nurse-maid was saying to Tony, 'No, you can't have ginger beer at one in the morning even if the Thames has overflowed!'

Next morning, although the flood had subsided, the ground floor and basement of the house were in an appalling state. Margaret Benn recalls, 'The kitchen was like Neptune's cave with potato peelings hanging everywhere.' In the basement, which was still awash with sewage sludge, her husband's flood-sodden papers and files lay in total disarray. Outside, the pavements and huge chunks of the road had been lifted up and smashed by the force of the flood waters. As the embankment was severely breached the affected area was being evacuated and fenced off. Margaret Benn and her two sons had to take refuge in a hotel.

As over 450 houses had been badly damaged, Westminster City Council faced such a major task of cleaning and repairing that it would obviously be a long time before the Benns could return home to Grosvenor Road. It was eventually decided, therefore, that the family should live in Scotland so that Wedgwood Benn would not need to travel constantly backwards and forwards. So in June they moved into Clydebank House in Greenock, close to Margaret Benn's home-town of Paisley.

Unexpectedly, Wedgwood Benn was invited to be the candidate for North Aberdeen in a by-election caused by the death of Frank Rose, the sitting Labour Member. Having obtained the consent of the West Renfrew constituency, Wedgwood Benn readily accepted the invitation and threw himself energetically into his first campaign as a Labour candidate, boldly asserting in his election address, 'The Labour Party is a Socialist Party, and I am standing as a Socialist.' On 16 August he was triumphantly elected.

Naturally the Benns were delighted. Knowing that their London home could still not be reoccupied, Margaret Benn decided, in the children's interest, to make an important change to the household – she applied to the Norland Institute for a qualified children's nurse to join the family. She was put in touch with Olive Winch, who was then twenty-eight years old. After some correspondence, Nurse Olive, as she was known by the family, travelled to Scotland early in September. The two women liked each other immediately and Nurse Olive, whom Margaret Benn has described as 'the most wonderful colleague a mother ever had', played an important part in bringing up the Benn children. Always orderly, conscientious and caring, she was to be in the Benns' employ for over eleven years and was afterwards to remain a close and loyal friend to all members of the family.

Returning to the Commons, Wedgwood Benn joyfully resumed his parliamentary life. His considerable experience and formidable debating skills were welcomed by the Labour leaders. His mastery of parliamentary procedure was instantly put to use and he soon became a popular and admired member of the Parliamentary Labour Party. He succeeded in antagonizing neither his fellow backbenchers nor the Opposition, because he was never doctrinaire nor sanctimonious. Like the Labour Party itself at that time, he was far more interested in people's welfare than in economics. Not being a theoretician, he was concerned with the heart rather than with the head.

Having left London for the Christmas recess he was at home in Scotland on 28 December 1928, when Margaret Benn gave birth to their third son, who was called David.

Some months later, it became possible for the Benns to return to their flood-damaged house at 40 Grosvenor Road, soon to be renamed Millbank. So, just after Easter in 1929, Wedgwood and Margaret Benn, with their three children and Nurse Olive, again took up residence in their five-floor house overlooking the Thames.

Even before they had settled in, a General Election was called and Wedgwood Benn returned to North Aberdeen to defend the seat he had won only ten months earlier. Voting took place on 30 May. It was the first election Tony Benn remembers. He asked to be told the result and when he woke up in the morning there was a note at the end of the bed saying that his father had been re-elected.

Nationally the Labour Party scored a remarkable victory, increasing its representation from 151 to 288. Although not having an overall majority, it was the largest Party in the House and Baldwin's resignation was inevitable. Ramsay MacDonald agreed to form a Government and decided to include Wedgwood Benn in the Cabinet, realizing that the appointment would considerably augment the debating strength of the Front Bench. Unfortunately Wedgwood Benn was at Stansgate when MacDonald's unexpected telegram arrived and so he did not receive it until the next day. Returning to London as quickly as he could, Wedgwood Benn went to 10 Downing Street where he was asked to sit down and wait outside the Prime Minister's office. Shortly afterwards, Ramsay MacDonald put his head round the door and invited him in.

'Have you ever made a speech on India?' the Prime Minister asked.

'India? No, I've never spoken about India,' Wedgwood Benn replied. 'I'm interested in it, but it's not a subject on which I've specialized.'

'Well, in that case, will you take the India Office? Get a silk hat. Saturday, Paddington at 11.30 – special train to Windsor. Kiss hands with the King.'

So Wedgwood Benn was appointed Secretary of State for India, a prestigious but, in the face of the growing unrest in the country, extremely difficult post to fill. For the next two years he was fully occupied with the minutiae of Ministerial work, much of which now seems absurd. Given the impossible task of running the Indian Empire by remote control from London, the Secretary of State was forced to spend time on such trivial questions as whether women teachers from the LCC should be allowed to travel first class, like nurses, or whether they were to go third class and dine in the Sergeants' Mess and not in the Officers' Mess. In Parliament Wedgwood Benn was constantly caught in the cross-fires between supporters of the aristocratic Viceroy, Lord Irwin (who was popular in India because he was thought to be a man of integrity), the staunch pro-imperialist position of Churchill, the wobbly position of the Labour Cabinet which did not really want to be involved in anything as dangerous as giving India its independence, and the very radical position of the Labour left led by Fenner Brockway.

Despite the difficulties, there were some significant achievements. Following discussions with Lord Irwin during his home leave it was agreed that on his return to India he would publish a declaration that 'the natural issue of India's constitutional progress is the attainment of Dominion status'. This move was supported by Baldwin, who had appointed Irwin as Viceroy, but it was bitterly opposed by Churchill and Lloyd George. Stopping Wedgwood Benn in the Lobby one day, Churchill emphatically stated, 'While remaining personally friendly, I shall make your life as difficult as possible!' On 7 November, an initially acrimonious debate followed the publication of the declaration. Lloyd George in a mischievous speech referred to Wedgwood Benn as 'this pocket edition of Moses'. He was momentarily silenced by roars of laughter which greeted Wedgwood Benn's scathing response: 'But I never worshipped the Golden Calf.'

A further success was the Round Table Conference on India which was held between 10 November 1930 and 19 January 1931. By bringing together Indian politicians and princes with representatives of both the Government and the Opposition, the existing tensions in India were reduced. In achieving this, Wedgwood Benn was surprisingly helped more by Baldwin than by either MacDonald or Sankey, the Chairman of the Round Table Conference, who suffered from critical indecision under the constant pressure of his Liberal colleagues.

Throughout his period of office, Wedgwood Benn frequently met and entertained Indian visitors. It was a responsibility that affected the whole household. When Margaret Benn visited Court for the first time she had to present to the King twenty-four Indian women, quite an ordeal for someone who, aged only thirty-two, was by far the youngest wife of a Cabinet member. One of the Indian guests at the Benns' home presented a complete Maharajah's outfit with a turban, jacket and sandals. It is now in Tony

Benn's possession for, as a child, he was fascinated by it and by the many Indians he met.

Because of their father's position, the young Benn children met many other important people. At the age of five, Tony was taken to see the Trooping the Colour from a balcony at the back of 10 Downing Street overlooking Horseguards' Parade. As he was sitting there an elderly gentleman leaned down and spoke to him. It was Ramsay MacDonald. Having been asked what he thought of the day's events, Tony replied, 'I expected to see soldiers and the Prime Minister, but I didn't know I was going to have chocolate biscuits!'

By this time, Tony was attending his first school in Graham Street. He recalls:

'There was a headmistress there called Miss Morrison and another teacher called Miss Babcock. I was a very boastful little child and before I went to school I claimed I would give Miss Morrison a cow-bite, which is a pinch. I never actually gave her one. She was a kindly old lady. But I got into terrible difficulties there because of the religious lessons. Miss Babcock and I used to argue. I had been so used to discussing religion at home, that I assumed I would be able to do it at school. Ultimately I had to be taken out of Miss Babcock's class after my mother had talked with her about how I should receive my religious education. Miss Babcock said, "The trouble is, Mrs Benn, that when I begin, he begins!"'

At home Tony slept in a large upstairs front room which he shared with Nurse Olive and his younger brother, David. Michael had a room of his own. The boys spent most of their time at home in the nursery on the first floor below. There they ate the meals which were brought up from the kitchen by the nursery-maid. If their parents were in they would join their sons for tea. It was the high point of the day and on the rare occasions when one of the boys had misbehaved the severest punishment he could be given was to be excluded from the meal with his parents. As Wedgwood Benn was in his mid-fifties, he was much more of a genial grandfather to his sons than an authoritarian father. Margaret Benn and Nurse Olive brought up the children: their father was able to enjoy their company. At meal-times they would watch his deep brown eyes and when they lit up they would gleefully cry, 'Joke coming!'

Tony was always fascinated by his father's work, and began as early as he could to help in the basement office, where each day the two copies of *The Times* were cut up and filed, using the elaborate system his father had invented. A large guillotine cut the paper lengthways. The pieces passed on rollers driven by a small electric motor past another guillotine which cut the columns to the required size. The pieces of paper then ran over a little sticky roller onto a sheet of paper. By lunch-time, *The Times* had been read, arranged according to Wedgwood Benn's own decimal classification, stuck on paper, and filed in the appropriate volumes.

The children's lives were just as organized as the office. Bedtime was fixed, with one late night permitted each week during school time and two during the holidays. Pocket money was two pence a week when they went to school, plus another penny providing a detailed statement was made of how the money had been spent. Tony's accounts include the fascinating entry 'Vice – 6d.', which in fact relates to a carpentry tool he bought in Woolworth's because he wanted to copy his father, who had a life-long penchant for woodwork.

There was also a routine for the holidays. Each Christmas continued to be spent at Ernest Benn's home where there was some jollity, although the children were somewhat constrained by knowing that they had to be on their best behaviour. They far more enjoyed the Easter, Whitsuntide and summer holidays which were spent at Stansgate, where they rode bikes and sailed a little dinghy in the estuary.

The summer vacation of 1931 was different. For Wedgwood Benn and his Cabinet colleagues it was a hectic, worrying time. The country's worsening unemployment and financial situation had caused a crisis with which MacDonald seemed incapable of dealing. While at the theatre to see a performance of *The Yeomen of the Guard*, Sankey spoke to Margaret Benn about the Cabinet discussions. Wedgwood Benn was horrified, because he accepted totally the confidentiality of his office and had said nothing to his wife.

The crisis, however, soon became public. On 24 August, the Cabinet resigned and MacDonald formed with the Conservatives and Liberals a National Government. Having fought so long against the undemocratic nature of coalitions and parties formed around a non-elected leader, Wedgwood Benn would not join MacDonald's handful of Labour defectors. There was some delay before a General Election was called, but when it did take place on 27 October all but fifty-two of the Labour candidates were defeated. Wedgwood Benn after only three years in Parliament as a Labour Member was one of them. He was later to recall that in none of the campaigns he fought were the crowds at meetings so great, so attentive or so silent as they were in 1931.

His defeat surprised and disappointed Wedgwood Benn, who found himself once again in the political wilderness. He was to be out of Parliament for six years. It was an unsettled and worrying period, even though there were activities in which he was involved, including the Second Round Table Conference towards the end of 1931. This was attended by Mahatma Gandhi, and Wedgwood Benn took Tony and Michael to meet him. Tony recalls that he somehow expected to see a magician who materialized things out of the sky. Instead he saw a gentle old man sitting cross-legged on the floor who made a profound and lasting impression on him.

With their father out of Parliament, Tony and his brother had more contact with him. At every meal-time there were intensive discussions with him and with their mother, who, pursuing her interest in theology, had enrolled as a part-time student at King's College where she studied Hebrew and Greek. So by the time he was five or six, Tony was familiar with many political and religious ideas through this regular contact with his parents' formidable minds. Because of his father's long political experience, Tony obtained a political memory at least thirty years greater than his own chronological age. From his youngest days he wanted to be in Parliament, not just to follow his father or his grandfather, but because he was genuinely interested in and concerned about the national and international situation.

Among the subjects the family discussed were Wedgwood and Margaret Benn's foreign travels. In 1932 they went to Germany and witnessed the growing power of Hitler and the Nazi Party. From 25 January to mid-April 1933, they travelled through the United States of America. The following year they went again, but having decided to visit some of the states they had previously missed they arrived in California and gazing at the Pacific decided to sail on to Asia. Before they returned home in July, some seven months later, they visited Hawaii, Japan, Manchuria, Mongolia, Siberia and Moscow. In a book entitled *Beckoning Horizon* they recorded their impressions and conversations, including those with Henry Ford in the United States and General Chiang Kai-shek in China.

While the Benns were away, Nurse Olive had the entire charge of the house, answering letters with a postcard saying the Benns were abroad and would be back later. She also looked after the three boys both in London and, during the holidays, in Stansgate where in the summer of 1933 Wedgwood Benn had bought from the widow of the previous owner, Captain Gray, the house that his father had built. Naturally, Nurse Olive knew the children well. When I met her she recalled: 'Tony was the most friendly and most helpful one. His father used to call him "The Serving Brother".'

Less academic than his younger brother and not as self-contained as Michael, Tony was neither a scholar nor a sportsman of note, even after his transfer in 1934 to a private school called Gladstone's, which was owned by a great-nephew of the old Liberal Leader. Some time later the school moved nearer Eaton Place and was renamed Eaton House Preparatory School. One of the few things of interest to happen during Tony's stay there was the visit made by the American Ambassador, Joseph Kennedy, who wanted to see if it would be a suitable place to send his son John. It obviously did not reach the required standard, for the future President of the United States did not become a fellow student of Tony Benn's.

The year after Tony started at Gladstone's, 1935 was a disastrous one for the Benns. In the spring, Michael caught scarlet fever, and, in April, Tony had his appendix removed. Things appeared to be improving when, after several disappointments, Wedgwood Benn found a new constituency to fight. On 7 May 1935, he was adopted as the prospective parliamentary candidate for Dudley, which had in 1931 been won by a Unionist. This did not deter him, however, for it seemed likely that MacDonald's Coalition Government would soon fall and that the Labour Party would make considerable gains.

Not only was Wedgwood Benn looking forward to the next election, but also to the birth of his fourth child, which was due in August. Deciding that the baby should be born at Stansgate, the Benns gathered in the family cottage. Unfortunately the infant was still-born. In the Stansgate cottage where they had spent so many happy days, the whole Benn family was subdued by sadness.

That evening David, who was six and a half, was taken seriously ill. For a while it was assumed that he had cancer, but eventually tuberculosis was diagnosed. It seemed possible that he would die, but the whole family was determined that he would be nursed back to health. And so he was. For four years Nurse Olive looked after him at Stansgate, her own home in Harlow, and in boarding-houses in Bexhill. Although confined for a long time to a spinal carriage, David was ever cheerful and studied constantly. As his doctor was an émigré from the USSR, David when he was nine learnt Russian from him with the help of a primer. (His linguistic ability and knowledge of Eastern Europe continued to develop, and David Benn subsequently became the Head of the Yugoslav Department of the BBC.)

David's illness and subsequent absence broke up for a while the unity of the family. There was to be a further reverse in the unhappy year of 1935. At the General Election, held on 14 November, Wedgwood Benn was defeated by 2449 votes at Dudley. With 167 MPs, the Labour Party under its new leader, Clement Attlee, began to reorganize and rebuild. Out of Parliament, Wedgwood Benn could play no part in this process, for he had no political base either in a trade union or a constituency. Still questing for action, he undertook lecture tours for the British Council, travelling in December 1936 to Central Europe and the Balkans where he spoke to English Clubs on such subjects as 'The Place of Parliament in British History'. It was almost as though he had retired. His own political wilderness was threatening to obscure him.

But, as is so often the case in the Benn family saga, there was a sudden change of fortune. Wedgwood Benn was invited to contest a by-election in Gorton, Manchester. After an energetic campaign in which he was aided by his wife and his elder son, he was again returned to Parliament as a Labour MP on 18 February 1937. He was determined to throw himself once more into the thick of the battle, but things and people had changed considerably during his absence. The mastery of intricate parliamentary procedure was not considered important by the new, more radical Labour MPs. With the rise of Hitler and the alarming situation in Europe, Members were more concerned about the rivalry of political ideologies than about policy differences over such matters as free trade. Although never doubting his decision to join the Labour Party, Wedgwood Benn felt after his return to the Commons a little unsettled. Yet his presence in Parliament was widely acclaimed by his fellow MPs, as the results of the elections for the executive Parliamentary Labour Party show. In 1937 he was elected, coming seventh with 97 votes (Shinwell was tenth and Bevan, who received only 25 votes, was not elected); in 1938 he was fifth in the ballot; and in 1939 he was second.

With the Benn household returned to its normal hectic life, the vacations were valuable times for the family. In the summer of 1938, Wedgwood Benn took Tony and Michael abroad for the first time – on a day-trip to Boulogne. During the return journey the boys were arguing with their father. This disturbed a lady sitting close by who rebuked them sharply, 'Now come on. You're to do as your grandfather tells you!' Father and sons found this highly amusing.

In the autumn of 1938, Tony went to Westminster School, which was a short walking distance from the house in Millbank. It did not seem anomalous that a Labour MP, especially one from the upper middle class, should send his children to a private school. Nor at that time did it seem strange to Tony. One day when he was walking to school, he came across two men unloading a truck who were having a heated political discussion. Tony joined in and announced seriously that he was a Labour supporter. The men stared at him, wearing, as was the school's custom, a top hat, and they laughed. Tony, who was then thirteen, could not understand why. It was only in retrospect that he realized how privileged were the pupils at Westminster School, for they were being trained to become the ruling class, as officers in the Army, managers in industry, ambassadors and politicians.

At school, Tony did his best to fulfil his father's charge that he should show 'the Tories'. The big division in the school was between the Scouts, which was a centre of pacifism, and the Air Cadet Corps. Tony joined the Scouts. He also became an active member of the Debating Society, which immediately after the Munich Agreement of 30 September 1938 discussed the motion that 'This House supports the Government's attitude towards the present international situation'. The defeat of the motion, the school

The Rev. Julius Benn, 1826–1883

The Rev. Julius Benn's children *c* 1890s: front row: Irene Benn, William Rutherford Benn; back row, left to right: Robert Davis Benn, George Anthony Benn, John Williams Benn, Julius Taylor Benn, Henry Pringuer Benn

Wedgwood Benn MP, Junior Lord of the Treasury, 1910

Margaret Eadie Holmes, aged nineteen, 1919 – the year before her engagement to Wedgwood Benn

GENERAL ELECTION, 1906.

Wedgwood

BENN

For

St. George's

and

Wapping.

NO TAX ON FOOD.

Printed and Published by The Whitfield Press, Ltd. (t.u.), Singer Street, E.C.

At the 1906 General Election, Wedgwood Benn became the youngest Member of Parliament

Low's cartoon of Wedgwood Benn MP, 1921

Tony Benn, aged six, outside the Houses of Parliament, June 1931

Tony Benn and his father sailing off Stansgate, summer 1933

Tony Benn and Peggy Rutherford on the beach at Bexhill, summer 1939

Air Commodore the Rt Hon. Viscount Stansgate, DSO, DFC, with his eldest son, Michael, who shortly afterwards died in an air crash, 1944

Tony Benn just after obtaining his pilot's wings, March 1945

On the Oxford University debating tour of America – Tony Benn with Edward Boyle and
Kenneth Harris, 1947

Tony Benn and Hugh Gaitskell (centre), 1 May 1955, with (left to right) Will Coldrick,
Stan Awbery and Will Wilkins

aroline Benn addresses a conference on
Education into the 1970s' held in the
Royal Festival Hall, January 1970

Tony Benn at work in his Bristol constituency, 1974

ony Benn with Yorkshire miners' leader, Arthur Scargill,
4 February 1976

Tony Benn with Neil Kinnock, Joan Lester and, in the background, a smiling Dennis Skinner at the Labour Party Conference, October 1979

Hilary and Sally Benn with their son, Michael, and his admiring grandfather, 1982

magazine, *The Elizabethan*, records, was 'largely the result of an excellent speech by a new member, Wedgwood Benn'.

While the debate was taking place, Tony's parents were in Germany. At Marburg they stood on the roadside and watched the German Army returning from the rape of Czechoslovakia. People were rushing up to the troops with flowers and on the tanks there were placards: 'The War is Over. Home to Mother.'

At home the Benns fervently discussed the worsening international situation. Listening to the radio, they heard Hitler's demonic ranting at a Nuremberg Rally. Tony was on the platform of a Labour meeting in the East End which Mosley's Blackshirts tried to disrupt. As the countries of Europe sped towards an apparently inevitable war, Wedgwood Benn in Parliament and Tony Benn at Westminster School fervently denounced the rise of Fascism. In the House on 10 November 1938, Wedgwood Benn stated:

'After six or eight months of the policy of appeasement we find France weakened, Czechoslovakia gone, Spain with Italian intervention condoned, Germany with 10,000,000 more people to draw upon for her armed forces, and our own armaments not in the most satisfactory position.'

In a school debate, when a speaker was claiming that Hitler was improving the conditions in Germany, Tony interrupted with the comment, 'By providing better conditions in concentration camps, I suppose.'

Immediately after war was declared on 3 September 1939, Westminster School was evacuated to Lancing, the public school near Shoreham in Sussex. Tony, like his father, was neither a jingoist nor a militarist, but he did believe that the fight against Hitler was necessary and just. Intending like his elder brother to volunteer for the Royal Air Force as soon as he was old enough, Tony resigned from the Scouts and joined the Air Cadet Corps.

His father too was determined to battle against Hitler. Even though he was nearly sixty-three, he was contemplating rejoining the Royal Air Force. First he went in February and March 1940 on a British Council lecture tour of Yugoslavia, Bulgaria, Rumania and Italy.

On 10 May, Chamberlain was dethroned and replaced by Winston Churchill as the leader of a Coalition Government. Although supporting the united stand against the Nazi evil, Wedgwood Benn was unhappy about political coalitions and, as in the First World War, felt that he could serve more usefully outside Parliament. But when Viscount Halifax on 29 May offered him the Chairmanship of the British Council, he declined. He had already enlisted in the Royal Air Force as a pilot officer.

It was a brave, if foolhardy, decision, for his health was poor. Knowing that his wife would be opposed, Wedgwood Benn did not consult her. The first she knew of it was when he phoned her to say, 'Meet me at St James's Park tube station at three o'clock this afternoon.'

She went, wondering what she was going to find, and was shocked to see him dressed in officer's uniform with several rows of medal ribbons.

'It's no good,' he said. 'I have to go. I've got no choice. I couldn't live with myself if I didn't throw myself in with these boys.'

With Wedgwood Benn living at the Air Ministry, Tony and David away at boarding-school, and Michael entering the Royal Air Force to train as a fighter pilot, only Margaret Benn continued to live in the house at Millbank. It seemed that the family might be even further dispersed, because the large-scale evacuation of children to Canada was being discussed. Despite Churchill's opposition to the idea, it was supported by several of his Ministers. David Benn, then eleven years old, wrote to his father: 'I am writing to beg you not to let me go to Canada ... I would rather be bombed to fragments than leave England.' Margaret Benn sent the letter anonymously to *The Times*. Churchill was so impressed that, when he heard who had written it, he sent David an autographed copy of his book *My Early Life*. To Wedgwood Benn, Churchill wrote: 'A splendid letter from your boy. We must all try to live up to this standard.'

But war made it impossible for the family to keep together. In October 1940, the house at Millbank caught fire after an air-raid and Margaret Benn spent the next couple of months clearing it out, staying most nights in a public shelter in Thames House. As the Stansgate cottage was requisitioned, the Benns had no family home and Margaret Benn during the rest of the war lived either in rooms or for a short time with relatives. The family gathered together when arrangements could be made, but such meetings, although much valued, were very rare.

Tony spent his last two years at school near Bromyard in Herefordshire, the final place to which Westminster was evacuated. The war, rather than academic work, occupied most people's thoughts. Sports were replaced by the cultivation of land, and with the ever present threat of a German invasion considerable attention was given to Home Guard activities. He still vividly remembers one eventful joint exercise with other Home Guard units in the area:

'We were using live ammunition and so it was really extremely dangerous. Each unit had to prepare its own map, but one of the machine-gun groups that came from Bromyard thought there were 2240 yards in a mile instead of 1760 yards. So they paced out the area and drew a map which didn't in fact fit in with anyone else's. That was the first hazard. The second hazard was the Lewis gun which was a really lethal piece of equipment. As we were using live ammunition, it had been arranged that everyone living in the area would be evacuated. Unfortunately the people using the Lewis gun arrived late and, in order to fit into the timing that was required (that they would open fire at 14.04 or something like that), they fired before they had put pins into the four legs of the Lewis gun. As a result, they shot quite a few tiles off a nearby cottage, because the gun was vibrating madly. That caused great anxiety.

Another hazard was created when some of the handgrenades we threw didn't blow up and Mr Murray Rust, the chemistry master, was sent in as the Bomb Disposal Officer to explode the things. It was really quite dangerous! Then we had a sticky bomb (that is a bomb covered with glue on a broomstick handle) which we were meant to stick on a wooden reproduction of a German tank. Well that didn't work, and Murray Rust had to blow that up with a detonator.

Then a man called Colonel Blacker was at this exercise. He had invented a machine of his own called the Blacker Bombard. It was a type of mortar, made from a piece of tubing with a pin in the bottom. You dropped a special bomb down the tubing, it hit the pin at the bottom, and blew the thing out again. But it didn't work and poor Blacker had to tip the bomb out again.

It was all very colourful, but it was exciting because we didn't know whether or not it would all be necessary. It wasn't a game. We were waiting in the English countryside for the Germans to arrive at any time.'

While Tony was still at school, his father was asked by Churchill to accept a peerage so that the Labour Party's representation in the House of Lords could be increased. As there were no life peerages at that time, the title would be hereditary. Wedgwood Benn, assuming that he might be too old to continue his career in the Commons after the war, discussed the matter with his wife and then with Michael, his eldest son. 'Now look,' Wedgwood Benn said to him. 'If you don't want to go to the House of Lords, I shall turn it down.'

Michael, who had already decided that he wanted to be an Anglican clergyman when the war was over, replied, 'Well it doesn't matter to me. I can make a disturbance in the Lords and Tony can make a disturbance in the Commons. We'll have a marvellous time. It certainly doesn't matter to me.'

The subject was not discussed with Tony, who was astonished and angry when he heard on 22 December 1940 that his father had been created a Viscount, the automatic rank for someone who had been a Secretary of State. Tony's concern was not allayed even though the official citation stated that his father's title was bestowed not for political services but 'as a special measure of state policy ... to strengthen the Labour Party in the

Upper House, where its representation is disproportionate, at a time when a coalition Government of three parties is charged with the direction of affairs'.

Wedgwood Benn decided that he would take the title Stansgate after the holiday home in which he had enjoyed so many happy times. He had no intention, however, of sitting out the war in the House of Lords, and on 9 January 1942 it was announced that with the acting rank of Air Commodore, he had been appointed the Director of Public Relations at the Air Ministry.

Already a member of the Labour Party, which he joined on his seventeenth birthday, Tony left school in the summer of 1942 politically committed. Too young to join the RAF, he was accepted as a short-course cadet at New College, Oxford, to read Politics, Philosophy and Economics, but because he had an operation on his ankle he did not go up until December 1942. Although he knew that he would be there for only six months or so, he immediately became involved in the Oxford Union Society, proposing in March 1943 the motion: 'That in the opinion of this House, reconstruction in Europe and in Britain is impossible unless all the major production resources entirely ceased to be owned by private individuals.' The *Oxford Magazine* commented on his contribution, 'This was the evening's best undergraduate speech, and excellently delivered.'

On 24 July 1943, Tony Benn entered the RAF as an Aircraftsman Second Class and was posted for pilot training to Stratford on Avon, moving later to the Elementary Flying School at Elmdon in Birmingham. In October he was sent to a transit camp at Heaton Park outside Manchester. While waiting to be posted abroad, there was very little to do. He recalls:

'The way they tried to occupy us was to send us on route marches around Heaton Park. I remember once I was put on guard duty to stop people jumping over the wall and leaving the camp. It was ludicrous and I climbed over the wall myself to go into Manchester. Then out of the fog, about five yards away, came the route march. It was all a sort of game.'

There were, however, valuable lessons to be learnt. Through discussion with his fellow airmen who came from a variety of backgrounds, Tony Benn's political education continued. He soon realized that his belief in the political nature of the war was not shared by his senior officers who saw the conflict as an unhappy incident in which the national army of Britain was fighting against the national army of Germany. They believed that afterwards the world would be restored as it was before; Tony Benn was convinced that in post-war Britain a new society would have to be built. Having set sail from Glasgow on 11 January 1944, in a troopship bound for South Africa, he and a man called Whitehead, who had been a junior trade union official, decided that they would address the troops on the aims of the war. Tony Benn was called before the Commanding Officer, who said, 'Benn, I hope this is not in any way political.' Realizing that this was an example of the old military attitude that the troops should be allowed to discuss nothing other than how to defeat the enemy, Tony replied that he failed to see how the war aims could be anything but political. The public meeting, the first he had addressed, was packed.

After arriving in South Africa, Tony Benn was posted to Bulawayo in Rhodesia. His father was then based in Southern Italy as the Deputy Head of the Allied Control Commission which was responsible for reconstituting a democratic Italian Government. Tony Benn's elder brother Michael, who had served as a fighter pilot in North Africa as well as in Britain, was on duty at Chichester.

At 11 p.m. on 22 June, Michael Benn set off from there on what was to have been his last mission before becoming the ADC to the Air Marshal Commanding in the Far East. By a terrible misfortune, the aircraft mechanic had forgotten to check the air speed indicator. The plane, fully armed, set off. When the speed indicator proved to be inoperative, Michael Benn radioed to his base and was told to return immediately. Not being able to check the speed, he overshot the runway and in the crash the seat hit his neck, breaking it. The gunner with him was not hurt. On being taken to the hospital, Michael Benn said, 'Please don't worry my mother.' She was, however, telegraphed, and arrived at 3.20 p.m. on 23 June, after her eldest son had lost consciousness and shortly before he died.

Among Michael Benn's papers was a letter addressed to his family:

'So may I now take my leave of you.

Father, from whom I inherited those qualities which I hoped would play their part later in my life and who was always a friend I could trust and who was everything a friend could be. If he knew how true his first words had come.*

Mother, from whom I inherited the precious gift of religion. Time alone would have shown what I intended to do with that.

James [his pet name for Tony], who would have been a helping friend and who shared so many interests with me. We might have done great things together.

The little prof. [David Benn], to whom I am devoted. Take care of him.

Last, but by no means least, [Nurse Olive], who has contributed to the family more than she can ever realize.

To you all I say au revoir.

It was my dearest wish to see us all united after the war. I wanted then

---

*When Michael Benn was born, his father said, 'He's going to be a great friend of mine.'

to settle down to do what I could to prevent the suffering of another war from descending on the lives of our children. How I longed to see a world when people could be as free and happy as we were in our family. The toast is then "The Future". God bless you all, my family.'[1]

Lord Stansgate set off for home as soon as he received the tragic news of his son's death. Arriving two days after the funeral, he collapsed with exhaustion and a severe attack of malaria. Essentially a family man, the loss was almost too much to bear for one who was always deeply emotional, easily moved to tears. Characteristically, he resolved after a few weeks' rest to deal with the situation by becoming even more active. He resigned from the Allied Control Commission and applied to train as an air-gunner. When his request was rejected, he set out on a lecture tour of RAF bases, carefully selecting mainly those where air-gunners were trained. He even succeeded in flying on a number of operational missions and had the unusual distinction of being, at the age of sixty-seven, again mentioned in an official dispatch. This recognition of his activities led, however, to his unofficial missions being stopped.

Tony Benn received the news of his brother's death in a telegram delivered just before the start of a training class in Bulawayo. He had to sit throughout the lesson without revealing his feelings. It was a very painful experience, for he had always felt very close to his brother. The tragedy also made him heir to his father's title. Viscount Stansgate wrote to him, 'I'm afraid I've dropped you in it.'

Continuing his training in Bulawayo, Tony Benn flew regularly over vast stretches of unoccupied territory. It was often dangerous and a couple of his friends were killed. On one occasion, when he was in a plane, loaded with smoke bombs, that was being flown by an instructor, one of the engines cut out. The plane was crash-landed in the boulder-strewn bush. All the bombs exploded, filling the plane with smoke. Fortunately Tony Benn and the instructor escaped unscathed, apart from their smoke-filled lungs. Several hours later they were rescued.

In Rhodesia, Tony Benn also continued his political education. He stayed in Salisbury with a trade unionist called Auld, whose daughter, a nurse, took him to a hospital where the marvellous facilities for white patients were in marked contrast to the wooden hut where the blacks were treated. The iron bedsteads had no mattresses; there were patients sleeping on the floor; mental patients were handcuffed to their beds. This convincing proof of the brutality of colonialism deeply affected Tony Benn. Determined to see more, he went with a kindly missionary, Peter Ibbotson, to visit several African settlements, where the appalling conditions made him a convinced anti-colonialist.

Having been awarded his wings and RAF commission on 10 March 1945, Tony Benn was posted to Alexandria in Egypt, from where he wrote to the Jewish agency asking if he could stay on a kibbutz during his next leave. So it was that he was at Shaar Hagolan, by the sea of Galilee, on VE day. It was a memorable celebration.

He returned home in June 1945, just before the General Election. While on home-leave he campaigned in the Westminster constituency for the Labour candidate, Jeremy Hutchinson, who was then married to Peggy Ashcroft. One of Tony Benn's tasks was to drive the famous actress around the Pimlico estates, where she would descend from the car and harangue her somewhat bemused audience about the need for a National Theatre, which would certainly be built if the Labour Party was elected. He also went with the candidate to canvass the electors living in 10 Downing Street. All the servants were lined up in the street and Hutchinson introduced himself as the Labour candidate. The butler said, 'We're all Conservatives in this house.' A maid standing at the back then exclaimed, 'And we'd lose our jobs if we weren't!' Within a fortnight the unexpected had happened. The Labour Party was victorious and Churchill was replaced at 10 Downing Street by Clement Attlee. Lord Stansgate was appointed to the Cabinet as the Secretary of State for Air, a post he was to hold for fourteen months.

Still keen to be where the fighting was, Tony Benn applied for a transfer to the Fleet Air Arm, for RAF pilots were not required in the Far East. He was sent to Bootle in Cumberland and was there when the first atomic bomb was exploded. That great turning-point in history led to the surrender of Japan and shortly afterwards Tony Benn was given his release. He returned to Oxford and again became immersed in the activities of the Labour Club and the Oxford Union, of which he became in turn secretary, treasurer and, in 1947, president.

A committed supporter of the Labour Party's policies, Tony Benn became at Oxford a skilled and incisive debater. In September 1947, he went with Kenneth Harris (later a journalist) and Edward Boyle (who became a Conservative Minister of Education) to the United States for an Oxford Union debating tour, during which they visited sixty universities in forty-three states. Everywhere they encountered a self-confident belief in the virtues of private enterprise and an unreasoned suspicion of anything thought to be socialist. Tony Benn faced all such attitudes with an uncompromising advocacy of the socialist cause, stating, 'The nationalization of the basic industries is the first serious attempt to make ourselves the masters of the economic situation and not its slaves.'

In February 1948, he returned to Oxford to prepare for his final examinations, which he was to take in December. During the summer vacation he received a letter from T. George Harris, a friend he had made at Yale during the debating tour, saying that a young woman he knew, called Caroline Middleton De Camp, was visiting Oxford for a summer school and suggesting that Tony Benn and she should meet. So he accepted an invitation to have tea with Caroline De Camp on Monday, 2 August 1948.

They had much in common. Like the Benns, the De Camps were a very close family and this absorbed a large part of their lives. They had emigrated to the new world in the seventeenth century and by the nineteenth were successful carpenters and stonemasons, noted for their hard work, frugality, truthfulness and temperance. By the twentieth century the family had prospered and both Caroline De Camp's grandfathers and her father were successful lawyers. Unlike the Benns, her family was not politically active, but, as Caroline describes, they had their own tradition:

'My family was not political in the party political sense. They were good conservatives in the mid-twentieth century who had earlier in the nineteenth century been founder members of the radical movement to preserve the Republic. They were followers of Lincoln, and were opposed to slavery. Earlier still in the eighteenth century they had fought the British in the Revolution of 1776. I can still go to a local graveyard and see carved on the gravestone: "Moses De Camp – Revolutionary".'

Caroline, who just before her visit to Britain had obtained a BA with first class honours at Vassar College, kept the radical tradition going:

'I had political instincts, but such interests were not well developed. For example, when I was very young I had definite views on the question of racial equality, which not many people articulated in the 1930s. As people didn't generally take much notice of what young people said, it was probably thought to be something that would just fade away. But as I got older, my views got firmer, and, of course, public opinion did too, as in the Civil Rights movement. When I went to college I met for the first time women who were politically committed. I was not politically knowledgeable at the time, and I did not spend a lot of time on political issues, but I was able for the first time to talk face to face with people about radical issues.'

During the week that followed their meeting, Caroline and Tony saw a good deal of each other. She recognized that he shared her social and political commitment. He appreciated her strength of character, impressive intellect, obvious sympathy, apparently limitless vitality, and genuine sense of fun.

On the evening of 10 August, the day before she was to leave Oxford, Caroline went for coffee to Tony's rooms at 2 Church Walk. On the way back to her college, Tony realized that he would never see her again unless some proposal was made. It was just after midnight, and he decided to act. Stopping at a telephone kiosk by Plantation Road, he rang his brother to say he would not be returning to London that night. From that moment, as they walked along, he was looking for somewhere suitable to propose. At the point where the Woodstock and the Banbury Roads converge there were three benches. Picking on the centre one, Tony sat down next to Caroline and asked her to marry him. Although it was only nine days after they had met and the proposal was unexpected, she accepted. (Later Tony Benn bought for £10 from Oxford Council the bench on which he had proposed. It stands now outside the Benns' home.)

Almost immediately after becoming engaged, the couple separated. Accepting that after her marriage she would live in Britain with her husband, Caroline returned to the United States. As it had been agreed that Tony would join her there after he had completed his degree, Caroline decided not to take up her fellowship at Columbia University in New York but to study instead at the University of Cincinnati in her beloved hometown.

Corresponding frequently and voluminously, Tony and Caroline described to each other their families, their backgrounds, interests, and their views. Everything they wrote reinforced their affection and confirmed the wisdom of their decision.

When he had completed his examinations, Tony set sail for the United States, where he was to sell magazines for Benn Brothers until Caroline had completed her second degree. After spending a few days together with her parents he set off on his travels as a salesman. From January to June 1949, his was a miserable, lonely life staying at nights in one little hotel after another, while during the days trying to sell British trade magazines in a country that was full of its own glossy ones.

At the end of the academic year, Caroline was awarded her MA for a thesis on the poetry of John Milton. On 17 June 1949, she and Tony were married at the Church of the Advent in Cincinnati. Their honeymoon was spent on Lake Michigan but their stay there was interrupted. Sharing his father's dislike of leisurely holidays, Tony took Caroline, just as his father had taken his mother on their honeymoon, to an international congress. It was the Summer Institute for Social Progress held at Wellesley College, where Tony took part in a debate with a Polish Communist on the future of post-war Europe.

They sailed for Britain on 30 July. For a while they stayed with Tony's parents at 40 Millbank, but it was not long before they had organized their immediate future. Tony obtained an appointment as a talks producer for the BBC North American Service, with an annual salary of £475; Caroline enrolled for a second post-graduate degree at University College, London; and they moved into a flat at Stamford Court, Chiswick.

Although having their own friends and interests, the couple still saw a good deal of Tony Benn's parents, who were themselves fully involved in their individual activities. Lady Stansgate was much occupied with religious affairs. With her husband she visited Israel several times. Later she became a member of the Executive of the Council of Christians and Jews. She was also a founder member of the inter-denominational Society for the Ordination of Women. With her encouragement, her husband in 1946, when he was Secretary of State for Air, appointed the Rev. Elsie Chamberlain as the first woman chaplain in the forces.

Despite his uncertain health, Lord Stansgate in the years after the war remained extremely active, pursuing new goals. In April 1946, he was sent to Cairo to head the British delegation for the Anglo-Egyptian talks about the renegotiation of the 1936 Treaty, which gave Britain the right to maintain troops in Egypt – an arrangement that was no longer acceptable to Egyptian public opinion. Although Stansgate conducted these negotiations on behalf of the Labour Government, he did not conceal his strong sympathy with the cause of Egyptian self-determination. At the end of the talks, Attlee announced in the Commons on 7 May that British troops would be withdrawn, although no agreement had been reached on the future of the Sudan, then under an Anglo-Egyptian condominium. The negotiations paved the way for the final withdrawal from Egypt of British troops which had been stationed there since 1882. Thereafter in Egypt, as in India, Stansgate was always recognized as a friend and supporter of the country's national aspirations.

Having been asked by Attlee to resign from the Cabinet in October 1946 to make way for a younger man, Stansgate assumed that his political career was over. 'Well, it's happened now,' he told his wife. 'I've retired.' But it was not to be. Shortly afterwards he was elected the President of the Inter-Parliamentary Union, an organization based in Geneva which was devoted to furthering international understanding, especially among politicians. During his ten years of office Stansgate revitalized the IPU and, largely through his dedication and lobbying throughout the world, its active membership was doubled. Among the new members he was instrumental in recruiting were the USSR, Spain, India, Pakistan, Burma, Thailand, Libya, Tunisia and Israel. To his regret, he failed, in the face of unrelenting opposition from the United States, to obtain the admission of the People's Republic of China.

His fervent internationalism, which Tony Benn shared, was not in tune with the times, in which the immediate post-war suspicion of Communism had been intensified into the Cold War and witch-hunts against anyone suspected of Communist associations. In his opposition to this paranoia, Stansgate often stood alone. On 10 May 1949, he asked in the Lords a question about the decision of John Lewis Partnership to dismiss employees who were members of the Communist Party. (As a protest, his wife closed the family's small account at the store.) On 2 May 1950, he proposed a motion of censure on Lord Vansittart who had made allegations in the Lords about Communist infiltration of the Civil Service and the Church of England. Although outrageously accused by Vansittart of having 'taken his ticket and labelled himself as a fellow-passenger of fellow-travellers', Stansgate spiritedly announced:

> 'My Lords, we nonconformists have a hymn:
> "Dare to be a Daniel, dare to stand alone."
> That is what I propose to do.'

And he did stand alone. No member of the Lords was prepared to second the motion, even though one of those present, the Bishop of Bradford, had been accused by Vansittart of being a Communist sympathizer.

The willingness 'to be a Daniel' had been the hall-mark of the Benn family for generations. As a dissenter, the Rev. Julius Benn had been prepared to fight alone for his faith, his family, and the East End poor; Sir John Benn had been prepared to fight alone so that the people of London could have cheap public transport, parks and free libraries; and Wedgwood Benn had been prepared to fight alone first to ensure the radical beliefs of the Liberal Party and then to improve international understanding. Yet they were never really alone. Each had a strong supportive wife, (and, therefore, a strong supportive mother) who made their own work possible and who provided the family organization in which they all found such succour that the approbation of others, even their political colleagues, was unnecessary.

Being prepared to stand alone in public for a principle is then part of Tony Benn's heritage. There is much more. Not only did he benefit from his father's political memory that stretched back to the beginning of the century, he had also acquired many of his father's attitudes. Like him, he deplored wasting time and organized all his work meticulously, having already begun to amass the files and diaries which, like his father's, provide a most valuable archival resource for political students. He also shared his father's internationalism, his support for colonial independence, his unwavering belief in parliamentary democracy, and his distrust, born of the Benn family's early experiences, of a legal system that appeared to buttress the establishment rather than to dispense justice equitably.

Most importantly, Tony Benn like his father was determined to play the fullest part in the work that was seen as being for the greater good. Aware that his had been a privileged life, he felt deeply committed to the building of a more egalitarian society, not just in Britain but also in its colonies. To fulfil his long-term ambition of becoming a Member of Parliament, he wanted but the opportunity. It was soon to be provided.

5
TONY BENN AND THE PEERAGE
1950-1964

With the post-war economic recovery well under way, it was generally assumed that Attlee and his Government would easily win the 1950 General Election. Yet on 23 February the Labour Party obtained an overall majority of only five. It clearly had been unable to counteract the virulent anti-nationalization campaign waged in the press or the growing fears that Communist expansion in Asia threatened world peace. Also the implementation of its more socialist policies had been made more difficult by the constraints on social spending demanded by the United States as the price for its Marshall Aid, which in April 1949 began flooding into Britain after the Government, in a badly miscalculated bid to retain the country's status as a world power, had overcommitted its military resources and had consequently been forced into dependence on the financial and strategic assistance of the United States.

Believing that he had no mandate to implement his policies after the election, Attlee marked time and his ageing, exhausted Government began to crumble, just as Asquith's had done after 1911. In October 1950, Sir Stafford Cripps, the Chancellor of the Exchequer, was forced by ill-health to resign both from the Cabinet and from the Commons, in which he had represented Bristol South East since January 1931.

As the Labour Party had such a slender majority, it was essential that the seat be retained, although that did not appear difficult, for in the 1950 election it had been won by Cripps with a majority of nearly 17,000. Naturally, the General Management Committee of the constituency was inundated with applications from would-be candidates, including several who had lost their seats at the General Election.

To his surprise, Tony Benn received a message from Mervyn Stockwood, then Vicar of St Matthews, Bristol (and later the Bishop of Southwark), asking if he would like to apply to be the candidate in Bristol South East. He had apparently been recommended by Tony Crosland, his ex-tutor at Oxford, who had just become the Labour MP for South Gloucester. A few months earlier Tony Benn had been short-listed for Birmingham Northfield, the seat held by Raymond Blackburn, who in August 1950 had resigned from the Labour Party; but as the selection conference had not been held, he accepted a nomination from Bristol.

Tony Benn was one of three people on the short-list. The others had both been defeated at the General Election. They were Arthur Creech-Jones, the former Secretary of State for the Colonies, who had been born in the constituency, and Muriel Wallhead Nicholl. As Creech-Jones was certain, if elected, to be restored to the Cabinet, he was Transport House's choice and the National Agent, Dick Windle, attended the selection conference to support his candidature.

On 1 November 1950 – the day of the conference – Tony Benn arrived in Bristol for the very first time. Each prospective candidate had to speak for ten minutes and answer questions for five. Naturally, Tony Benn had prepared his speech meticulously. Even at the beginning of his political life, his remarkable gifts of oratory were well evident, and what he said made a considerable impact. He declared:

'Socialism is not just a question of material progress. It isn't concerned only with wages and taxation. Nor is a socialist policy a sort of Christmas stocking of a policy with a little bit for everyone. It is a faith and a way of life and a way of thinking that can find its expression in every city and every community and every home. We are trying to build the sort of society where everybody "counts for something" and no one is neglected or left out, where "love your neighbour as yourself" finds practical expression. We must never get so bogged down by detail that we lose sight of that wider vision.'

He was then asked questions, two of which he vividly remembers:

'One was, "If we select you, will you give money to the constituency?" I knew that Stafford Cripps before the war had been giving £500 a year and that as Creech-Jones was a trade union sponsored candidate there would be some contribution from him. But I replied, "This is not a Tory selection conference. If I had any money to give, which I haven't, I certainly wouldn't tell you before selection." I got a tremendous cheer for that.

The second thing they asked was, "If we select you, will you live in Bristol?" I said, "No, I won't. I'm just married. I hope to have a family. My work as an MP will keep me in London, and if I were to live in Bristol I wouldn't see my family except at the weekends and I'd be very unhappy. But I promise you that I'll be in Bristol whenever you want me."'

When the voting took place, Tony Benn was elected on the first ballot, receiving forty votes to Creech-Jones's eleven and Muriel Nicholl's four. The following day he had to resign from the BBC which had a rule that producers could not participate in politics.

The by-election campaign was not easy, for the Labour Government was unpopular and the outbreak of the Korean War in June had spawned a desire, carefully nurtured by the press, to see Churchill, the acknowledged war leader, restored as Prime Minister. The fear of war was heightened by Truman's announcement, on Polling Day, that he was willing to use the atomic bomb in Korea. Refusing to be diverted by such hysteria, Tony Benn campaigned for the socialist policies of public ownership and the redistribution of wealth. And, even though the Labour majority fell by nearly 10,000, he was elected on 30 November as the Labour MP for Bristol South East. Aged twenty-five, he was, like his father when he was first elected, the youngest Member of Parliament.

Yet when Wedgwood Benn had become an MP in 1906, he had joined his father in the Commons. Tony Benn was in a different position, for his father was in the Lords and, as the heir to an hereditary peerage, his career as a Member of Parliament seemed limited. Indeed the people of Bristol South East had elected a man who was at the time effectively seventy-three years old, his father's age.

This did not distress Tony Benn, however, for he was convinced that it would not be difficult for him to renounce the title. As she explains, Caroline Benn also took this view, regarding the peerage as an irrelevancy that could not possibly become an impediment to an active political life:

'When I heard the first time that his mother had a different name, I assumed that there had been a remarriage. I didn't understand anything about the peerage. It came up first only as a very minor matter, as a sort of curiosity and not as something that was very important. It's so old-fashioned, and for an American it's part of all that was renounced on behalf of the new republic of 1776 – you renounced the devil and all his works, socially speaking. Part of freedom was freedom from hereditary rule and state religions. For years I didn't believe that anyone living in a twentieth-century democracy could put a title before the other principles by which you swore, such as a representative electoral system.'

Not accepting then that his parliamentary career might be brief, Tony Benn threw himself wholeheartedly into his work as an MP. In his maiden speech on 7 February 1951 he firmly attacked the Opposition's motion condemning the nationalization of the steel industry. The speech was well received, but its central plea that the Labour Government should stick to its socialist policies was to go unheeded. In April, Hugh Gaitskell introduced his deflationary budget to meet the £4,700,000 cost of the Korean War. Objecting to the imposition of health prescription charges and distressed by rearmament and the associated dependence on America, Aneurin Bevan, Harold Wilson and John Freeman resigned from the Government.

This split between the left and the ruling right in the Labour Party was to dominate its affairs throughout the decade. Tony Benn was invited to join the Bevanites, but refused, firstly because the group had its own whipping system which he would not accept, and secondly because he did not wish to be a member of a parliamentary group that was smaller than the Labour Party as a whole. Instead he met daily with a loose grouping of like-minded radicals: Fenner Brockway, Leslie Hale, Reginald Paget, Ian Mikardo and Geoffrey Bing.

Although his parliamentary and constituency work frequently took him away from home, his chief political confidante was Caroline Benn who involved herself fully in all his activities. Although she had known little about practical politics when they first met, she learned quickly and soon became a far-sighted and incisive political analyst whose opinions Tony Benn always valued, even though he did not always accept her advice. A very private person, she was, at least initially, willing to shelve her own ambitions to become a university lecturer because, coming as she did from a large and happy family, she wanted to have children of her own. Stephen, her first, was born in August 1951. As they then needed more space, the Benns moved into another flat in Stamford Court which had an extra bedroom.

Shortly afterwards, Attlee, faced with dissension in his Party and a series of minor parliamentary defeats, called a General Election for 25 October 1951. A small swing to the Conservatives throughout the country gave them an overall majority. The Labour Party lost thirty seats, although Tony Benn easily retained his, nearly doubling his previous majority.

As his parliamentary seat was at least temporarily secure, the Benns in 1952 purchased for £4500 a four-storey house in Holland Park Avenue in which they have lived ever since and where Stephen, his two younger brothers and sister grew up. (Hilary was born in 1953, Melissa in 1957, and Joshua in 1958.) Theirs has been a comfortable existence, free from financial anxiety, for in addition to his parliamentary salary Tony Benn has always received some income from his shares in Benn Brothers and from his occasional work as a broadcaster and journalist. In addition, Caroline Benn could look forward to being left money by her own parents. This sum, which is a matter of public record, has been wildly exaggerated by the British press, and stories of vast wealth, usually associated on Tony Benn's side with imagined aristocratic connections, vast private estates and secret multi-million pound trusts, are untrue. Moreover, much of the family's additional money has been used, as Tony Benn's father's was, to support political work and to maintain an efficient office at home.

During his early days in Parliament, the only cloud on Tony Benn's horizon was the chance that he would be unable to rid himself of the peerage. He deemed it advisable, therefore, to work for the introduction of enabling legislation. The first attempt was made on 11 February 1953, when Reginald Paget introduced in the Commons the Peers Bill which stipulated: 'That no person shall exercise the privilege or suffer the disqualification of the peerage until such a time as they have taken the oath in the House of Lords.' After a short debate, the Bill was defeated by 238 votes to 145. Concluding that no such general change was likely to be acceptable, Tony Benn determined to study the peerage law so that he could make a personal application. He did not, however, see the peerage issue merely as a personal matter. From the start it was for him a wider question of individual freedom. He was determined not to be deprived of his democratic right to stand for election as a Member of Parliament by an hereditary title that he did not want to accept.

Because of his fight and the interests he had acquired before entering Parliament, he was eager to take up the cause of others whose civil rights and personal liberties were being attacked. In March 1954, both he and his father sought to obtain the reinstatement of Paul Garland who had been dismissed from the Bristol Boy Scouts because he was a Communist. After Stansgate had spoken in the Lords, the Bishop of Southwell said of him:

'Everybody holds him in honour for the way in which he is always ready to support the unpopular opinion, the minority cause and the under-dog. Indeed, all through his public life he has made himself a kind of knight errant of freedom of conscience; whenever he sees the damsel in distress, out comes his sword and to the rescue he rides.'

The following month, Tony Benn received a letter from Dr Joseph Cort, an American lecturing at Birmingham University, who, because of his previous membership of the Communist Party, had been called back to the United States for military service, even though he had previously failed the medical test. The Home Secretary had agreed to the American authorities' request that he should not renew Cort's residence permit. Tony Benn lobbied Ministers and moved in the Commons an adjournment motion on the disturbing case, but the Government would not relent, refusing to acknowledge that there were any political factors.

Tony Benn was concerned not only with such cases involving individual liberty, but also with the wider movement for colonial freedom of which he had for long been an advocate. In the fifties the Benns' home in Holland

Park became a centre of the anti-colonial movement and a safe-house for many exiled African and Arab nationalists. The Benns struck up many lasting friendships, including one with Ruth and Seretse Khama during his long exile from Bechuanaland. At four o'clock one morning, after a long night's political discussion, both Ruth Khama and Caroline Benn, deciding to give up smoking, agreed that they would only smoke another cigarette if they first obtained the other's permission. Neither has ever smoked since.

With Fenner Brockway, Tony Benn formed the Seretse Khama Defence Council and served on the Central African Committee which sought to arouse public opposition to the formation of a Central African Federation. In Parliament he consistently advocated self-government for the individual colonies and fiercely criticized the Government's repression in Kenya which had helped cause the Mau Mau rebellion.

Radical support in Britain for colonial independence gave rise to many fragmented pressure groups, which clearly needed to be brought into a co-ordinated movement. On 8 March 1954, Tony Benn was involved in the launch of 'a new organization to rally public opinion in favour of a change in colonial policy'. At the inaugural conference of the Movement for Colonial Freedom, Fenner Brockway was elected as Chairman and Tony Benn as Treasurer. Over a hundred MPs, thirty-eight constituency Labour parties and twenty-two trade unions gave their support.

Through his work with the MCF, Tony Benn realized that not all aspirations were represented in the political system and that extra-parliamentary groups were essential to represent mass movements rightly demanding change. In Parliament he kept up a constant flow of questions and adjournment motions that were highly critical of the Conservative Government's limited concept of justice and equality. In part, through his substantial efforts and those of colleagues, especially Fenner Brockway, the previously less than enthusiastic Labour Party committed itself by the mid-fifties to a policy of speedy decolonization.

Another movement with which Tony Benn at that time was actively involved was the H-Bomb National Committee which he founded on 11 April 1954 with Sir Richard Acland, Fenner Brockway, Anthony Greenwood and Donald Soper. Appalled that the development of the hydrogen bomb had taken place without the consent of Parliament, Tony Benn was determined that public pressure should prevent further nuclear tests and encourage disarmament. Speaking at a May Day rally in Bristol, he declared: 'The whole battle for parliamentary control [over nuclear weapons] has been a battle for the rights of people to govern their own destinies.' At the end of the campaign, 357,000 people had signed the petition calling for arms reduction, and Tony Benn, Anthony Greenwood, Sidney Silverman and George Thomas (later to become the Speaker in the House of Commons) presented it at 10 Downing Street on 31 December 1954.

Earlier that month Tony Benn had presented to the Personal Bills Committee his own petition, entitled 'The Wedgwood Benn (Renunciation) Bill'. In January 1955, the members of the Committee were named, including Lord Drogheda and the former Lord Chancellor, Lord Simmonds. Tony Benn prepared his own case, and the evidence submitted included the Instrument of Renunciation which stated:

'I, Anthony Neil Wedgwood Benn, do hereby declare my irrevocable desire to cease to be the heir male to the name, state, degree, style, dignity, title and honour of the Viscount Stansgate of Stansgate in the County of Essex.'

It was witnessed by, among others, Clement Attlee, Aneurin Bevan, Jo Grimond and Julian Amery. One of the witnesses to Caroline Benn's Statement of Consent was Roy Jenkins.

The petition for leave to present the private Bill was heard on 18 February 1955. After surveying the whole gamut of peerage legislation, Tony Benn stressed the uniqueness of his case, declaring: 'I seek only to be allowed to continue to serve my constituents as their representative in the House of Commons. I am the first person in history who has ever offered to renounce the peerage for this reason.' As supporting evidence he presented a resolution signed by the Lord Mayor, aldermen and burgesses of Bristol asking for legislation allowing them to retain him as one of the city's Members of Parliament. Despite congratulating Tony Benn on 'the very able and attractive way' in which he presented the petition, Lord Drogheda, after a brief withdrawal, announced, 'The Committee does not feel able to report to the House that the objects of the Bill are proper to be enacted by personal Bill.' It was obvious that the Committee was afraid that Tony Benn's Bill, if accepted, would undermine the hereditary principle and the power of the second chamber, which had recovered from its wartime doldrums and, with a Conservative Government and increased volume of legislation, had been given a fresh lease of life.

Paradoxically, it was Lord Stansgate, as much as any individual, who had brought distinction to the House of Lords. His debating skills, parliamentary expertise and rapier wit were widely appreciated and reported. His individualism and his refusal to kow-tow to Party discipline heightened the level of debate above the insipid conformity usually expected. Even though his political position was seen as having moved further to the left in his old age, Lord Stansgate was much admired even by journalists who gently teased him for his views. Thus the Parliamentary Correspondent of the *Guardian* wrote:

'Lord Stansgate can be relied upon to introduce some red, or pink corpuscles into any House of Lords debate whether it is showing anaemic signs or not ... He is essentially a Bevanite in scarlet and ermine, though the only leader to whom he acknowledges allegiance is Lord Stansgate. This fiery particle does not mind treading on anybody's toes.'

As a protest against the rejection of his son's petition, Lord Stansgate reintroduced the Bill in the House of Lords on 15 March 1955. The debate took place on 26 April, but the Lord Chancellor, Viscount Kilmuir, declared that the constitution was more important than any individual grievance, and after an hour and a half the Bill was decisively rejected.

The only course of action apparently still left open to Tony Benn was to press for reform of the House of Lords, even though the possibility of a radical change seemed increasingly slight. In May the Conservatives were returned at the General Election with an even greater majority. Seven months later Attlee resigned as the Leader of the Labour Party and Gaitskell defeated Bevan in the election for the successor, thus confirming the Party's drift to the right.

While considering what constitutional reforms could be proposed, Tony Benn continued to be deeply involved in his twin activities of advocating colonial self-government and protecting individual freedoms. On 21 March 1956, during a debate on a Bill introduced by the Conservative Government to tighten the security vetting of civil servants so that Communist supporters could be excluded, Tony Benn stated that he desired informed civil servants capable of free thought and independent inquiry: 'Far from dismissing any member of the Foreign Office who had read Karl Marx, my inclination would be to dismiss anyone who had not read Karl Marx.' He concluded, 'The real security of a free society lies in its freedom.'

When the Suez crisis erupted in the autumn of 1956, Tony Benn saw the debacle as a cynical perpetuation of the colonialism he so vehemently opposed. All too aware of the imminence of war, and distressed by Gaitskell's initial support of Anthony Eden,* Tony Benn addressed on 16 September a rally of over 7,000 people in Trafalgar Square. Urging that the Conservatives' belligerence should be replaced by international peace moves, he stated, 'I am afraid to sit opposite 300 MPs who dream of an empire all their lives.' On 29 October, Israel attacked Egypt, and the following day France and Britain joined the invasion. Tony Benn spent a whole day with Gaitskell helping him to draft for a television broadcast his statement that the Labour Party would support any other Conservative Leader who stopped the war. Faced with joint American–Russian demands

*Eden had replaced Churchill as the Prime Minister in April 1955.

for a ceasefire and with widespread public and political condemnation at home, the British Government speedily complied and by 2 December all British troops had left Egypt. As a reward for his sustained attacks on the Government throughout the crisis, Tony Benn was appointed by Gaitskell to be Labour's second front-bench spokesman on the RAF.

As it was considered that he would become, like his father, an expert Parliamentarian, he also joined the Select Committee on Procedure, where he constantly urged the need for all power to be accountable.

In January 1957 (the month that Macmillan replaced Eden as the Prime Minister), Tony Benn's proposals for the reform of the House of Lords were published in a Fabian Society pamphlet, 'The Privy Council as a Second Chamber', which suggested that the Privy Councillors who opted not to sit in the Commons should form a body that would undertake the existing responsibilities of the Lords. It was an unsatisfactory, though original, compromise, falling short of advocating total abolition, although his most cogent passages were those which made that case:

'To claim that a House based on appointment and heredity should act as a mouthpiece for the opinions of the nation is not only dangerous because it is untrue, but it would be very undesirable even if it were true.'

No doubt concerned that would-be reformers might move towards the abolitionist view, Macmillan determined to undertake revitalization, announcing that he would introduce life peers in the parliamentary session of 1957/58.

It was not an innovation that appealed to Tony Benn, because it considerably reduced the possibility of radical reform and because any powers given to the Lords inevitably lessened those of the Commons. And that was something to which Tony Benn was bitterly opposed. So when in July 1957 the Speaker refused to accept Tony Benn's demand that there should be an emergency debate on the Government's decision to send troops, so soon after Suez, to Muscat and Oman, he tabled a motion of censure on the Speaker. In the debate he firmly asserted that, despite the Party system, it was the freedom to speak in the Commons that was the protector of freedom:

'The modern Party system, even at its most oppressive does not in any way limit our rights to speak. It may limit how we vote at the end of the day, although in my own Party and in the Party opposite we have the right of abstention on grounds of principle. That is a comfort which I draw from the restrictions of the Party system. "It is not what a man does that matters; it is what he says." It is not the vote at the end of the day that limits our rights. It is the right of free thought and free speech that is left unfettered by the Party system ... I am not forming an anti-Party faction ... I am one of the thousand flowers asking permission to be allowed to bloom.'

The speech attracted considerable attention and Bernard Levin in the *Spectator* wrote a congratulatory paean:

'It was eloquent beyond the farthest reach of all but a hand-count of his fellow-members; it was witty, graceful, modest, learned, pointed, and in some strange way deeply moving. More: it was magnificently constructed to make, by easy stages and gentle persuasion, his point – that the rights of backbenchers had diminished, were diminishing, and ought to be increased. Mr Benn, in his oration, struck a great blow for his view and for himself. But he did more: he struck a blow for Parliament.'

No doubt Tony Benn's ability to attract such a good press contributed to his election, in October 1957, as Chairman of the Labour Party's Advisory Committee on Broadcasting.

The following month, Macmillan, as he had promised, introduced the Life Peerages Bill. When it was debated in the Lords on 17 December, Lord Silkin introduced an amendment to allow all hereditary peers to become life peers. That would, of course, have permitted Tony Benn to remain a commoner, but the amendment was fiercely attacked, being described by the Earl of Macclesfield as 'detestable'. It was rejected by 75 votes to 25.

In the interval before the Peerage Act received the royal assent, which it did on 30 April 1958, Tony Benn introduced as a Private Member's Bill his own suggestions for parliamentary reform. He sought to:

(1) remove all hereditary peers from the Lords;
(2) permit commoners to be made life members of the Lords;
(3) abolish all the powers of the House of Lords over statutory instruments; and
(4) give the Commons the power to override any obstacles from the Lords.

The Bill, when it was presented on 28 February 1958, attracted little support. There was no longer real public interest in or support for further reforms of the House of Lords. Although his determination to renounce the peerage was not one whit lessened, his attempts to change the structure of the House of Lords were at an end, and it was perhaps better that it was so. Tony Benn was well aware that his father, who was over eighty, much enjoyed his work in the House of Lords. As the lease on the house in Millbank had expired, Lord Stansgate and his wife had moved into a small flat in Great Peter Street, almost opposite the Houses of Parliament which, for the best part of fifty years, had been his true home.

Tony Benn's attention moved to organizational work for the Labour Party, which under Gaitskell had ditched its socialist programme. Although somewhat bemused by this, Tony Benn was not then deeply distressed. 'I did have sound radical instincts,' he told me, 'but, when I look back, I realize that my understanding of the socialist position was very imperfect.' Inclined, like his father, to be more interested in action than ideology, he was at his happiest when fully occupied. In July 1958, he prepared a memorandum on the necessity for a tactical staff to advise the Party Leader on operations in Parliament. This was well received and, impressed by his unending flood of ideas and his considerable organizational ability, Gaitskell asked him the following year to help in the run-up to the next General Election. In the campaign before election day on 8 October 1959, Tony Benn monitored the daily progress of the Labour Party and masterminded the first ever political broadcasts on television. Acting as a linkman between famous personalities and Labour politicians, he was in his element, surrounded by gadgets and new technology. Throughout the campaign he did his best to portray the Labour Party as modern and progressive. It was certainly no fault of his that the majority of the electorate preferred the established, avuncular style of Macmillan. For the third successive General Election the Conservatives increased their majority. From 1945, when it won 393 seats, the Labour Party's representation had sunk to 258.

As a result of its ignominious defeat, the Party was wracked by self-doubt and dissatisfaction. Gaitskell's position as Leader and the policies he advocated were soon under attack. In an atmosphere of increasing tension, every faction suspected others of deviousness and self-advertisement. Even Tony Benn, who studiously avoided joining any group, was suspected for showing what was considered to be excessive zeal. Richard Crossman tetchily wrote in his diary on 19 October 1959:

'I gave Tony Benn dinner at the Athenaeum. He's as keen as anyone on a sensible reorganization, including effective co-ordination of Parliament and Transport House. He pullulates with proposals, including the names of the people to fill every job, from top to bottom. His enthusiasm is, for me, the reverse of infectious. The more names he names, the more cautious I get.'

At the annual Labour Party Conference, which took place at the end of November, Gaitskell, in an effort to revive the Party and to divert criticism from himself, sided with the revisionists like Roy Jenkins and Tony Crosland and initiated the debate aimed at abandoning Clause IV, the commitment to public ownership. Although remaining on the fringes of the debate,

Tony Benn, who had been elected to the National Executive Committee for the first time, supported the retention of the clause while pleading for the modernization of the Party so that it appealed more to the younger electorate whose votes it had so obviously failed to win in the General Election.

Although just failing to be elected to the Shadow Cabinet, Tony Benn was appointed by Gaitskell as the Shadow transport spokesman. At thirty-four, he was Labour's youngest Shadow Minister. Typically he threw himself energetically into a detailed study of a subject about which he had not previously known a great deal. In December he introduced a Private Member's Bill to initiate a comprehensive transport policy. Throughout 1960 he constantly attacked Ernest Marples, the Transport Minister, for his failure to provide adequate investment in public transport or to implement a satisfactory road-safety programme. Considerably ahead of his time, he advocated the compulsory wearing of safety-belts, annual tests of vehicles, and stiffer penalties for drunken drivers. Convinced that the chaotic road conditions were a result of priority being given to private rather than public interests, he campaigned for a programme of subsidies to modernize and extend the public transport system. After visiting Stockholm and Germany in July, he returned to condemn the British road system as outdated and to demand 'a twenty-year programme based on scientific study'. His efforts awakened such public consciousness that Marples was forced to exercise a greatly increased measure of centralized control.

Within the Labour Party, Tony Benn campaigned for decisive leadership, developed policies, and more efficient organization. He came to accept that such changes would be extremely difficult while Gaitskell remained as the Party's leader. Seeking for new approaches, he visited Russia in September, returning with renewed enthusiasm for public ownership. Politically estranged from Gaitskell, he attended the Labour Party Conference in October where events convinced him that a new Leader must be found for, when the unilateral disarmament motion proposed by Frank Cousins was overwhelmingly accepted, Gaitskell refused to accept it, declaring, 'There are some of us, Mr Chairman, who will fight and fight and fight again to save the Party we love.' Tony Benn, although not a unilateralist, had in the debate pleaded for Party unity, strongly feeling that the nuclear issue was being used as an excuse to permit the right to expel the left from the Party. Believing that Cousins and Gaitskell should have accepted a compromise rather than forcing a confrontation, he resigned from the NEC. The move, which Caroline Benn advised him not to make, was not well received and was indeed badly miscalculated for it served no obvious purpose. Although he stood immediately for re-election, he was not returned, being the runner-up in the constituency section.

After the Conference, Harold Wilson announced on 29 October that he would stand for the Party leadership. In the poll of Labour Members that took place a few days later Gaitskell was victorious with 166 votes, while Harold Wilson obtained the support of eighty-one MPs, including Tony Benn. No longer on the NEC. and with his Shadow Cabinet position in jeopardy because of his open opposition to the Party Leader, Tony Benn seemed to have spoiled his chances of further advancement and to have lost some of the support from the Party membership. Suddenly, however, he was catapulted into the epicentre of public attention.

After lunch on 15 November, Lord Stansgate, who was eighty-three, walked to the House of Lords intending to speak against the Central African Federation which he believed, like his son, was a device designed to perpetuate white rule in Rhodesia. Before he could make his speech, he suffered a heart attack. Tony Benn was called from the Commons and stayed with his father until the ambulance arrived. The following afternoon, with his wife by his bedside, Lord Stansgate died. That evening they had planned to go to the theatre – it was their fortieth wedding anniversary.

All the national newspapers carried tributes to the man known popularly as 'Little Benn' or 'Wedgie' who had been an ever-present figure on the political stage throughout the century. Under the headline 'Freedom was his passion', the *Daily Herald* described him as the 'Fighter Scholar'. The *Manchester Guardian* stated, 'Diminutive of stature, bright of spirit, and moved by strong conviction, he was of the very type to win popularity at Westminster and he did so in full measure.' *The Times* obituary said:

'By his death British public life is deprived of one of its most vivid personalities and the House of Lords loses one of its most endearing, irrepressible, provocative, and witty debaters.

"Wedgie Benn", as he was affectionately known, was a fighter to the end of his days. Age seemed only to sharpen the flashing blade of his scorn for injustice, indolence, equivocation, or woolly mindedness in high places. The spell of his charm could, however, vanquish the most acute exasperation which he might provoke, and even his victims forgave him. For his integrity of purpose was manifest. His physical bravery was matched by high moral courage, and he stood in awe of nobody.

It is as a Parliamentarian that he will best be remembered. Few could rival his knowledge of procedure or match his mastery of the niceties of debate. His sharp brown eyes could pierce to the heart of any sham; they could also blaze with righteous fury and twinkle with fun. He was relentless in exposing shoddy argument, hypocrisy, and inconsistency. With a vivacity which could electrify the dullest debate, he had a galvanic effect on the House of Lords.'

Further tributes to Lord Stansgate were made in the House of Lords when it next sat on Tuesday, 22 November. Viscount Hailsham was the first to speak. 'In Lord Stansgate,' he said, 'this House has lost one of its most remarkable and colourful figures, as well, I must say, as one of its most conscientious attenders; one who, despite reaching some of the highest positions to be held under the Crown, never became pompous or dull.' Next Viscount Alexander of Hillsborough and then Lord Amulree paid their tributes. The final speaker was Earl Attlee:

'What always struck me about "Wedgie" was that, although he was now well on in years, he still had the heart of a boy. He had an extraordinary zest for life and he was always a knight errant, ready at all times to take up a cause for anything or any person in the world whom he thought to be suffering injustice. He was a great character. We shall miss him very sadly. I know that our sympathy goes out to his family. I think that he himself would have liked to die in harness – the happy warrior.'

Naturally there was considerable media interest in Tony Benn's position, for immediately after his father's death he renounced the title. On 23 November he held a press conference at which he announced that symbolically he had returned unopened the letters patent to the Lord Chamberlain and that he was 'not a reluctant peer but a persistent commoner'. Requesting the formation of a select committee to consider his case, he said that if deprived of his seat he would stand repeatedly for election to the Commons, just as Charles Bradlaugh had done throughout his fight, as a militant atheist, not to swear the oath of allegiance.

The novelty of the occasion attracted much interest and, although not all Labour MPs thought it an issue worth fighting, the press were generally supportive. *The Times*, for example, concluded an editorial on 25 October by stating: 'Whatever turning it may be best to take in the constitutional and procedural maze in which he finds himself, Mr Benn deserves to succeed in his main objective.' Although agreeably surprised by such support, Tony Benn knew that he must convince his constituency party that his fight was not about an individual's right to reject privilege but about the need to transform archaic aspects of society. At a mass meeting in Bristol on 26 November he said, 'The fight is really just a small part of the struggle to bring Britain up to date. Tradition should breathe life into things that are dead; it should not breathe death into things that are alive.' Two days later the General Management Committee of the Bristol South East Labour Party unanimously agreed to affirm the right of the electorate to choose its MP and the right of the MP it had elected to sit in the Commons.

On 29 November, Sir Lynn Ungoed-Thomas, the Labour MP for Leicester North East and a former Solicitor General, presented to the Clerk of the House a petition from Tony Benn which stated fully his case and asked for a select committee 'to grant him such other relief as it may think fit and proper'. The proposal was, however, rejected by the Home Secretary, Rab Butler, who wished to refer the matter to the Committee of Privileges, a move that the Commons accepted without a division.

Butler's intransigence in the case contrasted sharply with his previously untarnished liberal image and typified the confusion and ambivalence generated by the issue. Although not deprived of his seat, Tony Benn was not permitted to enter the Chamber of the House of Commons; although as a kindly gesture Gaitskell had asked him to continue as the Shadow Minister for Transport until the end of the year, Tony Benn's parliamentary salary and allowances were stopped on the night of his father's death. His right to remain as an MP was widely recognized, and yet, because the machinery apparently did not exist for this to be achieved, many Parliamentarians seemed to hope that the issue would just fade away. There were also some, especially the representatives of the traditional establishment, who could not understand why anyone should so adamantly refuse an honour that so many others strove so desperately to achieve.

It was soon apparent that there would not be a speedy resolution to Tony Benn's petition. So when the Committee of Privileges, consisting of fourteen MPs from all parties, summoned him to appear on 12 December, he was asked to answer little other than factual questions; the examination of case histories and the intricacies of peerage law continued over ten long hearings. At its final meeting on 14 March 1961, the Committee considered the Attorney General's draft report which concluded that a peerage could not be surrendered because in 1626 Justice Dodderidge had decreed that it was 'an incorporeal heriditament affixed in the blood and annexed to the posterity'. Although accepting the verdict, the Labour members of the Committee, striving to find a remedy, forced divisions on a number of amendments. It was recommended that a joint committee with the House of Lords should consider reforms, but the amendment requesting legislation to redress Tony Benn's grievance was defeated by the casting vote of Butler, the Chairman. When the Committee's report was published on 21 March, it did not recommend any legislation. Tony Benn, incensed at being excluded from the Commons because of a judgment made almost 350 years earlier, declared, 'Far from being the end of the matter, it marks the beginning of a campaign of common sense, personal freedom and elementary democracy.'

The following day Charles Pannell, who though a right-wing Labour MP became a most active supporter, demanded in the Commons that Tony Benn should be permitted to speak from the bar of the House. The Speaker, Sir Henry Hylton Foster, deferred his decision. While it was being awaited, on 24 March, Sir Lynn Ungoed-Thomas presented a Bill 'to provide machinery whereby certain peerages may be renounced for life'. Marking the beginning of the all-party, liberal support that was to develop for Tony Benn's case, the Bill was supported by among others Lord Lambton and the Conservative MPs Gerald Nabarro, Gilbert Longden and Peter Kirk. The Bill got nowhere and three days later the Speaker announced that Tony Benn would not be permitted to address the House. Amid growing concern from many quarters that Tony Benn was being deprived of his rights without having a fair hearing, the Conservative Government, fearing that there might be a revolt in the Party, announced the imposition of a three-line Whip when the Report of the Committee of Privileges was debated on 13 April. This inept step at last rallied the full support of the Parliamentary Labour Party and on 29 March the Shadow Cabinet decided that it would give its wholehearted backing to Tony Benn's cause. Increasingly supported by the press, including the *Daily Telegraph* which in a leader demanded immediate remedial legislation, Tony Benn intensified his campaign before the parliamentary debate. The day before, he sent to each Conservative MP a copy of a letter he had received from Churchill in 1955:

'As I wrote to you confidentially in September 1953, I certainly feel yours is a very hard case, and I am personally strongly in favour of sons having the right to renounce irrevocably the peerage they inherited from their fathers. This would not of course prevent them from accepting another peerage, if they were offered one, later on.'

The same day, Will Wilkins, the Labour MP for Bristol South, presented to the Commons a petition signed by 10,357 electors of Tony Benn's constituency protesting 'that they may be unjustly denied their right of free choice in the member they have elected to represent them in the present Parliament'.

Before the debate on 13 April, the Speaker announced that he had received a letter from Tony Benn asking permission to address the House. Gaitskell then proposed a motion that he should be heard, adding, 'There is no single case in the history of the House of Commons where a member whose right to sit is in dispute and who has asked leave to address the House has been refused.' Butler, insisting that Tony Benn had ceased to be a Member on the death of his father and was not, therefore, eligible to speak, was all but shouted down. After a stormy debate, the motion was defeated by 221 votes to 152. Butler then proposed the Government motion that note should be taken of the report. Gaitskell moved an amendment, demanding immediate legislation to permit the renunciation of titles, but that too was rejected by 207 votes to 143. In the three hours of heated debate which followed, support for Tony Benn was expressed by MPs from all Parties, and there was much criticism of Butler for his inflexibility, but the Government's motion was accepted by 204 votes to 126, although fifteen Conservatives joined the Liberal and Labour MPs in opposing it.

Throughout the country there was a feeling of anger at the Government's stance, which left the Labour Party with no alternative but to request a parliamentary writ for a by-election in Bristol South East. On 17 April, Tony Benn was unanimously re-selected as the Labour Party candidate, and a week later he and Malcolm St Clair, the Conservative candidate, handed in their nomination papers.

Rarely can a by-election have received either such national interest or such local support. Although the constitutional issue was paramount in most people's minds, Tony Benn was determined that the wider social significance would also be aired. At his adoption meeting on 26 April he announced, 'It is given to Bristol in this election to wrench the Parliamentary system away from its feudal origins and pitchfork it kicking and screaming into the twentieth century.' Taking as the campaign's theme 'The New Generation', Tony Benn used a variety of new techniques, as he described in *Tribune:*

'The meetings were run like a sort of summer school and the speakers who came down were asked to use our platform to get across some of the fundamental things that have got to be done in Britain. Professor Blackett spoke about the scientific revolution, James Cameron about the press, and John Horner about the future of the trade unions. We held an architectural exhibition on town planning in our headquarters and took some exhibits around to our meetings. Afterwards we held seminars for young people from all over the city so that they could come and talk into the small hours with the speakers whom they had heard earlier.'

He even managed to step up the already hectic pace at which he worked at all elections. His agent, Herbert Rogers, reported:

'Our candidate has been referred to as a human dynamo; a more apt description would have been a power station. He was always on the ball. His energy and enthusiasm were untiring and became contagious as the campaign progressed. He would address bus queues at 6 a.m., and attend works canteens at 8 a.m., press conferences at 11 a.m., and spend his afternoons with a loudspeaker and canvassing. After the evening meetings he would be found with other evening speakers at the Hotel with groups of 30 to 40 young persons discussing politics. Tony Benn proved to be the type of candidate any constituency should be proud to have.'

Support for Tony Benn was given by people in all walks of life, including Malcolm Muggeridge, Frank Cousins, C.D. Lewis, Wolf Mankowitz, John

Osborne, Graham Sutherland and Sir Compton Mackenzie. Most reiterated the central theme of the campaign. Gaitskell wrote, 'As Labour candidate you are fighting against out-of-date, stick-in-the-mud attitudes everywhere.' Arnold Toynbee declared, 'Our country is a living community not a historical museum.' Richard Clements, the editor of *Tribune*, stated, 'Your fight in Bristol is the fight of all true radicals in this country against the mealy-mouthed Establishmentarians who try to turn every issue about which people argue into the trivia of gossip and personalities.' To reinforce his message and maintain public interest, Tony Benn issued a daily news sheet, *The Bristol Campaigner*. The local and national press gave their support, the *Guardian* declaring on 24 April that if Tony Benn was not elected it would be a national disaster.

Faced with such a campaign, the Conservatives could do little more than claim that the Labour candidate, whom they insisted on calling Viscount Stansgate, would be disqualified if elected and so votes given to him would be wasted. Apparently as a sop, the Government announced on 26 April that a joint committee with the House of Lords would be set up to consider the peerage law, including the right to surrender. The Bristol electorate was not, however, willing to relinquish its right to select its own MP. On polling day, 4 May, Tony Benn received 23,275 votes and St Clair, the Conservative, 10,231. The majority of 13,044 was over twice that which Tony Benn had obtained in the 1959 General Election.

St Clair refused, however, to admit defeat and the following day announced that he intended 'to petition the court of the Queen's Bench to declare that Viscount Stansgate is incapable of sitting in the House of Commons'. Tony Benn then went privately to see the Speaker.

'I'm turning up on Monday,' he said.

'Well you can't come in,' the Speaker replied.

'Well, I've got a certificate,' Tony Benn insisted. 'I am the duly elected Member and I'm coming.'

'Well I won't let you in the House because the House has unseated you.'

'Well, will you give instruction that force will be used to keep me out?' Tony Benn inquired.

The Speaker adamantly announced, 'Yes, I will.'

On Monday, 8 May, Tony Benn arrived at the door of the House with his two sponsors, Will Wilkins and Herbert Bowden, the Chief Whip. The Chief Doorkeeper, Victor Stockley, blocked his way and said, 'Sir, you cannot enter.'

'On whose instructions?' Tony Benn asked.

'On Mr Speaker's instructions, sir.'

'And have you had instructions to use force to keep me out?'

'Yes,' he replied. 'I have.'

As he had no intention of fighting with the Doorkeeper, Tony Benn handed over a letter he had already written to the Speaker protesting about being prevented from entering the Commons and asking to be heard at the Bar. From the Strangers' Gallery, Tony Benn heard his letter read to the House and Gaitskell's demand that he should be admitted. Again Butler was adamant in his refusal and Gaitskell's motion was defeated by 259 votes to 162. Tony Benn then issued to the press copies of the speech he would have delivered if he had been given the opportunity. In passionate terms it stressed that the rights of electors to determine their representatives were more important than the will of the Government of the day: 'The manifest absurdity of hereditary disqualification is widely recognized and overwhelmingly rejected. To enforce it today against the wishes of the electors will inevitably bring British parliamentary government into disrepute.'

Although he did not have the status of a Member of Parliament, Tony Benn was allocated a small room so that he could prepare for the hearing of St Clair's petition, a case he felt sure he would win. He recalls:

'It was a tiny little room and I was assisted by a young librarian called Michael Griffith-Jones and Michael Zander, who was a friend training to be a solicitor. We worked continuously eight or ten hours a day from 10 May to 10 July when the case began. Since the issue had never been to the court at any time, the whole of British history was available. The old scrolls from earlier peerage arguments, of which there were many, were available in the Victoria Tower. So we sat in the room and as the stuff came we analysed it and we photocopied it – one for me, one for each of the judges, and one for the other counsel. We did a really systematic job.'

The election hearing took place from 10 to 28 July in the Royal Courts of Justice. Tony Benn conducted his own case and his presentation, which was 125,000 words long, lasted some twenty-three hours. It was masterful, and Tony Benn was praised by the court for the 'magnificent way' in which he had conducted his case. But it was all in vain. It was ruled that succession to the peerage was in itself a disqualification from the House of Commons. As though that were not bad enough, the court then ordered Tony Benn to pay £8000 costs, a considerable sum which was actually paid for by a public appeal, organized by his supporters in all parties.

On 31 July, the Speaker declared that Malcolm St Clair was the duly elected Member for Bristol South East. All the Labour MPs walked out of the Chamber in protest as St Clair took his seat. On 14 August he announced that he would be prepared to resign if Tony Benn gave an assurance that he would not stand again for the constituency. It was a clever ploy, but Tony Benn would have none of it. He immediately replied:

'I can well understand Mr St Clair's embarrassment at the position he now finds himself in. Following his defeat at the by-election, he deliberately chose to get into Parliament by means of an election petition. It has now been explained to him that an MP ought to be elected by a majority vote - the very point on which the Bristol election was fought. He now asks me to solve his problems for him by abandoning the whole campaign so that he can withdraw from the difficulties into which the Government have led him. But it is not for Mr St Clair or the Conservative Party to decide who the Labour candidate at the next election in Bristol shall be or not be. To ask for that is to add fresh absurdity to the present law. Mr St Clair's duty is perfectly clear; he should ask an immediate public pledge from the Government that the law will be changed, and when it has been changed he should resign immediately. This is the honourable course open to him.'

At a press conference the next day, St Clair announced that he would not resign. The matter seemed closed: the press and the general public seemed to have lost interest; the Parliamentary Labour Party announced that it would not participate in an all-Party joint committee to consider reform of the peerage law; and Tony Benn was under considerable pressure to give up the fight. He was summoned to see Ray Gunter, the Chairman of the Organizational Committee of the Labour Party, who told him, 'If you stand again we will not support you.' George Brown was extremely hostile and said, 'As you will appreciate, I'm totally opposed to the whole thing. It's an absolute disaster that the Labour Party ever got involved in it.' Gaitskell called him in and said, 'Why don't you get your wife to stand next time?' That ludicrous suggestion incensed Tony Benn for it made it obvious that the Party Leader saw the issue as being about keeping the seat in the family and not about the right of electors to select their own MP.

Caroline Benn was also concerned about the apparent inability of people and the press to differentiate between the personal and the wider political issue:

'I felt that people were not interested in it at all because of the wider democratic issue: they were only interested in the personal. Therefore the lesson wasn't coming home generally. And so from that point of view I thought it was a waste of time.'

But Tony Benn did not accept her analysis. Having made the connection between the personal and the much wider, democratic issue, he had a vital principle for which he was prepared to keep on fighting. While others, battle-weary, might be distressed by defeat, the Benns were made of sterner stuff. And Tony Benn was not the first in his family to be deprived of his seat by an election petition. It had happened to his grandfather, John Benn, in 1895.

Although determined not to give up the fight, Tony Benn, having lost his income as an MP, had to earn his living. As his father had done when he lost his parliamentary seat, Tony Benn worked as a journalist and a broadcaster. (A collection of the weekly articles he wrote for the *Guardian* was later published as *The Regeneration of Britain*.) He also gave many lectures, including three tours of the United States. He attended the Goa Conference in Delhi and the Anglo-German Conference at Königswinter. Visiting Berlin in April 1962, he talked with Willy Brandt, and in December he attended a symposium in Jerusalem on Arab-Jewish relations. Despite his work and travels, he did not ignore his constituency, for regardless of the court's ruling he considered himself to be its Member of Parliament. In June 1962 he founded the New Bristol Group which over the next three years published pamphlets and held seminars on such civic issues as town planning and race relations. It strongly supported comprehensive education and advocated the municipalization of all development land. His work with the group was for Tony Benn a stimulating experience of true community politics.

In Parliament things moved slowly. After the Labour Party had eventually agreed to participate in a joint committee examining peerage law, meetings were held at intervals throughout 1962. When the final report was published on 5 December, it recommended legislation enabling peerages to be surrendered for life on execution of an instrument of renunciation, just as Tony Benn had tried to do. But any pleasure he felt was short-lived, because it soon became obvious that any such reform was not considered a priority by the Government.

It was not long, however, before it became so. In February 1963, Gaitskell died and the election for the new Leader of the Labour Party was won by Harold Wilson, who seemed more inclined to tackle radical causes than his predecessor. As Macmillan had by that time faced a series of misfortunes, including the Profumo affair and de Gaulle's refusal to allow Britain to enter the E.E.C., there was doubt about his survival as Prime Minister, and at least two of the possible replacements, Hailsham and Home, were in the House of Lords. Wilson on 2 May asked how soon the Government would introduce the Peerage Bill. On 9 May it was promised and on 15 May the parliamentary timetable was announced. The Bill was published on 30 May and received an unopposed second reading in both Houses of Parliament. On 31 July it became law. Immediately after hearing the Royal assent being given, Tony Benn, Caroline Benn and Lady Stansgate rushed to the office of Sir George Coldstream, the Clerk to the Crown in Chancery, and handed in the instrument of disclaimer. At the press conference which followed, Tony Benn happily announced that he was 'the first man in history to be prevented by Act of Parliament from receiving a hereditary peerage'.

The same day St Clair resigned. In the by-election that followed neither the Conservatives nor the Liberals put up a candidate, although Edward Martell stood for the National Fellowship. On 20 August, Tony Benn won a widely acclaimed victory with a majority of 15,479, but his expected triumphant return to the Commons was unexpectedly muted. In October, during the recess, Macmillan fell ill and resigned. So before Parliament reassembled both Hailsham and Home announced that they would renounce their peerages. When Parliament reassembled on 24 October, the strange situation existed that the new Prime Minister, Sir Alec Douglas-Home, as he had become, did not have a parliamentary seat. The business of the day was, therefore, a debate to discuss the postponement of the new session. Tony Benn seized the opportunity, in making what could be regarded as his second maiden speech, to berate the Government for seeking to maintain the privileges of the House of Lords and thus allowing the position of the Commons to be demeaned. He ended with a warning that such a happening was likely to cause the British people to lose faith in parliamentary democracy:

'There are people outside the House who look upon us as the instrument of change, who see that the only hope of realizing their dreams is for this country to have a modern, effective, lively, vital Parliament. They know very well that privilege and backwardness are inextricably bound up one with another, and when they see the Government pursuing through each of these stages a policy dictated by the desire to use the Prerogative to help themselves, to maintain the privileges of the other House, they will lose confidence in the ability of this House to do the job which has to be done.

This is not an attack upon tradition, for tradition is not the Beefeaters and Mr Speaker's wig and silver buckles. The true tradition of this country is the ingenuity of its people, the creativeness, the inventiveness, the innovating skill of the people, represented at the best periods in our history by the same sort of leadership given in this House. If we are now to slip back into practices long since past, from the seventeenth, eighteenth and nineteenth centuries, we must not be surprised if the British public loses faith in this Parliament as an instrument by which they can participate in the future of their own country.'

His speech showed how dramatically his views had changed during the three years he had been excluded from the House of Commons. Before his father's death he had been a committed Parliamentarian, although determined to ensure that those who exercised power should be accountable to those over whom they exercised it. On his return, his faith, as he explains, rested in people rather than in institutions:

'However the peerage issue has been for me the turning-point in my political life. On every issue since then I've always gone out and won support and come back and then the people at the top have had to capitulate because of public pressure. So the whole political process for me became totally transformed by that experience. I also discovered that when I went round all the clerks of the House that there was nothing particularly democratic at all in the Lords and the Courts and the Commons. They were running a little game of their own. The idea that there was a real, vibrant right to be represented never occurred to them. They were amused by what I was doing, because I was putting an interesting problem to them, and some of them were personally friendly, but the general impact of it all was that this was a vulgar intervention. And if I'd been a dustman who'd tried to prove that I was a Duke, they would have treated me with much more courtesy, because at least I would have wanted what they'd got to offer me. What really incensed them was that I didn't want what they had to give. I never went to the House of Lords. I never went in the place.

So for me it was a very interesting experience, because it radicalized me. It taught me a lot about parliamentary democracy, which is what we are now told is the litmus paper by which we must all be tested. It taught me a lot about how the political process works and the need for a power-base, not in a personal sense, but a power-base on a principle, for that simply broke the whole resistance down. The game wasn't worth the candle. The Government capitulated the way Tories always do. They gave away enough to safeguard their main interest, which was preserving the House of Lords, by conceding one minor point.'

So in the end, as Caroline Benn states, the opposing views she and Tony Benn held on the fight to renounce the peerage were both vindicated:

'I felt they were not going to let him win. But in one way he was right; in one way I was right. They did let him win in terms of getting on with his career, but in terms of the peerage we didn't win at all. The peerage is still entrenched, the House of Lords is still going on from strength to strength. We didn't really make a dent in it; we just alerted them to threats that might be made on the House of Lords so they could bolster it up some more.'

6

TONY BENN

· I 1964-1975

Despite failing to initiate a popular movement seeking the abolition of the House of Lords, Tony Benn in his fight against the peerage turned what could have been a substantial personal defeat into a public success that changed the law, establishing the rights of individuals to reject hereditary titles and of constituents to elect the representatives of their choice. His struggle not only gave him new opportunities but strengthened his radical views. Convinced by his prolonged encounter with the establishment of its inherent unfairness and the inevitably resulting corruption of privilege, he became an enthusiastic advocate of the democratic system, a subject that was by most politicians indifferently regarded on the mistaken assumption that in Britain democracy had achieved perfection. Thus his attacks on the unrepresentative nature of the House of Lords were extended to a searching criticism of the whole system, a theme on which he concentrated in his weekly *Guardian* column. On 3 January 1964, he declared: 'The Honours system as it now exists serves to buttress the class structure in Britain, dividing people into social categories on the basis that there are superior and inferior human beings.' A few weeks later he wrote: 'We are on the eve of a period of revolutionary change in Britain ... The mood of reform goes far beyond a desire for fresh and vigorous political leadership. It reflects a growing dissatisfaction with the accepted institutions and methods in Britain today.'

The theme of national regeneration and the idea of getting together left-wing thinkers, as Tony Benn had done with the New Bristol Group, were eagerly expanded by Harold Wilson, who was seeking to model his Government-in-waiting on the task-force of intelligentsia recruited by President Kennedy in the United States. At the 1963 Labour Party Conference he had captured the public imagination by announcing: 'We are re-defining and restating our socialism in terms of the scientific revolution ... The Britain that is going to be forged in the white heat of this revolution will be no place for restrictive practices or outdated methods.'

With the Labour Party linked in the public's mind to the technological advances seen as necessary for the revitalization of the country's flagging economy, Wilson capitalized on the growing unpopularity of Home by identifying him as representing 'grouse moor leadership'. In the prolonged electioneering that took place while the announcement of the next General Election was awaited, Wilson was ebullient and frequently called for help on Tony Benn, who possessed both considerable public appeal and apparently limitless energy. In December 1963, Wilson asked Tony Benn to be his unofficial speech writer; on 9 January 1964, Wilson summoned him to discuss the election campaign; on 3 March, Wilson and Tony Benn began a series of meetings to plan the Labour Party's television broadcasts; and, in May, Wilson took Tony Benn with him to the *Guardian* luncheon.

Tony Benn was also developing ideas of his own. Early in July he published in the *Guardian* an article outlining his Post Office Development plan, a matter about which he had already submitted a paper to Wilson, who at the Durham Miners' Gala in July intimated that, if Labour won the election, he would appoint Tony Benn as the Postmaster-General. As an erstwhile journalist and the Chairman of Labour's Broadcasting Advisory Committee, Tony Benn was deeply interested in the media and, stemming from the reporting of his stance on the peerage, increasingly concerned about the way in which issues were trivialized in the popular press. In his *Guardian* column on 24 July, he wrote:

'Perhaps the greatest defect of the press is its failure to provide within its own pages the sort of confrontation of rival views that is necessary to allow the readers to make a wise choice. Fact and comment are now so hopelessly mixed that no one who relies on a popular newspaper - or even some serious ones - is ever brought up against the full weight of the argument advanced by the other side.'

He also condemned 'the personality cult in politics', stating, 'The whole business has got totally out of control and there is a serious danger of burying the real issues under mounds of personal trivia which envelop the principal figures on either side.'

In the long campaign that extended throughout the summer until polling day on 15 October, Tony Benn was a victim of the trivialization to which he had referred. Almost as though punishing him for mounting an attack on them, the popular newspapers harshly criticized Tony and Caroline Benn over the education of their children. Although the usual media criticism of Labour politicians at the time was that they argued for state education but sent their own children to private schools, when the Benns decided to move all four of their children from private education to state education in the local primary and comprehensive schools, the media criticized them for sacrificing their children's education to their own political principles. Later the media shifted their attack to concentrate upon the original choice of private schooling with the insinuation that the Benn children were being educated privately. When this false claim could no longer be sustained (as all four attended Holland Park Comprehensive School until they were eighteen), it was even more absurdly suggested that the Benn children went to a comprehensive because no private or grammar school would accept them.

Almost no mention was ever made in the media of Caroline Benn's own distinguished and extensive professional work in education – as a teacher and lecturer – nor of her work as one of the founders of the successful comprehensive education campaign in Britain. Editor of the journal *Comprehensive Education*, she has written on comprehensive education in many professional journals and lectured about it on university courses. Her research work on secondary reorganization, which she wrote jointly with Professor Brian Simon and which was first published in 1970 as *Half Way There*, is still the definitive work on the subject.

Within the Labour Party of the 1960s, many shared Tony and Caroline Benn's views that comprehensive education was a better education in itself, and that it provided the only alternative to the divisiveness of meritocratic or private systems. This belief was enshrined in the Labour Party's 1964 manifesto, which Caroline Benn suggested should be called 'The New Britain'. The title was unfortunately thought to be too snappy and so was extended on publication to 'Let's Go with Labour for the New Britain'. Despite the apparent good intentions, the document contained many platitudes which sought to establish the Labour Party's right to govern, but which in fact proposed few significant changes to the organization of society. Socialism was packaged as a form of planning that would make capitalism work. So the Labour Party's policies under Wilson were not too different, except in style, from those which had been expounded by Gaitskell.

In the event, the manifesto did not bring the expected sweeping victory. After thirteen years of unadventurous Tory rule, the Labour Party managed to win, but with an overall majority of only four. Although able to recruit only three experienced Ministers into his Cabinet and facing a severe balance of payments deficit, Wilson proved to be a wily political juggler who, while balancing the rival claims of the Labour Party's disparate factions, made several adventurous appointments. Tony Benn, as Wilson had earlier suggested, was appointed the Postmaster-General, a position not in the Cabinet but with responsibility for a Government Department that employed over 400,000 people.

Aged only thirty-nine and having had no previous experience in government, Tony Benn was determined to become a most efficient Minister. He was, therefore, somewhat taken aback when, on the day he assumed office, his Private Secretary asked, 'How do you intend to play it, Postmaster-General? How often do you intend to turn up?' It transpired that Reginald Bevins, Tony Benn's predecessor, had usually put in an appearance only on Tuesday, Wednesday and Thursday mornings during parliamentary sittings, when he had signed all the necessary papers which had been placed around a large circular table. That was certainly not how Tony Benn intended 'to play it'. To his new responsibilities he applied all his substantial energies, as Marcia Williams, Wilson's secretary, records in her memoirs, *Inside Number 10*:

'He is a man of fantastic imagination and inventiveness – what would be called in the business world an "ideas man". He is one of the most hard-working people I've met, rising at an early hour and entering his office at the crack of dawn, much to the astonishment of his civil servants. This quickly instilled in them the idea that they were perpetually late for work. For Tony it was not an act of pretence or a demonstration, it was how he operates.'[1]

Resolutely and enthusiastically, Tony Benn set about transforming the Post Office from an old-fashioned, inefficient bureaucracy into a modern re-equipped public enterprise with model staff relations. He began by circulating the Labour Party's manifesto to all the senior officials, drawing their attention to the passages affecting the Post Office. He then saw each of them separately. Every week he held a meeting of a different branch, and each Monday he met his chief officials over cups of tea and a sandwich lunch. Numerous memoranda were issued, demanding answers to questions and solutions to problems. Having become the first Postmaster-General ever to visit the headquarters of the Union of Post Office Workers, he also set up a trade union liaison committee that met regularly. Concerned about the interests of the consumers, he established a Post Office Users' Council and introduced a new system of dealing with complaints.

Yet far more had to be done than establishing better relationships between customers, workers and officials, for the Post Office was in such dire financial difficulties that necessary technological innovations had been limited. Tony Benn both secured considerable increases in Government investment and took the unpopular step of putting up postal and telephone charges. During his twenty months in office, he was able to accomplish a great deal, including the introduction of advanced electronic sorting equipment, postal codes, the new STD telephone-exchange system, National Giro (the Post Office's own banking system), the National Data Processing Service (NDPS), the regular issue of commemorative stamps, and the Philatelic

Bureau. Although it had been planned by the previous Government, he also opened London's spectacular Post Office Tower. Nor was his unending supply of ideas restricted to his work as Postmaster-General. Immediately after the election he suggested to Harold Wilson a scheme that became the Queen's Award to Industry. In the autumn of 1965, he met with Crossman and Tommy Balogh to work on the manifesto for the next General Election, and, as a member of Wilson's kitchen cabinet, discussed electoral strategy at the regular meetings.

Although naturally iconoclastic and innovative, Tony Benn has always been guided by the social consciousness that is firmly rooted in his family's traditions, and so he used the Post Office as a means of implementing social policies, including phones for the disabled, a scheme for postal workers to check on the housebound, and subsidies for remote rural telephone kiosks. He was also guided in his responsibilities by the socialist ideals which, although not fully formed, were becoming ever more meaningful to him. He was concerned about relationships with the trade unions; through Giro and NDPS he introduced new public enterprises; and he sustained a concern about the international dimension, visiting his counterparts in such countries as Sweden and Japan. Significantly, he also succeeded in persuading the Cabinet to accept that the Post Office should be turned into a public corporation, a nationalized industry answerable to Parliament.

His experiences at the Post Office considerably increased his confidence and knowledge of how government works. They also, as he relates, continued the process of radicalization, for he saw that people, excitedly responding to the opportunities they were given, preferred to participate in change rather than passively accept a Government's dictates:

'When in answer to a parliamentary question I said that I'd be very interested in receiving new designs for stamps, there came this absolute flood of exciting designs. So the stamp policy showed me, not only that the Arts could be developed wherever you were, but also that the way to proceed was to trap the talent that was there. Having said I was ready to receive new stamp designs, immediately, like putting oil rigs in the North Sea, the stuff poured out and all you had to do was to capitulate to the pressure you had helped to create. It's like building the wooden horse of Troy and then popping in to open the gates so that you were there to welcome it when it arrived. As a method of social change that idea enormously impressed me.'

But such public response and enthusiasm are considered extremely dangerous by those who oppose any social change. The more radicalized Tony Benn was seen to be, the more he was attacked in the reactionary press. He says:

'From 1964 onwards, I became a much less popular public figure, partly, I think, because people who came up against what I was doing began to realize that, though it was to be strengthened later, there was a genuine radicalism emerging from the administration. And the Post Office continued my own radicalization, because I saw society for the first time from the top and when I saw it I realized how unsocialist and undemocratic it was.'

There were sacrifices that had to be made for the intensity with which Tony Benn applied himself to his work. Constantly busy as a Minister, a constituency MP, and a rising star in the Labour Party, he was able to spend little time at home, as Caroline Benn recalls:

'At the time it didn't matter. We had a really good time. I loved bringing up the kids, even though it was always so busy and every time you went out you had to put forty fingers into forty glove-holes. It didn't leave much time to think about the bigger questions.'

But as the children were growing up, Caroline Benn was able to go back to work. In 1965 she started as a tutor preparing extra-mural students for the London University degree course in English and, with several colleagues attached to the National Extension College, helped run courses and tutorials in the London area. She has continued with this work, and now prepares adults for entry to degree courses at London colleges and the Open University.

Unfortunately the socialist principles underlying the work of both Caroline and Tony Benn did not guide the policies pursued by Wilson's first Government, which immediately after its election faced a sterling crisis engineered by overseas capitalists who feared that socialist measures might be introduced. Such moves were, however, effectively prevented by the consequent rise to 7 per cent in the bank rate and by the strings attached to the £1071 million loan from the International Monetary Fund. In such circumstances it was unwise to prolong unnecessarily a Government with such a slender majority, and as the Tories, led uneasily since July 1965 by Edward Heath, were in disarray, it seemed sensible for Wilson to call an early General Election. After a subdued campaign, during which Tony Benn again co-ordinated the political broadcasts, the Labour Party won a resounding victory on 31 March 1966, capturing 363 seats, an overall majority of ninety-six.

Although offered the post of Minister of Works, Tony Benn opted to stay at the Post Office, but he was to be there only a short time, for following the resignation on 3 July of Frank Cousins as Minister of Technology, Tony Benn was appointed in his stead, much to the chagrin of

Crossman, who felt he should have been given the post. It was a difficult time for the Government. The forty-seven-day strike begun on 16 May by the National Union of Seamen had encouraged international speculation against sterling. So at the first Cabinet meetings Tony Benn attended there was presented a package of spending cuts and increased taxation. These were accepted, although Tony Benn supported George Brown's minority view that as an alternative sterling should be devalued.

The Government's deflationary policies proved to be inadequate, and there followed considerable overseas borrowing, further spending cuts, and eventually, on 18 November 1967, devaluation. The Prime Minister was faced with growing discord in the Labour Party, for the left objected to policies being determined by international bankers, while the right saw salvation in joining the Common Market, whose members enjoyed greater economic stability. Wilson, ever a pragmatic opportunist, sought to retain Party unity by ruling with a presidential style that ignored discontent but thrived on crises. His passion for secrecy made him often appear devious and distrustful of both colleagues and the media.

Yet, for at least his first eighteen months in office, Tony Benn was no rebel in the Cabinet, concentrating on making public enterprise work at a time when British industry was entering a recession and holding an ever declining share of the world market. Despite heading a Ministry clearly unpopular with many civil servants, Tony Benn was determined to develop it into a powerful, united organization that would ensure co-operation between Government and industry. Events proved the necessity of such an ideal. In the autumn of 1966, Rootes Motors faced bankruptcy and, on 17 July 1967, it was announced that the Government had agreed that Chrysler would purchase the ailing company and in return would receive an investment of £1.6 million. This uneasy compromise between nationalization and complete closure ensured the firm's survival, but only for a while because in 1975 Chrysler collapsed.

In February 1967, Tony Benn introduced the Shipbuilding Industry Bill which planned to establish an independent board to supervise the reorganization of, and the granting of credit to, all the major yards. This too was a compromise, providing state help without effective control. That further action was necessary was proved in April, when only Tony Benn's personal intervention rescued from liquidation the Firth of Clyde's modern dry dock.

The main reason why the motor, shipbuilding and, as Tony Benn had proposed, the aircraft industries were not nationalized was that the Cabinet adamantly refused to accept the idea. And Tony Benn went along with that rejection, still enthusiastically praising the virtues of the mixed economy. So, in a speech on 'The Government's Policy for Technology' which he delivered at Imperial College, London, on 17 October, he said: 'There will always be arguments about how profits should be distributed as between customer, employer, worker and the community, but the profitability of a mixed economy is an essential prerequisite of economic growth and commercial success.'

His attitude was soon to change. Following the devaluation of sterling on 18 November, Roy Jenkins was appointed as the Chancellor of the Exchequer, and introduced a severe deflationary package, including vast cuts in public expenditure. As a consequence, private companies soon suffered. The Industrial Expansion Bill, which Tony Benn introduced on 1 February 1968, was bitterly attacked by Callaghan and by Conservatives as a socialist measure, but it did little more than extend Government assistance to private industries, a measure proved essential by the troubles which faced Rolls-Royce in March, when the company was given £9 million to launch the Lockheed Tristar.

The drastic cuts in public spending, the increases in taxation, the rising level of unemployment, and the problems facing British industry created considerable resentment, and the Government became very unpopular throughout the country. Within the Labour Party, members began to express deep concern about the direction the Government was taking and its obvious abandonment of socialist policies. Ignored by Wilson, the Party membership became separate from the Parliamentary Party and discontent grew.

Tony Benn was one of the first Labour MPs to understand and to sympathize with the anxieties being expressed by Labour Party members. In February 1968, he wrote to his constituents an open letter in which, although he appealed for loyalty to the Party and to the Government, he acknowledged the need for greater consultation:

'This dialogue between Party Leaders and Government Leaders – if you can really disentangle them – is essential both for the health of the Party, and for the health of the Government ... What we need to create are more opportunities for dialogue. We have got to build up the idea of a Party leadership, performing a distinct role as such. The debates that ensue, so long as they do not involve personal attacks, or systematic attempts to defeat the Government in the Commons, are altogether healthy and desirable.'

He did not then realize the full implication of his plan, for in the same month he delivered in Bonn a speech on a subject about which the British people, never mind Labour Party members, had not been consulted – membership of the EEC, which at that time he supported, claiming, 'The full benefits of an integrated European technology can be achieved only when Britain is a member of the EEC.'

Having begun to consider the need for greater involvement of the people in government, Tony Benn was, however, soon to return to the theme which was to become central to his thinking throughout the ensuing decade. On 25 May 1968, during a wave of student unrest, he delivered at the Annual Conference of the Welsh Council of Labour, held in Llandudno, a most important speech, entitled 'From Parliamentary to Popular Democracy'. Stating that the role of Parliament in a changing society had to be examined, he said:

'Much of the present wave of anxiety, disenchantment and discontent is actually directed at the present parliamentary structure. Many people do not think that it is responding quickly enough to the mounting pressure of events or the individual or collective aspirations of the community. It would be foolish to assume that people will be satisfied, for much longer, with a system which confines their natural political role to the marking of a ballot paper with a single cross once every five years.'[2]

The speech, especially its conclusion that a new popular democracy must be formed to replace parliamentary democracy, created a furore and fractured the hitherto friendly relationship between Tony Benn and Wilson, whose attitude was later described by Tony Benn as being 'people want to go on playing cricket and let me run the country'.

Undeterred by those who reacted adversely, Tony Benn refused to soften his demand for the greater involvement of people in government. At the Labour Party Conference, held at Blackpool during the first week in October, he proclaimed: 'In a modern democracy, people want to be invited to participate more fully ... Without the Party, the Cabinet is powerless and without the people the Party is powerless, and here is the message, without the Party the people of this country are powerless to control their own destinies.'

A fortnight later, on 18 October, at a meeting of the Hanham Labour Party in Bristol, he made an even more controversial speech on 'Broadcasting and Democracy', in which he critically examined the role of the BBC as the prime national instrument of broadcasting. Having clearly stated that he was '*not* proposing direct or indirect Government control of the mass media', he examined the inadequate treatment of news items by the BBC, quoting as an example the scant attention given to the views of both trade unionists and employers during industrial disputes:

'Almost all we see of trade unions or business leaders are hurried little street interviews when they are pinned against a wall by a battery of accusing microphones, wielded by interrogators who have just come from covering an air crash and are on their way to the hospital where some quins have been born. Is it any wonder that so few of us really understand the complexity of some current problems in industrial relations which are really going to condition our prospects of economic success or failure?'³

He went on to plead that access to broadcasts should be given to far more people, concluding, 'Broadcasting is really too important to be left to the broadcasters, and somehow we must find some new way of using radio and television to allow us to talk to each other.'

The popular press rallied to the defence of the BBC and castigated Tony Benn for his temerity. Pouring scorn on wider access to the media, the *Sunday Times* sternly proclaimed: 'Let Mr Benn imagine the untold suffering that would be inflicted upon innocent people by the endless procession of self-esteeming, flatulent and unedited worthies.' Labour MPs were equally hostile. Ray Gunter called for Tony Benn's resignation. Crossman was angry because he felt the speech stole the thunder from his forthcoming Guildhall Granada Lecture on broadcasting. Having received from the BBC a complaint about Tony Benn's alleged interference, Wilson sent him a warning note.

But Tony Benn was not to be silenced by the Prime Minister's disapproval. On 5 November, at a meeting of Fabians, he considered the emergence of special interest and pressure groups, pointing out: 'This phenomenon of a myriad of political action groups is not really new. What is new is the realization that they have now become an integral part of a new style parliamentary democracy, and may, in the process, be undermining the monolithic character of the parties and in part supplanting them.'⁴ As a consequence, Tony Benn then stated, it was essential for the Labour Party to assert its popular leadership by utilizing the expertise of such special groups while offering them a worthwhile ideology which in the increasing pragmatism of the times was being underestimated. So he appealed for a renewed study of Karl Marx and other socialist thinkers so that the current discontent could be diagnosed and the underlying power struggle could be properly understood.

To the horror of most of his Cabinet colleagues and all the popular media, Tony Benn, the Minister of Technology, had declared himself to be a committed and evangelical, although as yet only theoretical, socialist. He did so rationally and sincerely. Perhaps it can be seen as being to his credit that he also did so somewhat naïvely, for the essential nature of socialism is such that it seeks to destroy the privilege, inequalities and injustices of the capitalist system, but those who possess the power, wealth and privilege within it cannot be expected to surrender what they have amassed readily or by the force of argument. To them and their minions, Tony Benn came from that point on to be seen as an enemy.

But locked as he was into a heavy programme of daily Ministerial business throughout 1969, Tony Benn was unable to develop his socialist ideals into practical, well-planned policies. So it was a year of some confusion in which his actions at times fell short of the full-blooded principles he had come to hold. Faced with a Cabinet refusal to provide sufficient funds to rescue the incompetently managed Upper Clyde Shipbuilders, Tony Benn did not advocate nationalization but initiated a change of management and an injection of capital that was soon to prove inadequate. Accepting the general view that trade union reforms were necessary, he initially supported Barbara Castle's White Paper *In Place of Strife*, which proposed a conciliation pause of twenty-eight days for unofficial strikes and a ballot for official ones. Furiously opposed by the trade unions, the measures were rejected and replaced by an undertaking that the TUC would vet all disputes. Revealed as being without implementable policies, the Government appeared confused and uncertain. The disputes with the unions, concern about the potential costs of entering the Common Market, and rising unemployment added to the Government's difficulties and made defeat at the next election seem certain.

Yet Tony Benn continued working tirelessly, his ardour apparently undiminished. Despite their disagreements, Wilson asked him in August to help co-ordinate and plan Labour's election campaign. In the memorandum he submitted, Tony Benn drew attention to the break-up of traditional party-loyalties and the ever-growing sense of apathy: 'The progressive post-war collapse of national self-confidence is now a major problem that has got to be overcome if people are to be persuaded that anything can be achieved.' He suggested that the Labour Party should carry its campaign to the grass roots in the country and should, while emphasizing its strengths, 'be as candid as possible about our disappointments'.

Clearly impressed by Tony Benn's unflagging energy, which so contrasted with the dispirited attitude of most of his Cabinet colleagues, Wilson on 5 October announced in his Government reorganization that Tony Benn had been put in charge of an expanded Mintech, which absorbed the Ministry of Power and some of the responsibilities of both the Board of Trade and the Department of Economic Affairs. It was in effect a Department of Industry that with an extensive system of grants was intended to stimulate industrial development throughout the country. But as Britain went further into a deepening recession in which declining investment could not provide for workers' increasing expectations, there was no real hope of the new Mintech propping up with Government grants a private sector that was being deserted by the capitalists. Unemployment, which many including Tony Benn at first saw as being but the inevitable consequence of the technological revolution, began to rise rapidly, and the Government seemed incapable of dealing with the problem. Growing uneasy about the industrial policies of which he had once been a major advocate, Tony Benn began to extend his belief in the people's right of involvement in government to the right of workers to be involved in their industries. At a lecture on 'Technology and the Quality of Life' that he gave to the Manchester Technology Association on 25 February 1970, he stated: 'As the implications of scientific and technological decisions become more and more the subject of public interest, people will insist on having a greater say in these decisions.'

Showing few public signs of his increasing disenchantment with the policies by then ineffectively being pursued by the Labour Government of which he was a part, Tony Benn entered during the early summer of 1970 into the General Election campaign. An attack he made on Enoch Powell's pronouncements on racial issues was widely, although unfairly, credited with having helped produce the defeat of the Labour Party. No such help was necessary. Student demonstrations, civil war in Ireland, and widespread disillusionment had created a general desire for a change which, for once, Heath turned confidently to the advantage of his Party. At the polls on 18 June, the Conservatives won an overall majority of thirty. The Labour Party lost seventy-six seats.

At first shocked by the scale of the Labour Party's defeat, Tony Benn quickly saw that a period in opposition was necessary both for the Party to be reunified and for him to order his ideas. Realizing that the Conservative victory marked the end of the post-war consensus in British politics, he saw the parties returning to fundamentals, later stating: 'The Tories went back to Adam Smith, the Labour Party to Clause IV, and the Archbishop of Canterbury to the Ten Commandments.' His own first salvo in the battle to revitalize and make socialist the Labour Party was soon fired. Early in September his Fabian pamphlet, 'The New Politics', was published, with the subtitle 'A Socialist Reconnaissance'. Still concerned, as he wrote, with 'the method of politics rather than the conduct of specific policies', he acknowledged the alienation of Parliament from the people, and advocated the extension of democratic principles into the organization of industry so that there was real workers' control: 'It cannot, almost by definition, be imposed from above, having to grow from below in discussion between those concerned, creating a new leadership in the process of discussion, negotiation and conflict which must accompany such a radical change in the relationship between workers and owners of capital.' He also pointed out that the need for a greater involvement of people in decision-making should apply equally to the Labour Party, which should see 'in this rising tide of opinion a new expression of grass roots socialism'.

Constantly willing to accept the wider implications of his own statements of general principles, he returned to the idea of people being consulted on major issues by referenda, something he had first advocated in May 1968, during his Llandudno speech. As no matter had for a decade divided the Labour Party more than the proposal to enter the Common Market, he was convinced that that was a matter on which the British people should be consulted. He had already made the suggestion at a Cabinet meeting in October 1968, but it had received no support. In November 1970, he wrote a letter to his constituents setting out the case for a referendum on British entry to the Common Market. Although deeply concerned about the possible and apparently ignored consequences for Britain of membership, Tony Benn was not at that stage committed to opposing entry. His main concern was that, as the issue cut across traditional party loyalties, it could not be resolved by a General Election. He firmly believed, therefore, that the people should have the right to express their opinion on the issue. It should not, he maintained, be left to a majority vote in Cabinet:

'The whole history of British democracy has been about *how* you take decisions; and this has always been seen to be more important than what the decisions were. All political parties in Britain are prepared to accept electoral defeat because they believe the machinery represented by the ballot box is more important than the result it produces. If the Common Market question is decided without consulting the people, it will split the country and both parties.'[5]

The proposal attracted much attention, but little support, among the Labour leadership, who felt that any sign of dissent damaged the Party's electoral chances. So when at a Shadow Cabinet meeting in December Tony Benn proposed holding a referendum there was not even a seconder; but he was determined to continue the campaign, for his appeal had so obviously struck a chord with many British people, whose strong objections to membership of the Common Market had hitherto been all but ignored. The force of these arguments was soon to help change Tony Benn's own position, so that he was to become the most committed of opponents to entry.

A similar modification of his opinions took place during the debate on the Industrial Relations Act which took place throughout much of the 1970/71 parliamentary session. As its proposals to eliminate unofficial strikes and make collective wage agreements binding were in essence not too dissimilar from those contained in Labour's *In Place of Strife*, they were not rigorously attacked by most members of the old Labour Cabinet, but Tony Benn came to see that the bitter opposition of the trade union movement stemmed from a valid desire to protect working people and not from a mistaken determination to retain out-dated practices. Coming to accept the class struggle inherent in implementing socialism, Tony Benn became increasingly identified with and a firm supporter of the trade union movement's struggles. On 26 January 1971, he opposed the Tories' plan to abolish the Shipbuilding Industry Board, saying that the Government was like 'an old-fashioned medieval surgeon who pulls out a hack-saw and cuts off a leg'. When the collapse of Rolls-Royce seemed imminent, he visited Derby on 7 February and promised a mass meeting that the Labour Party would defend the workers' right to work. The following day in Parliament he warned the Government of how dangerous it would be to make 45,000 people redundant from the country's most famous engineering company. On 29 April, in an attack on the Tories' incomes policy in the Budget and on the rising levels of unemployment, he stated:

'The fact is that the Government is deliberately gearing the economy down to a lower level of production. Unemployment is now seen by the Cabinet as a main instrument of economic policy. High wages do not explain unemployment in declining industries where wages tend to be lower . . . High wages do not explain redundancies where there is a market, nor do they explain changes in the structure of unemployment and its longer duration.'

In a key speech, delivered at the Glasgow May Day demonstration on 2 May, he coupled his earlier plan for greater access of people to the media with his growing support for and understanding of trade unions:

'The trade union movement stands today, as it has done since its earliest years, in the front line of defence of the ordinary family and its living standards. That is why the Government has chosen to launch a sustained attack on them through their Industrial Relations Bill. This campaign against the trade unions has been enthusiastically taken up by many newspapers and commentators on radio and TV . . . The time has come when the trade union movement should demand the right to regular programmes of its own on the BBC and ITV to allow it to speak directly to its members without having everything they say edited away by self-appointed pundits and producers.'[6]

Yet it was not only an increased understanding of the class struggle and of why people should be involved in decision-making that resulted from Tony Benn's deepening analysis of socialism. His determination to work for a more egalitarian society made him aware of the injustices suffered by women at school, home and work:

'Now new options are beginning to open up for women. This is the stuff of which revolutions are made, because it involves a change of values which threatens the existing pattern of male domination . . . If women are to be allowed to lead fuller lives there will have to be a lot of changes made, and most of them will require a complete re-education of men.'[7]

In the atmosphere of mounting social and industrial unrest, Tony Benn often seemed to be at the centre of controversy, and that was certainly so in the summer of 1971 when the Upper Clyde Shipbuilders faced collapse unless the Government gave a substantial grant to cover losses. On 22 June, Tony Benn unsuccessfully introduced a Private Member's Bill seeking to take UCS into public ownership. The following day, he led a march through Glasgow of 30,000 workers who had struck in sympathy with their UCS colleagues. Faced with the Government's apparent unconcern, the ship-workers began a work-in on 30 July. Jimmy Reid, the men's leader, announced, 'This is the first campaign of its kind in trade unionism. We are not strikers; we are responsible people and we will conduct ourselves with dignity and discipline.' Co-operating with the management and the police, the workers still in employment were joined by those already made redundant to complete the existing contracts that the receiver wished to abandon. It was an historic moment in industrial development, for without violence or struggle the workers at UCS successfully undertook the organ-ization of their own labour. Alone of the Labour Party's senior Parliamen-tarians, Tony Benn gave the workers his full support. Widely attacked for supporting what was said to be an unlawful act, Tony Benn defended himself in a Commons debate on 2 August. Having admitted that it was a mistake when he was a Minister not to have pushed for the nationalization of UCS, he praised the action of the shipbuilders:

'Over the years I have seen the labour forces on Clyde about-turn from a defeated, demoralized and divided group engaged in demarcation dis-putes and unofficial strikes into a determined and responsible body of men welded into unity, into defending the public assets which have been made available to them by this House . . . The men have rediscovered by what they have done their self-respect which they never had under private management in the past. They want a future in shipbuilding and they mean to have a say in that future. They have shown the way to responsi-bility in industry by assuming responsibility in industry.'

Following Tony Benn's speech, support rallied behind the UCS workers. Nearly half a million pounds were quickly raised for the work-in, and on 18 August some 70,000 people attended a demonstration of support in George Square, Glasgow.

The workers' heroism and lack of self-interest did not last, and within two years the work-in collapsed. It was an exciting experiment, but not a long-term success. Yet it was the first British example of large-scale workers' control, and quick to recognize its significance Tony Benn stated: 'The workers in UCS have done more in ten weeks to advance the cause of industrial democracy than all the blueprints we have worked on over the last ten years.'

His tribute was part of a speech delivered at the Labour Party Conference held at Brighton in early October 1971. There the delegates rejected, but only by 3,082,000 votes to 2,005,000, a motion demanding a referendum on Britain's entry to the Common Market. Shortly afterwards, during the five-day debate in the Commons which ended on 28 October, Tony Benn again urged that the people had a right to decide the matter, but entry was endorsed by a majority of 112, including Jenkins and sixty-eight other Labour MPs who had rebelled against the Party's three-line Whip.

The Labour Party was clearly deeply divided on the Common Market as well as on other issues, so that the fundamental differences between the revisionist social democrats and the democratic socialists were already very evident. On 31 October, Tony Benn, the new Chairman of the Labour Party, and Michael Foot both announced that they would stand for the deputy leadership of the Party in opposition to Jenkins who, although the Deputy Leader, had headed the rebellion.

In his statement explaining his candidature, Tony Benn asserted three principles: (1) The British people were entitled to expect that Parliament would not give away their basic national sovereign rights without expressed authorization from the electorate; (2) the Labour movement was entitled to have its agreed policies presented in the Commons by its elected leaders and not to have them absolutely ignored; and (3) Labour MPs were entitled to a leadership loyal to their majority decisions. The statement concluded: 'These basic issues must be discussed and resolved if we are to restore respect for Parliament, rebuild the confidence of the Labour movement, and heal the divisions between Labour MPs during the coming year.'

As the debate about what direction the Labour Party should take became more open and more acrimonious, Tony Benn in a Fabian lecture delivered on 3 November considered 'The Labour Party and Democratic Politics'. He gave five instances of where the Party's rank-and-file had been correct and the Labour Government had been wrong – Vietnam, *In Place of Strife*, the East-of-Suez policy, prescription charges, and devaluation. This led him to plead for the introduction of a system which would allow popular thinking to influence policies:

'Democratic change starts with a struggle at the bottom and ends with a peaceful parliamentary victory at the top. That is what I call Popular Democracy . . . This is not an appeal for violent revolution or even systematic and sustained civil disobedience. In Britain we don't need them. It is an appeal for the strategy of change from below to make the parliamentary system serve the people.'

The result of the first ballot for the deputy leadership was announced on 10 November. Tony Benn came third with a creditable forty-six votes. He immediately withdrew and a week later Jenkins was declared elected with 140 votes to Foot's 126. Yet this was not the end of Tony Benn's struggle and he intensified his campaign for a referendum, much to the anger of the right-wing Labour MPs like Jenkins, who believed that the matter had been finally decided and a victory won. At first Tony Benn received little support. On 15 March 1972, he succeeded in attracting only three other votes for his motion demanding a referendum put to a meeting of the Party's National Executive Committee. But the following day, President Pompidou announced that there would be a referendum in France about Britain's application for entry. Shortly afterwards, an opinion poll in the *Daily Mail* showed that 78 per cent of the British people were in favour of a national referendum, just as there was to be in Denmark, Norway, and Ireland over whether each of those countries should apply for admission to the Common Market. At the next meeting of the NEC, on 22 March, Tony Benn's referendum motion was accepted by thirteen votes to eleven. A week later, the idea was also accepted by the Shadow Cabinet.

The pro-Marketeers were incensed, and Jenkins, Owen, Lever and Thomson resigned from Labour's front bench. They had not, however, given up their campaign. When the referendum was debated in the Commons on 18 April, the right wing of the Labour Party formed a cosy coalition of fierce opposition with the Tories and the Liberals. Tony Benn in his speech fervently advocated the people's right to be consulted over a matter that involved a loss of parliamentary and legal sovereignty:

'Freedom began before the House of Commons was set up. Freedom was forced on the House by people outside it. Freedom is defended by the ballot box and not by the division lobby. The arguments against the referendum are the very same arguments as have been used against every extension of the people's rights for 140 years. I believe they will be ashamed at their blindness in failing to see that what they opposed in the name of parliamentary democracy was the flood-tide of popular consent without which parliamentary democracy cannot survive.'

The referendum was rejected and, on 13 July 1972, the European Communities Bill became law by the narrow margin of 301 votes to 284.

In the same month, in an attempt to implement the Industrial Relations Act, five dockers from the Transport and General Workers' Union, who had picketed a coldstore employing non-union labour, were sent to Pentonville Prison. Immediately Tony Benn sprang to their defence, and there was a storm of protest about the imprisonment leading to a threat by the TUC to call a general strike before the dockers were eventually released. On 22 July, on the eve of the annual Tolpuddle Martyrs' rally, Tony Benn compared the five imprisoned dockers to the six agricultural workers who had been transported to Australia in 1834 for trying to form a trade union:

'For centuries, Britain's democratic liberties have been won and upheld with the help of men and women who stood up for their beliefs and took the consequences. The right to worship freely, to organize trade unions, to vote – for men and women – in Britain were all won against powerful people who sought to maintain their privileges by stirring public fears about anarchy whenever anyone challenged these privileges. That is what the Government is now trying to do.

The British people are the most law-abiding people in the world. It would be quite wrong for anyone to tell others to break the law. But we cannot forget that, in the end, each man is answerable to his own conviction as to what is right and wrong. If a man's conscience lands him in jail the bars that keep him there imprison part of all our freedoms.

The law which has put these men in prison is an evil law, drawn up by a Government which hates the trade unions, and is being enforced by lawyers who have no experience of the problems of working people and their families.'

This total support for the Pentonville Five provoked bitter attacks on him in the media and intensified his conflict with Wilson, but Hugh Cudlipp, the editor of the *Daily Mirror*, offered Tony Benn the paper's centre-page spread to put the dockers' case. On 3 August his article was published. In it he stated:

'According to the Prime Minister, Britain has been taken to the brink of anarchy because five dockers disobeyed the law. If that was true the situation would be serious. But it is not true. No five men could undermine our country. What has really frightened the Cabinet is that millions of people who did *not* break the law expressed their sympathy and support for the dockers. One of them was me.'

Following the article, over 11,000 people wrote to the *Daily Mirror* supporting Tony Benn's view by a majority of eight to one.

Because of the obviously widespread support given to Tony Benn by vast numbers of trade unionists and Labour Party members who had for over twenty years had no effective socialist spokesperson in the higher echelons of the Labour Party, the attacks on him in the media and by those who held power greatly increased. No longer seen as a harmless visionary fascinated by new technology, he was presented as a dangerous revolutionary determined to seize power by deliberately provoking social unrest. Having already achieved one change to the constitution by his rejection of the peerage and apparently determined to initiate another over the introduction of the referendum, he was seen by the establishment as being, as described to me by one of his ex-Cabinet colleagues, 'the most dangerous man in Britain'. And he was dangerous to the establishment, but not for the reasons that were given. Although never making a secret of his willingness to lead the Labour Party if called upon, he was not motivated by personal ambition. If he had been, he would have set about things very differently, capitalizing fully on his already established reputation of being the only bright star in a less than glittering Labour firmament. His advocacy of the greater involvement of people in the decision-making processes of both government and industry stemmed not, as often claimed by his opponents, from a belief that by so doing he would be swept to power on a wave of popular support, but from a deep conviction, born of his own knowledge of and experiences in government, that the Labour Party had jettisoned any semblance of being either a socialist movement or one representing the interests and aspirations of working-class people. This had been done so that while in power the Labour Party could survive the joint onslaughts of capitalists' criticism and the declining state of the world economy by propping up rather than reforming the system to which it should have been opposed. Because it had been a course of action that he too had earlier been prepared to take, his change of views was even more resented by the Party leadership than it was by his political opponents. But his conversion to socialism came just in time to save the Labour Party from at worst disintegration and at best dilution into a broad coalition dominated by its right-wing social democrats whose main tenet was a rejection of Party democracy. That was why he was dangerous, for the Labour Party at the time of its defeat in 1970, having become estranged from the trade unions and from its grass-root supporters, was in the hands of a social democratic faction that, with its anti-socialist position, was seen by most industrialists, bankers and newspaper barons as being an acceptable, even though slightly less palatable, alternative Party of government to the Tories.

But because Tony Benn, like his father and grandfather, was a man of principle who refused to take the easy way, all that had changed by the summer of 1972. His time in opposition had been spent in an unending round of meetings and visits during which he had stimulated a new-found enthusiasm among Labour Party supporters. The Participation '72 Campaign, of which he was the prime mover, directly involved over 10,000 Party members in discussion about policy. Already Shadow Secretary for Trade and Industry, he was also actively involved in many bodies considering new policy ideas. In 1972 he became the Chairman of the NEC's Industrial Policy Committee; he served on the Home Policy, Human Rights, Science and Education, Information, and Transport Committees of the NEC; and in 1972 he was the Chairman of the Labour Party. His influence was, therefore, considerable, and was nowhere used to more important effect than in bringing the trade union movement firmly back into the Labour Party fold. Not only did he do this by his consistent championing of its causes, but also by direct appeals. Thus, on 5 September 1972, he addressed the TUC Annual Congress as the Labour Party's representative: 'The trade union movement must seek its political objectives as an integral part of an organized, democratic Labour Party in Parliament with a socialist programme . . . The unions and the Party must shape policy together at every level.' As his influence with trade unionists increased, Tony Benn established himself as a unique figure in the Labour Party, for he was a socialist with substantial support from both trade unionists and constituency members. Without the powers of patronage enjoyed while in office, Wilson could do little to stem the enthusiastic tide of support for him within the Party – and so he bided his time.

The media, however, did not; and with the approach of the 1972 Labour Party Conference, to be chaired by Tony Benn, his every word and move were screechingly berated as extremist acts. When in a speech at Tiverton on 23 September he made a call for Conference resolutions to be seen as guiding Party policy, he was accused by the press of attacking the Party's leadership. So in his opening address to the Conference as Chairman, Tony Benn stated: 'Conference never has and never would want to dictate to a Labour Government, but they do expect Labour Governments to take Conference decisions seriously and not deliberately reverse or ignore them.'

Tony Benn's handling of the Conference was monitored by and frequently abused in the media, especially innovations such as the use of request-to-speak cards. But on one point the press and Tony Benn agreed – as he said in his concluding remarks, the Conference marked a remarkable movement to the left in the Labour Party:

'What did this Conference say? ... It said we want the Party to turn towards socialism in the next government. It said we want socialist answers to the problems of industry, to the problems of land, to the problems of homes, to the problems of health, to the problems of education, and that unmistakably came from the floor and from the platform . . . This week we have spoken for Britain, but more than that we have demanded the right of the working people of this country to speak for themselves. We have demanded that they should have access to the public to speak of the dignity of labour, to raise the problems that concern them in their life and work. We have demanded that they should be given the right to govern Britain for themselves, which is what democracy is all about.'

Because of the swing to the left, the 1972 Conference also marked the beginning of the desertion from the Labour Party of the anti-socialists. Dick Taverne, who was at odds with his Party members in Lincoln, announced on the last day of the Conference his intention to resign and to stand as a candidate for his newly formed Democratic Labour Party, a step widely applauded in the press. Referring to this in his final speech, Tony Benn attacked the already hostile media, concluding:

'I sometimes wish the trade unionists who work in the mass media, those who are writers and broadcasters and secretaries and printers and lift operators of Thomson House, would remember that they too are members of our working, class movement and have a responsibility to see that what is said about us is true.'

Wilson was incensed by the off-the-cuff comment, and issued a statement declaring that the Labour Party was 'totally opposed in all circumstances to the use of industrial action for the purpose of impeding the printing or dissemination of news, or the expression of views'. Tony Benn issued a similar statement.

The incident prompted him to concentrate further on the fundamental problem of differentiating between anarchy aimed at overthrowing parliamentary democracy and law-breaking because of a conscientious desire to improve the representation of people. It was a pertinent matter at a time when the Conservative Government was making 'the preservation of law and order' a major issue. On 31 October, Tony Benn prepared for the Shadow Cabinet a paper on 'Law and Order', in which he argued that any law which lessened the natural sovereignty of people had no moral authority:

'Democracy and socialism in Britain are built upon three principles which we have struggled to establish over the years, and which have formed the basis of consent on which our system of government rests. The first is the supremacy of conscience over law. The second is the accountability of power to the people. The third is the sovereignty of the people over Parliament. These three principles are now under attack. The Tory campaign on law and order is designed to get us to accept the idea that all laws made by the State must be blindly obeyed.'

Almost as if to provide an example of the kind of decision that Tony Benn was highlighting, Heath on 17 January 1973 announced, not in Parliament but at a press conference in Lancaster House, the second stage of his prices and incomes policy, which imposed severe wage restraints and a statutory Pay Board and Price Commission. Considering such moves to be undemocratic, Tony Benn proposed unsuccessfully in the Shadow Cabinet that there should be a militant course of action to oppose the measures, culminating in a one-day national strike. In Parliament on 29 January he warned: 'If we are to recreate a social contract in this country, upon which agreed economic policies can rest, there has got to be a marked shift of power and wealth to the working people.'

Continuing his intensive dialogue with ordinary people, Tony Benn felt convinced not only that socialism provided the only cure for the country's many ills but that Heath, faced with a failure of capitalism, was introducing measures that, although designed to discriminate against working people, would permit a planned management of the economy. In an article entitled 'Heath's Spadework for Socialism', published in the *Sunday Times* on 25 March, he wrote: 'Heath has performed a very important historical role in preparing for the fundamental and irreversible shift in the balance of power and wealth.'

It was a shift that Tony Benn was determined that the next Labour Government would achieve by successfully managing the economy. How this would be done was spelt out in the Labour Party's Green Paper, *The National Enterprise Board*, which was published in April 1973. Among the many recommendations it contained was that the top twenty-five companies should be nationalized and operated on a self-financing commercial basis. At an acrimonious meeting of the NEC on 31 May, the commitment was accepted by only seven votes to six. Amid howls of protest from the press, Wilson immediately announced that he had a veto and rejected the decision, a move that led directly to the forming of the Campaign for Labour Party Democracy which was to have a vital role in subsequent events. On 8 July, the Party issued its *Programme for Britain, 1973*, which for the first time since 1945 was a genuine socialist policy, containing commitments on public ownership, the municipalization of development land and the taxation of private wealth. It stated: 'Labour's aim is no less than a new social order. The people must determine the nation's destiny and only by economic liberation can they have the collective social strength to decide that destiny.'

Convinced that the people could fulfil their proper role in a democratic society only if there was openness in government, Tony Benn proposed that the minutes of the NEC, including the record of how members voted on resolutions, should be published so that the rank-and-file could see how the Party was run. At a meeting of the NEC on 27 June, the motion was defeated by 11 votes to 9, and the same day the Shadow Cabinet rejected it by 12 votes to 1. In an article that appeared in *The Times* on 11 July,

Tony Benn expanded on his ideas about open government, stating: 'There is a growing public recognition that democracy itself cannot function unless the people are allowed to know a great deal more about what goes on inside government, even to the point of knowing when Ministers disagree on important issues coming up for decision.' In Britain, where secrecy in government has been taken to extremes, appeals for more openness receive surprisingly little support. It was, however, something for which Tony Benn continued to campaign, subsequently submitting a memorandum on the subject to the Home Policy Committee.

An exercise in consultation took place at the 1973 Labour Party Conference, which began on 1 October, when the delegates met to debate Labour's *Programme for Britain*. To the dismay of the popular press and to the delight of the majority of delegates, many socialist resolutions were carried. Advocating the acceptance of the nationalization programme, Tony Benn stated:

'The violence of the attacks upon our public ownership plans and on us for defending them launched by big business and by the media confirm our judgement that these plans are a serious threat, as they are intended to be, to the unaccountable privileges that they defend with that power ... We are saying at this Conference that the crisis that we inherit when we come to power will be the occasion for fundamental change and not the excuse for postponing it.'

Unexpected events were to bring the Labour Party into power far quicker than anyone at the conclusion of the Conference could have predicted. On Saturday, 6 October, the day after the Conference had ended, Egypt invaded Israel, precipitating a world economic crisis as the oil-producing states quadrupled the price of oil. With a rapid increase in inflation that made the Government's prices and incomes policy untenable, the coal miners, after months of fruitless negotiations, reached an impasse with the Government over their pay claim. As the confrontation worsened, Heath on 13 December declared a state of emergency and imposed a three-day working week. Suspicious that the moves had been introduced in order to break the miners' solidarity by turning public opinion against them, Tony Benn organized from his home a systematic collection of facts about fuel supplies and of opinions about the effects of the three-day week. The information received formed the basis of an intense campaign against the unprecedented measures introduced by Heath. In the Commons on 10 January 1974, Tony Benn declared:

'The Prime Minister's attempt to justify the three-day week was not concerned, as one would expect were it a genuine proposal, with husbanding the nation's fuel resources and protecting the people at a moment of shortage. It was an act of mobilization for a long war against the miners.'

As Tony Benn's attacks on the Government continued, it became obvious that there was a growing, widespread rejection of Heath's actions. Tony Benn on 27 January proclaimed:

'The Conservative Party and its allies, including the mass media, are prepared to sacrifice even free enterprise itself in order to preserve the pattern of power and wealth that corresponds with their class interests ... When historians come to write about this period of British history, Mr Heath will certainly be credited with having awakened people, who had never thought about class before, to what class means and how it relates to their own experience.'

On 7 February, two days before the miners' strike was to begin, Heath announced that a General Election would be held on 28 February. The Labour Party's manifesto of socialist policies, *Let Us Work Together: Labour's Way Out of the Crisis*, accurately described the situation: 'The Government called this election in panic. They are unable to govern, and dare not tell the people the truth.'

Tony Benn took no part in the national campaign, because a boundary revision had made Bristol South East a very marginal constituency. He was, however, easily victorious, obtaining a majority of over 8,000. Nationally the Labour Party did less well, winning 301 seats, with the Conservatives obtaining 296, the Liberals 14, and the various Nationalists 24. Confusion reigned for several days, but on 4 March, having failed to persuade the Liberals to join with him in a coalition, Heath resigned, and Wilson formed the first minority Government since 1929.

As the Tories received their lowest share of the vote since 1906 and as the alternative parties (Liberal and Nationalist) had a dramatic increase in support, the election showed that many of the electors were discontented with the overlapping two-party system, which had been in decline since Heath's victory in 1970 and against which Tony Benn and others in the Labour Party had fought during the intervening four years. Yet the desire to re-establish consensus rather than confrontational politics was still widely felt by many politicians. Although the Labour Party had come to victory with a socialist manifesto, there were considerable forces already joined to ensure that it would not be implemented, and among the fiercest opponents of radical change were influential Labour MPs, including the new Prime Minister.

Because of Tony Benn's standing in the Labour Party and the special relationship he had established with the trade union movement, Wilson could not avoid appointing him to the Cabinet, and so Tony Benn was made Secretary of State for Industry and Minister of Posts and Telecommunications. Momentarily, he was concerned that in office his socialist ideals might be eroded, but it was not his own will and principles that were in question. It was the outright refusal of many around him to co-operate which was to prove the greatest and ultimately insurmountable obstacle. When Sir Anthony Part, his new private secretary, met Tony Benn, his astonishing greeting was, 'I presume, Secretary of State, that you don't intend to implement the industry proposals in Labour's manifesto!'

It immediately became obvious that the top officials in his department had no intention of working on the plans to establish the National Enterprise Board, refusing to participate in any scheme to take companies into public ownership on the grounds that it might be 'unconstitutional'. In an article 'Neutralizing the Industrial Strategy', Tom Forester states:

'The civil service was totally opposed to the interventionist strategy. Adrian Ham, who was Healey's special assistant, says there was a "Whitehall-wide conspiracy to stop Benn doing anything". This conspiracy included government ministers as well as the permanent secretaries, who meet regularly in their own unofficial inner Cabinet. "Some senior civil servants went so far as to brief anti-Benn ministers behind the backs of their own ministers," he says. "They had this obsession about defeating 'Bennery' – a term coined in Whitehall long before Fleet Street picked it up."'[8]

An early crisis Tony Benn faced was the attempt of civil servants to cancel Concorde, the Anglo-French aircraft. He recalls:

'I think that there is no doubt whatever that they reckoned whichever Government was elected, either Tory or Labour, the cancellation would follow immediately: The Tories having got us into Europe wouldn't care any more and the Labour Party with Denis Healey as Chancellor would be bound to want to kill it. So I took it to colleagues and I said: "Well, if the case is as bad as this, the figures are as bad as this, let's publish them. Then at any rate there will be some public understanding of the reasons for the cancellation!" They agreed to that, but when my officials discovered that I intended to publish them, they got into a great panic because they were afraid that the figures wouldn't stand up to examination. It was one of the strongest cases for open government.'

When the figures were examined it was clear that the costs of operating a limited number of aircraft were less than the cancellation costs, and so in

June it was announced by Tony Benn that the Concorde project would not be stopped.

Naturally, Tony Benn was also bitterly opposed by the Confederation of British Industry. In May, the newspapers gleefully carried a public warning to Tony Benn from Sir Michael Clapham, the President of the CBI, not to pursue 'interventionist' policies. Concluding that Tony Benn did intend to persist with his plans, the CBI's representative informed the Commons' Industry Bill Standing Committee that members of the CBI would refuse to abide by any clauses in the Act requiring them to disclose information. Aims of Industry, a right-wing pressure group, launched a £100,000 anti-nationalization campaign. The press too increased its campaign of vilification, castigating Tony Benn's every act as doctrinaire and extremist. In April his proposal to issue a stamp to commemorate the fiftieth anniversary of the General Strike provoked outrage. There were also signs of far more threatening opposition. Private armies raised by General Walker and Colonel Stirling for a national emergency were alleged to have been joined by 200,000 people.

It was fortunate for Tony Benn that he had considerable support in the Party and on his staff. Two of his Junior Ministers, Eric Heffer and Michael Meacher, were committed left wingers, as were the two advisers he recruited, Francis Cripps and Frances Morrell. He also met weekly with left-wing Ministers, including Foot, Barbara Castle, Peter Shore, Judith Hart and Lord Balogh, at a dinner which was called for 'Husbands and Wives' to allay Wilson's suspicions that it was a group in opposition to him. As a member of Labour's NEC, Tony Benn had regular contact with the officers of the Party and saw the committee as an ideal vehicle for keeping the Party informed of what the Government was doing. He also believed that there should be a sustained campaign of public education for, as he said in a memorandum on Party strategy submitted to the NEC in May: 'Apart from highly political comments in the context of the Labour Conference and the General Election, very few people really know what the programme says or what the argument is all about.'

But Wilson, bent only on limiting controversy so that he could call an early General Election to provide the Party with an overall majority, wanted neither openness in government nor the implementation of socialist policies. So he initiated a two-pronged attack on Tony Benn, aimed at silencing him and at rendering powerless the proposed National Enterprise Board. During the six months following the election, Wilson rigorously and simultaneously pursued these aims, believing that by so doing he would remove the fierce hostility of industrialists and banks towards the manifesto programme and hence the Labour Government.

Despite all obstructionism, Tony Benn, aided by Eric Heffer, pushed ahead with the production of a Green Paper on industrial policy. Knowing that the proposals would be bitterly attacked by the establishment, he maintained a series of discussions with trade unionists and in the NEC. Distressed by the level of interest this produced and concerned that policy-making was being removed from his personal control, Wilson sent to Ministers a minute, obviously directed at Tony Benn, about the collective responsibility of the Cabinet and containing a specific threat:

'It would be unfortunate if circumstances developed, perhaps later in the year, in which it proved impossible to deal with this situation except by means of a ruling that no member of the Cabinet might offer himself for election to the NEC ... Nevertheless, this situation could be avoided only if Ministers themselves recognized and accepted that, where any conflict of loyalties arose, the principle of the collective responsibility of the Government was absolute and overriding in all circumstances and that, if any Minister felt unable to subscribe to this principle without reservation, it was his duty to resign his office forthwith.'[9]

It was clearly an authoritarian move intended to muzzle others rather than to provide co-equal responsibility.

To a frenzied reaction from the CBI to his plans, Tony Benn presented on 20 May to the TUC-Labour Party Liaison Committee a progress report on his department in which he announced his ideas for the new Industry Act and for the introduction of a system of planning agreements with initially the hundred largest firms, which together controlled about half of Britain's manufacturing output. The next day *The Times* reported that the report had produced 'bitter comments from senior politicians who see it as electorally damaging'. Wilson was so enraged by the notion of publicly discussing ideas that he announced that he was taking charge and appointed himself, in place of Ted Short, as the Chairman of the Cabinet's Industrial Development Committee.

Aware that the struggle to implement the policies on which the Labour Party had been elected could be won only outside Parliament and the Cabinet, in which there was an anti-socialist majority, Tony Benn was determined to continue his exhaustive programme of public consultation and dissemination, despite the Prime Minister's attempts to silence him. Reacting to Wilson's minute on collective Cabinet responsibility, he issued to his Ministers his own guidelines in which he stated:

'We are not just Labour Ministers confined in our interests to the batch of responsibilities allocated to us in our departmental work. We are elected Labour leaders who must think, and act, and speak politically over the whole range of political issues that touch our people, or stir our convictions. All Ministers are individuals with personal convictions that have brought us into political life; and we have been elected, and appointed because of our convictions and not in spite of them. In the end it is our loyalty to what we believe that offers the only ultimate safeguard on our conduct.

We are also members of the Labour Party and the Labour Movement, owing loyalty to its policies and the people in it upon whose efforts we relied for our electoral strength before we became Ministers and upon which we shall rely long after our departure from office.'

During the summer, the political storm created by his proposals continued to capture the headlines. The Tories, sensing an early election, seized every opportunity to lambast Tony Benn, who in turn continued in his frequent speeches to inform people of his thinking. On 7 June at a Nottinghamshire miners' gala, he announced that in an effort to reveal the extent of the public funding of private industry his officials were examining the accounts of the twenty largest companies and their 4000 subsidiaries. It was then erroneously claimed that he was intending to bring all of them into public ownership, and on 26 June a headline in the *Daily Express* proclaimed: 'BENN WIDENS HIS GRAB NET: READY TO POUNCE ON 4000 LITTLE FIRMS.' Further hysterical condemnations in the press greeted Tony Benn's announcements in July that his department was to give financial help to the workers' co-operatives which had taken over two companies that had closed – the Triumph motorcycle factory at Meriden and the newspaper, previously owned by Beaverbrook Press, which was to be replaced by the new *Scottish Daily News*. It had not been easy for Tony Benn to secure the necessary funding for these projects, because his civil servants were obstructive, especially in the case of the Meriden workers. He later related in the *Sunday Times*:

'Everything was brought to bear. The Industrial Advisory Board rejected Meriden's application more or less outright. The Department of Industry, the Cabinet, and the Prime Minister's Offices each referred the issue to the Central Policy Review Staff, which gave a critical and pessimistic report. Finally, the Treasury, the most powerful office of all in Whitehall when it comes to providing funds, opposed the plan.'

The result was that the projects were underfunded, much of the cash being paid directly to the shareholders of the previous company.

However angry Tony Benn's actions may have made him, Wilson did not react officially until Tony Benn made clear his refusal to accept the Prime Minister's softening of the Party's commitment to initiate a renegotiation of the terms for continued membership of the Common Market before submitting them to a national referendum. Before Callaghan's meeting on 4 June with the Council of Ministers in Luxembourg, Tony Benn tried to put amendments to the Foreign Secretary's speech, but was ruled out of order. To the delight of the pro-Marketeers in the Cabinet, when Callaghan reported back to the House on 11 June he stated, 'We do not propose to renegotiate the Treaties ... Why should we go out of our way to make trouble if our objective can be served without it.' It was an astonishing *volte-face* from the Party's official position. Tony Benn, appalled, tabled a motion at a meeting of the NEC that led to the formation of the NEC Monitoring Committee of Renegotiation, of which he was elected Chairman. Wilson was indignant. He had already ordered that there should be no public discussion about the Common Market by Ministers until the renegotiations were complete and so on 3 July he wrote a personal minute to Tony Benn, in which he said: 'I do not regard this as acting as a member of a team.'

That night there was a farcical incident which further angered Wilson. As there was a difficulty in dealing with the multitudinous regulations sent from the European Commission while renegotiations were still taking place, the Government initiated two debates to 'take note' of those thought important enough to require discussion. When in the first of the debates anti-Market backbenchers unexpectedly demanded a division, Tony Benn, who was waiting to speak in a debate on regional policy, abstained. Bob Mellish, the Chief Whip, was so upset that he ordered the Labour Party's backbenchers to go home. As there was no longer a Labour majority present in the House, Tony Benn was forced to talk out the debate on regional policy. In the Cabinet meeting the next day, Wilson rebuked Tony Benn, who pointed out that he had been the only Cabinet member present during the debate; but he received no support for his actions from his colleagues. That day, Wilson wrote again to Tony Benn: 'Your conduct was damaging to the Government and inconsistent with the ordinary rules of collective responsibility. I should be grateful if you would let me know your explanation of why you behaved as you did.' In his reply to this magisterial command, Tony Benn stated:

> 'This episode – which like you I greatly regret – was undoubtedly caused by general uncertainty about the new scrutiny procedure which put me in a real difficulty . . . I hope the Cabinet can now re-consider how to handle divisions on points of substance which may arise on motions to "take note" before a collective Ministerial decision has been taken.'

In the ensuing weeks, which were clearly a run-up to a General Election, considerable pressure was put on Tony Benn to say nothing more about socialist policies. Wilson insisted that Tony Benn's industrial proposals should be published not as a discussion paper but, in the hope of ending the debate, as a policy statement, which Wilson then went on to dismiss as 'a sloppy and half-baked document, polemical, indeed menacing in tone, redolent more of an NEC Home Policy Committee document than a command Paper'. The later White Paper, called at Wilson's suggestion *The Regeneration of British Industry*, included such a small allocation of funds to the proposed NEB that extended public ownership was made all but impossible. Wilson resorted to every stratagem he could devise to ensure that the private industrial sector would neither feel nor actually be under threat. Terry Coleman, later reporting an interview with Wilson in the *Guardian*, gives an example:

'He said a sub-committee of a sub-committee of the executive proposed to nationalize certain insurance companies. Now, I might think this was cynical, but he ... dictated a letter first to himself and then a reply from himself. He sent both to the insurance people saying they might like to send him his own letter and that his reply would then be published to show that the proposal was not government policy.'

But to win the election, Wilson also needed the support and co-operation of the trade unions. For this, Tony Benn's assistance was vital and in meetings of the Liaison Committee with the TUC during the summer, he helped forge the Social Contract which, contrasting with the disastrous statutory pay policy of Heath's Government, was to provide a central theme in the election campaign. Tony Benn, supported by the union leaders, was insistent that the Social Contract would not be, as he expressed it, 'solely nor even primarily about wages, but as a joint agreement to carry through economic, social and political changes'.

The General Election, which took place on 10 October, did not produce a really decisive result, giving the Labour Party with 319 seats an overall majority of only three. Reappointed as Secretary of State for Industry, Tony Benn discovered that the officials at the Department of Industry had prepared three different briefs: one in case the Conservatives won, one for a Labour Secretary of State other than himself, and one for him. His civil servants correctly assumed that he was to be isolated by Wilson, who could then more easily fulfil his main aim of ensuring that Britain stayed in the Common Market.

Within three weeks of the election, Wilson once more erupted with anger at a decision made by Tony Benn, for on 30 October he supported an NEC resolution censuring the Government for arranging naval exercises off Simonstown with South Africa. On 4 November, Tony Benn wrote to the Prime Minister explaining his action:

'... The exact interpretation and application of the principle of collective responsibility is difficult, despite all attempts to define it. Many things are done in the name of the Government which may not even be known to the Departmental Minister concerned, and if it were rigidly imposed on all official acts the situation would be impossible. All this requires further exploration.'

His confidence having been boosted by the newly won majority, Wilson in reply demanded from Tony Benn an unambiguous declaration of total support for the Government, stating:

'The fact that no Minister is in practice able to participate in the decision-making process over the whole range of Government policy does not alter the position. The obligations of collective responsibility are binding on all members of the Government, in the sense that it is unacceptable for any Minister publicly to dissociate himself from the policies and actions of the Government of which he is a member. If he feels impelled by reasons of conscience to dissociate himself, he must resign in order to do so.'

In his reply on 6 November, Tony Benn wrote:

'I made it clear in my last letter that I accept the principle of collective responsibility as applying to all Ministers and hence all the requirements that follow from it.'

But the matter continued to concern members of the Labour Party, and Tony Benn's constituency party passed a motion condemning Wilson's interference in Party democracy.

Tony Benn's main concern, however, was that Wilson's attempts to prevent both discussion and dissent should not be extended to the subject of the Common Market when the time came for the referendum. On 27 November, with Foot and Shore, he wrote a joint letter to the Prime Minister, which in part stated: 'It would be wise to agree, in advance, that Ministers should have the right to express their convictions publicly, in parallel with their accepted right to record them privately in the polling stations.' The matter was mentioned at a Cabinet meeting on 12 December, and Wilson sent a reply to the three Ministers on 24 December in which he promised further discussions, but demanded in the meantime silence under the guise of collective responsibility. Tony Benn's copy of the letter did not reach him until after he had published a New Year message to his constituents on 'The Loss of Self-Government', in which he endeavoured to explain the effects as he saw them of Britain's membership of the Common Market. In a letter, dated 2 January 1974, Tony Benn gave Wilson a detailed explanation of his action, concluding, 'I cannot, therefore, accept that my letter to my constituents in any way contravenes the Cabinet decision on 12 December.' In his reply, on 6 January, Wilson, while still holding out the prospect that an agreement to differ on the Common Market might be made, said: 'So I hope you will refrain from any further pronouncements of this kind until the Cabinet has taken the decisions which will provide the framework for our collective and individual approach to these matters in future.'

The same day, Tony Benn was elected unopposed as the new Chairman of the NEC's powerful Home Policy Committee. Typically the *Daily Mail* heralded this as 'BENN'S NEW POWER GRAB'. The apparently automatic way in which the media sought to distort and abuse any move involving Tony Benn was analysed by Paul Johnson in an article, 'Strange Case of the Anti-Benns', published in the *Daily Telegraph* on 4 January 1975:

'All his actions, irrespective of their intrinsic merits, are presented as offences against one or another economic law; and his public utterances, I notice, are described not as "speeches" but as "outbursts". The cartoonists hint, none too delicately, that he is a raving lunatic; though leader-writers are more inclined to suggest his participation – occasionally as a master-mind, more often as a deluded, or willing, dupe – in a deep-laid plot ...

Yet we know in our hearts – do we not? – that Mr Benn is probably right. Change, however uncongenial, is certainly coming ... You cannot live off history, or eat nostalgia. Mr Benn arouses enormous resentment because he tells us such plain truths. If we could dismiss his message as false we would find him much less offensive. So we ignore logic and reason, and take refuge in abuse.'

But the hostility of the establishment to Tony Benn continued unabated, and shortly afterwards he was warned by Sir Anthony Part, his senior civil servant, that financial support for workers' co-operatives might be beyond the legitimate realm of policy and that he would report Tony Benn to the Public Accounts Committee. Wilson demanded an explanation which Tony Benn gave, but the matter was leaked to the press where it was used as yet another stick with which Tony Benn was beaten.

The major differences arose from the Treasury's undisguised preference for dealing with the ever deepening industrial depression by the monetarist economic approach of cutting living standards and increasing unemployment so that inflation could be reduced and the balance of payments deficit eliminated. Tony Benn wanted to pursue the alternative economic strategy of preserving jobs and industrial capacity by large-scale assistance to industry and measures of control including selected import restrictions. In late January he circulated to the Ministerial Committee on Economic Strategy a paper prepared with Francis Cripps and his Junior Ministers. It was never discussed by the Cabinet, although a revised version of it, entitled *A Ten Year Industrial Strategy for Britain*, was published later in 1975.

Even though, on 21 January, Wilson at last agreed that Cabinet Ministers would be free to express their individual opinions during the referendum campaign, it was apparent that he intended to make few concessions to Tony Benn on the matter of industrial policy and was as determined as ever to emasculate the Industry Bill which Tony Benn introduced in the House on 17 February and which planned the establishment of the National Enterprise Board. The Bill revealed the concessions Tony Benn had been forced to make. No longer was the NEB to be given compulsory powers of acquisition and the planning agreements were to be voluntary. Nevertheless, the opponents of the Bill were furious, accusing Tony Benn of introducing a charter for workers' control, a reform he favoured but which was not contained in the Bill. That Wilson envisaged being able to limit even further the terms of the Bill was revealed by the *Economist*, which on 1 March reported that the Government was urging the European Commission not to react to the Industry Bill but to 'lie low until after the referendum'. With hindsight this can be seen as the first intimation of Wilson's determination to remove Tony Benn from office once the referendum had been held.

Britain's renegotiation of the Common Market terms was completed during a two-day meeting of the Commission at Dublin Castle on 10 and 11 March. A week later at a meeting of the Cabinet it was agreed by a majority, with Tony Benn voting against, that the announcement of the referendum, with the Government's recommendation that Britain should stay in the Common Market, would be given to the House. Hours later, Tony Benn issued a statement rejecting the renegotiated terms:

'I believe the recommendation made today is wrong for Britain and contains a tragic error of judgement. The new terms that have been renegotiated do not meet the clear objectives which we set ourselves and pledged we would achieve in our manifesto last year. It must be clearly understood that membership of the Common Market, even on these new terms, is fundamentally incompatible with the maintenance of parliamentary democracy in Britain and our capacity to safeguard our vital national interest.'

The next day he joined with five other Ministers – Castle, Foot, Hart, Shore and John Silkin – in a declaration against the Common Market. Amid some rancour and not a little confusion, the referendum campaign was mounted. As the Ministers went their individual ways, even the pretence of government through the Cabinet ended.

Inevitably, Tony Benn became in the eyes of the media the leader of the anti-Marketeers and at times the only spokesman reporters were prepared to acknowledge. Considerable efforts were made to discredit him. In early May he was scorned for refusing to accept the demand for 20,000 redundancies made by Sir Monty Finniston, the Chairman of British Steel Corporation. Allegedly bitter disagreements with Cabinet colleagues were widely reported, including one with Shirley Williams on 7 May. His plan, announced in mid-May, to save British Leyland from total collapse by taking it into public ownership was angrily criticized. So obsessed with Tony Benn did newspapers become that journalists took to camping out in the small garden at the front of his house, ringing the doorbell at all hours of day and night. On one occasion his younger children were hustled, and sworn at by 'gentlemen of the press'. Even the contents of his dustbins were for a while seized daily, presumably so that they could be searched for newsworthy items.

The verbal attacks made on him by pro-Market politicians were just as mindless and violent. Sir Keith Joseph likened him to 'Dracula'; Lord Watkinson demanded in the Lords that Wilson should sack him; Heath, who in February had lost the leadership of the Tories to Margaret Thatcher, said that 'before you could say "Viscount Stansgate", he would be leading us into his vision of the promised land, not flowing with milk and honey but swamped with ration books and state directives'; David Steel, who had never held government office, sank so low as to criticize 'upper class, public school and Oxford-educated sons of the peerage who seek to exploit mass grievances as the only means of obtaining political power for themselves – power which their own ability or record would deny them'; and Wilson, never one to be outshone, compared him to 'an Old Testament prophet without a beard who talks about the New Jerusalem he looks forward to at some future time'. Ominously Wilson added: 'Policy is decided quite clearly by the Cabinet. After 6 June there will be one Cabinet and one Cabinet view.'

With no real attempts being made to refute Tony Benn's arguments, the press bayed for his blood with, for example, the *Daily Mail* declaring in a headline: 'WEDGIE – HIS DAYS ARE NUMBERED'. On 5 June, the referendum predictably decided by a majority of two to one that Britain should stay in the Comon Market. Subsequently it was revealed that the pro-Marketeers had raised and spent on their campaign nearly £1,500,000, a remarkable contrast to the £133,630 used by the anti-Marketeers. Tony Benn accepted defeat gracefully, declaring: 'I have just been in receipt of a· very big message from the British people. I read it loud and clear ... I am sure everyone would want to accept that. That has been the principle of all of us who have advocated the referendum.'

Four days later, the Questions in the Commons were broadcast live for the first time. Tony Benn took part, but it was to be his last appearance in the House as Secretary of State for Industry, because a few hours later Wilson summoned him from a meeting of the Home Policy Committee and, announcing a Cabinet reorganization, asked him to go to the Department of Energy. Indignant at being asked to accept immediately, Tony Benn demanded and was granted a day in which to consider the matter.

The next day, 10 June, the newspapers were full of congratulations for Tony Benn's broadcast performance. 'BIG BENN IS THE STAR OF THE AIR!' announced the *Sun*. Even the *Daily Telegraph* agreed, declaring: 'BENN A HIT IN RADIO COMMONS'. So it was on the day that Tony Benn received such unusual press acclaim that he informed Wilson that reluctantly he would accept a move to the Department of Energy. Although Tony Benn was the hero of the Labour left and the chief proponent of socialist policies within the Party, there was no escaping the fact that Wilson, having willingly become the puppet of the Party's right wing, had given him the sack.

11 1975–1984

The heady days during which Tony Benn had attempted to introduce socialist planning into the tottering capitalist economy were over. He had failed, not because his plans did not work, but because Wilson had from the beginning been determined to sabotage them. Then, having destroyed the alternative economic strategy, Wilson set about destroying Tony Benn, its chief architect. Responding to the clear signals made by the Prime Minister, the popular press intensified the anti-Benn campaign which had already sunk so low that, at the height of the referendum campaign, the *Daily Express* had published Tony Benn's photograph daubed with a Hitler moustache.

The referendum defeat and Tony Benn's dismissal brought confusion to the Labour left. The trade union leaders, running scared, felt sure that, unless the Labour Party showed to the public an inoffensive, moderate face, the Tories were certain to be returned to power at the next election. As they felt that any Labour Government was preferable to a Tory one committed to the monetarist solutions propounded by Thatcher, most of them jettisoned their socialist beliefs and offered their full support to Wilson. Their decision led directly to the harsh treatment their members were almost immediately to receive from Wilson, and subsequently to the Labour Party's defeat at the next election.

In mid-June a concerted attack on the unions was mounted in the press. The crisis in British industry was blamed solely on wage demands – no mention was made of the failure to improve either management or production methods. There was harsh criticism of the crippling effect on the economy of workers withdrawing their labour, but not of investors withdrawing their capital to seek more profitable outlets overseas. As early as 18 June, the Cabinet discussed the introduction of an incomes policy. Increasing speculation imposed growing strains on sterling, and Tony Benn, who had been informed by senior civil servants weeks earlier that a financial crisis would follow the referendum, suspected the Treasury mandarins of encouraging the difficulties so that their policies could be implemented. Certainly there was soon a general acceptance of their view that the only way in which the slide in the value of the pound could be halted was by rigidly limiting wage increases. Wilson offered the trade union leaders the choice of a voluntary incomes policy or an economic collapse. Despite Tony Benn's appeal that it was not the responsibility of a Labour Government to nurse an unjust and inefficient system through yet another crisis, a maximum wage increase of £6 a week was agreed by the Cabinet and supported by the trade union leadership. Ten years after being rejected because of the united opposition of the trade union movement, an agreement along the lines of *In Place of Strife* had been accepted. It brought to an end the wider implications of the Social Contract envisaged by Tony Benn, and effectively constrained the militancy of workers which naturally centred on wage demands and collective bargaining.

The limited socialist gains of the previous eighteen months also began to be whittled away. On 24 July, for example, the Department of Industry refused to give the Meriden Motorcycle Corporation any further financial support. Constantly growing in confidence, the Tories fiercely opposed the proposal, presented in the House on 29 July, to establish the British National Oil Corporation, intended to give the Government an active role in the exploration and development of North Sea oil. But the objections raised were mostly unfounded, because the original policy of full public participation in the oil industry had already been effectively destroyed by Tony Benn's predecessor at the Department of Energy – Eric Varley, the Labour MP for Chesterfield. Nevertheless, the oil companies refused to co-operate with the Government and another anti-Benn campaign was mounted. An editorial in the *Daily Mail* on 31 July was headlined 'BENN, THE DEMON "MUGGER" UNMASKED'.

The anti-socialist measures of the Government continued apace. At a Cabinet meeting held at Chequers on 5 November, it was decided that available funds should be used to assist the modernization of private industry rather than to extend public ownership. In December, faced with

Chrysler's announcement of its withdrawal from Britain, Wilson persuaded the company to stay by offering £162.5 million, despite Tony Benn's protest that public ownership provided the only sensible answer.

Although more muted than before, such disagreements between Tony Benn and Wilson continued. On 28 January 1976, the NEC passed a motion criticizing Wilson for having awarded a life peerage to the Chairman of Guest, Keen and Nettlefolds, which was the largest contributing company to Conservative Party funds. Tony Benn then announced that he intended to resubmit at the next meeting of the Home Policy Committee a paper on the reform of the Honours System which he had written ten years earlier. Wilson at the time must have been working on what was to become generally accepted as a most controversial and inept Honours List. That perhaps explains the irritation that made him write to Tony Benn on 4 February:

'You must be aware that it is my responsibility to advise the Queen on matters relating to honours; and I cannot accept that it is appropriate for you as a Minister in the Government to initiate a policy study in a Party Committee on a matter which plainly falls within the responsibility of Government itself ... I should like to have from you your immediate assurance that you do not intend to proceed in this way in respect of the Honours System.'

In his reply, Tony Benn stated that the press reports on which Wilson had based his assumption were inaccurate, and that his paper had already been submitted in January 1964.

Wilson was not satisfied, and on 8 March further complained about a motion, proposed by Tony Benn and accepted by the NEC, authorizing the chairpersons of its sub-committees to make statements about meetings to the press. Wilson adamantly stated:

'I cannot agree that you, or any other Minister who is a member of a Party Committee or Sub-Committee, should make statements, or become identified with statements made on behalf of the Committee, in a non-Ministerial capacity. This is all the more undesirable where such statements affect the responsibilities of other Ministers, including myself. Ministers cannot speak publicly in a non-Ministerial capacity. In all cases they speak as Ministers and the principle of collective responsibility applies. Matters which raise major issues of policy or are likely to occasion public comment or criticism must engage the collective responsibility of the Cabinet ...'

What was to be the final attack in the anti-Benn campaign waged by Wilson while he was the Prime Minister occurred on 11 March when he sacked Joe Ashton, who was Tony Benn's Parliamentary Private Secretary, for voting against the projected £3 billion public expenditure cuts. Four days later, to the astonishment of the media, Wilson announced his resignation as Prime Minister. The congratulatory eulogies that appeared in the press suddenly ended with the publication of his resignation Honours List.

On 17 March, two days after Wilson's resignation, Tony Benn announced his decision to contest the leadership, declaring: 'I am standing for one reason and one reason only: to put forward policies in which I believe.' These he detailed in a mini-manifesto, entitled *A New Course for Labour*, in which he unambiguously stated: 'Given the nature of the crisis, the only possible leadership for the people of Britain at this moment lies in an active socialist programme.'

As there was an anti-socialist majority in the Parliamentary Labour Party, there was no possibility of Tony Benn winning, for then only MPs voted for the new leader. However, he did far better than even his supporters expected, receiving 37 votes, which was more than Healey and Crosland, but less than Foot with 90, Callaghan with 84, and Jenkins with 56 (a remarkable slump from the 133 votes he had obtained in the 1970 deputy leadership contest). Tony Benn immediately announced that he would not stand in the second round and that he would support Foot. On 5 April, Callaghan was elected the Leader of the Labour Party and became, therefore, the Prime Minister. He asked Tony Benn to stay on as Secretary of State for Energy, and it appeared as though a new beginning was possible, especially as Ashton was reinstated as his Parliamentary Private Secretary.

Unfortunately the economic situation continued to worsen, and Callaghan soon embarked on a programme of further controls. On 5 May an agreement with the TUC. was reached to limit wage rises to 5 per cent during the following year. But that was not enough for the bankers or the Tories who wanted to blame the slump on public ownership and trade union strength. They would not be satisfied until both had been overturned. On 7 June, the Government obtained a standby credit for six months of $5.3 billion from the International Monetary Fund on condition that there would be further substantial cuts in public expenditure.

Deeply concerned by what he believed to be a policy that would destroy the country's industrial base, Tony Benn attacked the deflationary moves in a series of political meetings. As Chairman of the Home Policy Committee, he was largely responsible for the production of Labour's *Programme for Britain, 1976* which, unlike the actual policies of the Government, was concerned with a planned, socialist economy that envisaged an extension of public ownership to the banks, insurance companies, and construction and pharmaceutical industries. In late September, the programme was overwhelmingly endorsed at the annual Party Conference in Blackpool.

But the 1976 Conference was an unhappy occasion. Searching desperately for reasons why the Government was clearly so unable to solve the country's economic problems, the Party split into factions that accused each other of betrayal or incompetence. In his tough-talking speech, Callaghan, in the name of expediency, not only rejected socialism but insisted that the maintenance of profits was the only way in which industry could be made to prosper. But even while he was speaking, the value of sterling was continuing to fall and the Government's future was increasingly in doubt. Booking into a hotel on 1 November under false names, representatives of the IMF investigated the country's finances. Their diagnosis that the financial difficulties were caused by excessive public borrowing was accepted by Callaghan, and cuts of £4 billion out of a total of £9.1 billion were demanded. While this was too much for most Ministers, after prolonged discussions the Cabinet on 9 December rejected Tony Benn's alternative economic strategy and accepted that there should be cuts of £2.5 billion. In exchange, the Government obtained from the IMF a seven-year loan of $1.5 billion.

Confidence in sterling returned, but the manifesto plans and underlying philosophy of the Labour Party had been all but destroyed. As tensions within the Party grew, many people, both inside and outside it, began to express the view that the Labour Party itself might be destroyed. As the calls for a government of national unity grew, the first of the social democrats, sensing defeat, made their escape. In December, Reg Prentice resigned to join the Conservatives. Jenkins left to become President of the EEC.

Tony Benn felt strongly that it had not been necessary to accept the harsh terms imposed by the IMF, for a loan could not have been withheld without severely damaging the Western alliance. In any case, the Government could have countered by threatening to reduce its defence commitments unless necessary funds were made available. As it was, however, Callaghan allowed the IMF to dictate Government policy and, as Tony Benn predicted, the reduction in public spending led inevitably to rising unemployment and a reduction in real living standards.

As he also warned, it brought about a coalition, for Callaghan, to ensure the continuation of his by then minority Government in a threatened No Confidence vote, entered on 23 March 1977 into a Lib–Lab pact with David Steel, the Leader of the Liberal Party. Sharing his father's repugnance for coalitions, Tony Benn considered resignation but, urged not to do so by his constituency Labour Party, he decided to remain in the Cabinet. There followed a most unhappy period for, as he relates, the Liberals were given consultative rights that made a nonsense of Wilson's earlier insistence that the principle of the Cabinet's collective responsibility precluded discussions on policy elsewhere:

'During the period when the pact was in force, Ministers were expected to discuss their policy proposals with their Liberal counterparts before bringing them to colleagues. Neither Labour MPs, even when organized in specialist groups, nor the NEC. policy committees, ever enjoyed such rights.'

Callaghan delivered a further blow to the principle of collective responsibility when in answer to a question from Thatcher on 16 June he announced: 'I certainly think that the doctrine should apply, except in cases where I announce that it does not.'

Thatcher's question had sought to discover whether Cabinet Ministers would be given the freedom to express their own views in the forthcoming Bill to set up direct elections for a European Assembly – a Bill which had been a condition imposed by Steel for joining the Lib–Lab pact. As the issue of the Common Market had again become a political one, Tony Benn, as its best-known critic, was once more subjected to a scurrilous press campaign, culminating in an item published in the first edition of *The Times* on 2 August:

'A member of Anthony Wedgwood Benn's family has been receiving medical treatment in the private wing of the Radcliffe Infirmary at Oxford. We all know Comrade Benn's views about private medicine. We are interested to learn, therefore, that when his son indulges in it, he does so under his mother's maiden name of De Camp.'

The story was completely untrue, and the following day *The Times* published an apology. Copies of the original item, however, were stuck on postcards and sent to many other newspapers. Each of the cards bore the mark of a postal franking machine which was later identified as belonging to the British European Movement, a pro-Common Market pressure group that had between 1964 and 1976 received substantial Government grants. Having listed this and several other fictitious stories about Tony Benn that had been carried in the national press, *New Society* on 11 August commented:

'It has long been obvious that Benn has been cast by the press as a "red bogeyman" – and in this journalists are often covertly encouraged by Benn's own colleagues in the Government. But the fact that these stories were not even checked with Benn suggests that an "open season" has been declared for Benn-baiting. No doubt Benn can look after himself. But should not the press take especial care to be seen to be maintaining their standards when reporting a politician with whose views they so obviously disagree?'

Despite such attacks and his feeling of distrust caused by Callaghan's abrogation of socialist beliefs, Tony Benn threw himself wholeheartedly into his work as Secretary of State for Energy. In 1977 he made 19 visits overseas, delivered 113 speeches, made 140 broadcasts, wrote 16 articles, attended 254 committee and 42 Cabinet meetings, voted 129 times in the Commons, and dealt with over 5000 letters from constituents. He was also the Minister responsible for North Sea oil, which by the end of 1978 was already producing half Britain's requirements.

Yet the revenue from oil was not sufficient to oblige Callaghan to curb his policy of severe economic constraints. Having decided not to call an autumn election, the Prime Minister faced growing opposition to his policies, which in October were rejected at the Labour Party Conference. The unrest caused by the rigid incomes policy escalated and the early months of 1979 became the 'Winter of Discontent' as many groups of workers, especially in the public sector, went on strike to press their wage claims. As the chaos grew, it was obvious that the Government, having totally alienated its own supporters, was certain to fall, and after losing a motion of No Confidence on 28 March the Prime Minister called a General Election.

Callaghan's betrayal of the Labour Party continued, for he refused to accept the draft manifesto prepared by the NEC and, using his position as Prime Minister, insisted that it was his right to decide the Party's policy. Callaghan's revisionist manifesto rejected all forms of socialist planning and offered the electorate little more than a further dose of wage restraints and belt-tightening.

As Callaghan was not seen as a threat by the establishment and the media, it was Tony Benn who during the election campaign was again identified as being the chief threat, and there were some people prepared to go to any lengths to prevent him becoming Party Leader should Callaghan retire suddenly. In an article, subsequently published in the *New Statesman*, Duncan Campbell states that, shortly before election day, Airey Neave, the Tory MP who was one of Thatcher's closest allies, discussed with Lee Tracey, an MI6 electronics expert, the possibility of assassinating Tony Benn should he become Prime Minister. Tragically, shortly afterwards, Neave was himself killed by a terrorist bomb. It was because Tony Benn did not wish to distress further Neave's family and because he did not believe the story that he raised strong objections to its publication, but the editor of the *New Statesman* insisted that the information given was correct and decided to publish it after Tracey had agreed to speak about his secret service activities on a *Panorama* programme on BBC Television. Campbell's article concluded:

'The fact that Mr Neave had conducted meetings of this sort just before his death was known to us in detail at the time, and has since been confirmed by another former security agent. In the immediate aftermath of the assassination, there was nothing we could or would have done to investigate further.

But Tracey's involvement with the *Panorama* programme, and his willingness to discuss the matter attributably, creates a new situation. To put the matter no higher, a man who has been frequently employed on Government intelligence work claims to have had a highly-dangerous conversation with a senior politician during the course of a general election. Ugly as the matter inevitably is, it would be difficult to argue that Tracey's evidence should be suppressed.'[1]

The story has never been denied.

The open anti-Benn propaganda in the press continued throughout the election campaign, as Caroline Benn recalls: 'The harassment got very bad. Everything centred on him rather than on the issues.' And Tony Benn had difficulties in expounding his cause which, although that approved by the Labour Party Conference, had been excluded from the Party's manifesto by Callaghan who, despite fighting on his own selection of policies, led the Party in the General Election held on 3 May to its worst electoral defeat for twenty years. In Bristol South East the electorate returned Tony Benn to Parliament for the twelfth successive time. But the country returned a Conservative Government, committed to a monetarist programme that would bring down inflation at the cost of rising unemployment and a decline in people's living standards.

With the majority of the Labour leadership at loggerheads with most Party members, Tony Benn decided that a period of Party reconstruction was essential. At the first meeting after the election of the left-wing members of the former Cabinet, he announced that he would not stand for the Shadow Cabinet. His plan was to spend eighteen months working for the structural reform of the Party necessary to make it far more responsive to the democratic wishes of the membership. So he went to the backbenches and immediately started his campaign to make the Labour Party accountable to its membership. On 7 May at a May Day rally in Birmingham he declared: 'We must rebuild the Labour Party as a mass party with a mass membership based upon the constituencies and upon factory and office branches, working closely at every level with the trade unions on policy and organization.' He identified three changes that were necessary: to ensure that the Party Leader was answerable to the Party, the constituencies and trade unions should be involved in the election and not just the Party's MPs, who relied upon the Leader's patronage for their own promotion; to ensure that MPs abided by the Party's policy, they should submit themselves to their constituency Labour Parties for reselection before each election; and to prevent a Labour Government reneging on the policies it had been elected to implement, the policy decision agreed by the annual Conference should be binding on the Parliamentary Labour Party. These reforms had already been demanded by several pressure groups within the Labour Party, including the Campaign for Labour Party Democracy, which Tony Benn joined.

He was not seen by the media, however, as being a member of or even the spokesman for a movement, but rather as a politician making a personal bid for the leadership of the Labour Party by advocating reforms seen as being more likely to achieve his ambition than the system which existed. It was a difficult accusation to counter. He made no secret of his willingness to lead the Labour Party, and yet he was not driven by personal ambition, for like his father he put principles before expediency and beliefs before promotion. Socialism was more important than personal success. Caroline Benn testifies to the strength of the conviction they both share and which throughout their life together has given them a common cause both have individually served:

'The cause is something in which your personal stake is nil. It cannot be about your own self-interest. It's about everyone's interests and the social good. It is not about yourself.'

Yet such commitment to a cause could not be understood by the newspaper reporters who continued to hound the Benns. Each pronouncement was interpreted only as a piece of self-publicity. So when it was announced that Tony Benn intended to deliver a lecture on 'The Case for a Constitutional Premiership' at Bristol University on 13 July, it was generally assumed that he intended to launch a personal attack on Callaghan. In response to the resulting furore, the Vice-Chancellor banned the lecture, which had to be delivered instead at the Folk House in Bristol. In his meticulously researched and well-reasoned speech, Tony Benn traced and analysed the development of prime ministerial power. He began:

'After eleven years' service as a member of four Labour Governments, I have reached the conclusion that the range of powers at present exercised by a British Prime Minister, both in that capacity and as party leader, is now so great as to encroach upon the legitimate rights of the electorate, undermine the essential role of Parliament and usurp some of the functions of collective Cabinet decision-making. In addition, a Labour Prime

Minister can neutralize much of the influence deriving from the party's internal democracy – which is necessary to serve the interests of its membership. In short, the present centralization of power in the hands of one person has gone too far and amounts to a system of personal rule in the very heart of our parliamentary democracy. The Prime Minister and party leader must be made more accountable to those over whom he or she exercises power, so that we can develop a constitutional premiership in Britain. To transform an absolute premiership into a constitutional premiership would involve making some fundamental changes in its functions comparable to those made, over the years, when the Crown was transformed from an absolute monarchy into a constitutional monarchy.'[2]

Throughout the year, Tony Benn enthusiastically continued his campaign, addressing in all 215 meetings. By the time of the annual Conference in October 1979, there was a considerable amount of support within the Party for organizational changes. Although bitterly opposed by Callaghan and his anti-socialist colleagues, motions were passed demanding that MPs should face mandatory reselection and that the NEC. should control the Party's manifesto. It was agreed that there would be established a Commission of Inquiry to recommend ways in which the Party Leader could be elected.

Knowing that the dominance they had assumed was being wrested away from them, the right-wing leaders naturally resisted, with the continuing support of the popular media. Every issue was reported as though it was a personal triumph for Tony Benn over the right-wing 'moderates' who sought only Party unity. Thus a BBC news reporter on 3 October stated: 'So Mr Benn won the two most significant of the three votes he needed to change the balance of power within the Party.' The capture of the Labour Party by Tony Benn and the left wing was the dominant theme in the media, accompanied by a hysterical outcry against the infiltration of the Party by 'extremists', 'Trotskyites', and 'Militants'. There was glee, however, when the national agent's office announced that because some drafting errors had allegedly been discovered it would be necessary for the motions to be considered again at the next annual Conference.

Fearing a bitter and destructive conflict within the Labour Party, the Transport and General Workers' Union persuaded the NEC. to call a special conference at Wembley in May 1980. The purpose was to prepare a statement of agreed policies, including the alternative economic strategy, unilateral nuclear disarmament, and withdrawal from the Common Market. This was agreed and issued as *Peace, Jobs and Freedom*.

During the special conference, a most significant event took place. Various left-wing pressure groups, concerned that the Commission of Inquiry might be used to prevent the introduction of the agreed reforms, decided to unite. On 31 May, Tony Benn addressed the inaugural meeting of the Rank and File Mobilizing Committee, which brought together such disparate organizations as the Campaign for Labour Party Democracy, the Socialist Campaign for a Labour Victory, the Labour Co-ordinating Committee, the Institute of Workers' Control, the Militant Tendency, the Labour Party Young Socialists, and the National Organization of Labour Students.

When the Commission of Inquiry submitted its report in June, it upheld mandatory reselection, proposed that there should be an electoral college to decide the Party Leader, and suggested that the manifesto should be drafted by the NEC. and then be endorsed by the electoral college. The Rank and File Mobilizing Committee rejected the proposed constitution of the electoral college, in which 50 per cent of the votes were to be held by MPs. It also reaffirmed its commitment to the control of the manifesto being held solely by the NEC.

At the 1980 Labour Party Conference in September, mandatory reselection was confirmed, but the motion giving the NEC the power to write the manifesto was narrowly lost. Various proposals about the electoral college were discussed, but it was agreed that the decision about how it should be formed would be deferred until a special conference was held at Wembley in January 1981.

It appeared as though the left had won a famous victory and that the right was in disarray, but the left's elation was soon to be over. Three weeks after the 1980 Party Conference, Callaghan announced his resignation as the Party Leader knowing that, as no electoral college had been formed, his replacement would have to be elected solely by the Parliamentary Labour Party, in which the right still had a clear majority.

Tony Benn considered standing in the leadership election, but decided against it and backed Foot, who was opposed by Healey, John Silkin and Peter Shore. Foot won the contest and Healey was unopposed when he stood for the deputy leadership. By the time the Wembley Conference took place on 24 January 1981, Foot had been installed as the Leader of a Labour Party that was anything but united. The left was well organized and had been conducting within the Party a vigorous campaign that was generally described in the press as being ruthless and over-aggressive. The right, having been saddled with a leader thought to be of the left, was in despair, and it was widely assumed that the Group of Three – David Owen, William Rodgers and Shirley Williams – would leave the Party to join Jenkins in some sort of coalition with the Liberals. After much debate and some acrimony, it was accepted that the vote of the electoral college should be made up of 40 per cent from the trade unions, 30 per cent from the Labour MPs and 30 per cent from the constituency parties. It was the formula advocated by the Rank and File Mobilizing Committee. Foot immediately displayed his inability to unite the Party and announced: 'I cannot pretend to you that absolutely all the results this afternon were the ones I wanted.' The following day, the Group of Three and Jenkins issued the Limehouse Declaration that led two months later to the launching of the Social Democratic Party, an event much publicized and lauded in the press.

Although active left wingers were not sorry to see the anti-socialists at last depart from the Party to which they owed their position in public life, many ordinary Labour voters were bemused. Like most other departing MPs, the Gang of Four said that it was not they but the Party which had changed. Although it was eagerly reported by the popular media, the claim that the Labour Party had suddenly lurched to the left was untrue; if anything it had under Callaghan lurched further to the right. The claim certainly made no sense to members of the Party, all of whom have printed on their membership cards Clause IV of the Labour Party's constitution:

'To secure for the workers by hand or by brain the full fruits of their industry and the most equitable distribution thereof that may be possible upon the basis of the common ownership of the means of production, distribution and exchange, and the best obtainable system of popular administration and control of each industry or service.'

It was this clause that Gaitskell had tried but failed to change twenty years before the formation of the Social Democratic Party. It was the clause which on joining the Labour Party and each year on renewing their membership the Gang of Four had agreed to accept.

Yet the desertion of the revisionists from the Labour Party worried the leadership, who claimed that a period of consolidation (or inaction) was essential for the survival of the Party. Trade Unions for Labour Victory, a group of trade union leaders, asked the Shadow Cabinet not to hold any leadership elections in 1981, threatening to try to stop any such attempt. The Tribune Group of Labour MPs also decided that there should not be an election. Yet this suggested moratorium did not prevent the organization of opposition to the construction of the electoral college, as established at the Wembley Conference. After 150 MPs had declared their rejection of the agreed formula, the Labour Solidarity Campaign was formed. No doubt encouraged by Foot's announced dislike of the electoral college's composition, moves began aimed at reversing the decision made about the method of electing the Party's leaders.

To prevent such a reversal, the left knew that an early election had to be held so that the agreed procedures would be used. As Foot was generally accepted as the Party Leader, it was far more sensible to contest the deputy leadership, for Healey was disliked by the left and had been returned unopposed only because it was thought by many that a contest should not take place until the electoral college had been established.

The only person of sufficient standing to make a worthwhile challenge was Tony Benn. As an election was not wanted by the leadership, it would obviously be a difficult campaign that there was a very real chance of losing, thus in all probability throwing away a later opportunity of being elected. For several weeks, Tony Benn discussed with friends and colleagues whether or not he should become a candidate for the deputy leadership. Naturally, he sought the advice of Caroline Benn, who recalls:

'I said, "If you want my opinion, the answer is no. I wouldn't do it." There was obviously going to be a confrontation, but I thought it should take place when the political omens were right.'

His constituency party discussed the matter twice, and approved a motion asking him to stand. Several trade union leaders also gave the same advice. Foot, however, urged him not to do so.

An early decision had to be made so that the different trade union conferences would have an opportunity of discussing the matter. On 2 April, Tony Benn announced his candidature for the deputy leadership and promised a six-month campaign during which the issues facing the Party would be fully debated.

Immediately there was launched a campaign in the media that can have had few equals for the vitriol, inaccuracy, and frequency of the attacks that were heaped on Tony Benn during the six months that preceded the election at the Labour Party Conference. On the day after his announcement, the hostility of the press was obvious: 'Mr Benn is plotting another power struggle' (*Daily Star*); 'SPOTLIGHT ON THE FANATIC' (*Daily Express*); 'A Benn victory will put the final nail in the coffin of Labour as a national, governing party' (*Daily Express*); and 'POWER-BID BENN' (*Daily Mirror*).

That was but the beginning; things were to get much worse:

'BENN IS A FANATIC WARNS ANGRY HATTERSLEY' (*Daily Mirror*, 4 April).

'Order of the Bennite Loon. For devotees of crazy political ideas.' (*Daily Mail*, 8 April.)

'He has finally blown his top, hepped up to the gills on tannin (he drinks 20 cups of tea a day) and is no longer a serious politician.' (*Daily Mirror*, 10 April.)

'Former Prime Minister Sir Harold Wilson dismissed Tony Benn's ideas for the future of the Labour Party as "barmy".' (BBC, 22 April.)

'WHY LABOUR LEADERS TREMBLE AT THE RELENT-LESS ADVANCE OF BENN'S ARMY. TORN APART BY POLITICS OF FEAR' (*Daily Express*, 22 May).

'MR BENN – IS HE MAD OR A KILLER?' (*Sun*, 22 May.)

'Left-wing maverick Tony Benn stepped up Labour's civil war early today by launching an angry attack on President Reagan.' (*Daily Mirror*, 23 May.)

'BENN THE DICTATOR. HE PUTS 200 MPs AT RISK' (*Daily Express*, 28 May). [This headline was the subject of a complaint to the Press Council, which in its adjudication stated: 'The headline "BENN THE DICTATOR" was unjustified, inaccurate and not supported by the text of the article. It reflected an editorial opinion rather than the substance of a news item.']

'BENN MEN PUT BOOT IN' (*Daily Mirror*, 30 May).

'The statement detailed the way Mr Benn is destroying the party's election chances with his maverick behaviour.' (*Daily Mail*, 4 June.)

'BENN GOES OFF THE RAILS AGAIN' (*Sun*, 4 June).

'THE MENACE OF MR BENN' (*Sun*, 24 July).

'FOOT MAY QUIT OVER BENN' (*Daily Mirror*, 3 August).

'Labour was falling deeper into the clutches of the militants last night ... The signs now read "Danger, Benn at work".' (*Daily Express*, 4 September.)

'BENN'S BRITAIN – WHAT IT WOULD BE LIKE UNDER WEDGIE'S BOOT IN 1984' (*Sun*, 7 September – in the week of the TUC Conference).

'The Marxist kingdom of Benn and Scargill.' (*Sun*, 10 September.)

'Benn's supporters are now sneering, hate-filled creatures.' (*Daily Mirror*, 10 September.)

Throughout the campaign, Tony Benn constantly said that he wanted the debate to be about policies and not about personalities, but the newspapers were concerned only with their hysterical and fictitious view of Tony Benn's personality. So the major point of the campaign was ignored – in all respects Tony Benn's policies were identical to those approved by the previous Labour Party Conference, whereas Healey did not support the most important decisions, including unilateral nuclear disarmament, withdrawal from the Common Market, and the establishment of the electoral college.

Halfway through the campaign, Tony Benn was suddenly taken ill and rushed to Charing Cross Hospital. The media showed little sympathy and reporters had a field-day speculating on the causes and nature of his illness. There was much talk about the amount of tea he drank, but little or no attention was given to the very real possibility that an attempt had been made on his life and that he had deliberately been poisoned. That certainly was the view of one of the doctors who treated him. The announced diagnosis was that he was suffering from Guillain-Barré Syndrome, a rare polyneuritis, the cause of which is unknown but the effects of which are shared by chronic mercury and arsenic poisoning.

Fortunately, Tony Benn made a speedy recovery, suffering no other effect than a temporary loss of sensitivity in his toes and the tips of his fingers. Returning to his campaign with all his usual industriousness and boundless energy, he undertook nineteen speaking engagements, including six radio and television broadcasts, between 3 and 26 September. As the election day approached, the hostility of the media towards him intensified. Any lie or rumour was grist to the anti-Benn mill, which was at work not only in the popular press. On 24 September, *The Times* wrote of his 'farm in Essex and the existence of a Stansgate trust in the tax haven of the Bank of Bermuda'. The following day, a letter of denial from Tony Benn was published with the statement: 'We accept Tony Benn's corrections and offer him our apologies.' On 27 September, the day of the election, the *Observer* ran a front-page story headlined 'WE FEAR A FIDDLE', which claimed that Alan Fisher, the Secretary of the National Union of Public Employees, was deliberately withholding from the union's delegates the results of the ballot of members, so that at the last minute they would be told it was so close that it was not binding, and thus be able to vote for Tony Benn. The claim was untrue, and on 21 December the *Observer* agreed in the High Court to pay appropriate damages and offer sincere apologies to NUPE and Alan Fisher - but that was, of course, after the election.

Foot too did not come out of the campaign period with credit. Goaded by the press, the Party Leader had in May challenged Tony Benn to contest the leadership. Naturally, he declined, pointing out that he had voted for Foot, unlike Healey and John Silkin, the other two candidates for the deputy leadership. Foot's ineffective huffing and puffing made him appear indecisive and uneasy. Quoted as saying that Tony Benn had destroyed Labour's chances of winning the next General Election, Foot showed by his apparent willingness to accept pressure from a press traditionally hostile to the Labour Party that he was incapable of effective leadership, having neither Callaghan's authoritarianism nor Wilson's pragmatism.

The trade union movement was also revealed by the campaign to be in some disorder. As those who had advocated a contest suspected, many union leaders had not even thought about the system that should be used to discover the wishes of the membership in the election. Hence there was confusion and a wide disparity of practice. NUPE consulted members individually. By contrast, the Transport and General Workers' Union consulted members through its regional organizations and, although the majority of the regions voted for Healey, the union's Executive Committee recommended a vote for Tony Benn on the grounds that this reflected the wish of the majority of voters. Despite this, the delegates decided to vote for Silkin in the first ballot.

Another issue that surfaced was the conflict between the constituency parties, the large majority of which supported Tony Benn, and their MPs, who in the main were opposed to his candidature. This led to considerable pressure being put on MPs to express the wishes of the local party members. When several MPs then announced that they would abstain, supporters of Tony Benn sent them a letter containing an implied threat that they might not be reselected: 'Abstain if you will, but do not expect the no doubt sophisticated reasons for doing so to be understood. That is asking too much.'

So in a tense and uncertain atmosphere, the MPs, trade union and constituency delegates met at the beginning of the Labour Party Conference, on 27 September, to vote for the Deputy Leader in the first ever electoral college. Viewed by a large television audience, the first ballot took place. Healey obtained 45.37 per cent, Tony Benn 36.63 per cent, and Silkin 18 per cent. Silkin was then eliminated, and on the second ballot Healey was elected with 50.426 per cent, Tony Benn receiving 49.574 per cent. So, despite the universal opposition of the press, Tony Benn came within a whisker of victory. Three important factors contributed to his defeat: the belligerence and over-zealousness of some of his supporters created animosity, allowing the debate on issues to be ignored; MPs who were almost immediately to defect to the Social Democratic Party voted for Healey; and a small but vital group of MPs abstained, led by Neil Kinnock, who had himself rejected the call of some constituencies to stand and, knowing that it was a contest he could not win, chose instead to become the darling of the media by contributing to Tony Benn's defeat and await a more opportune moment to seek (and achieve) election to an office from which he would otherwise have been excluded by his complete lack of Ministerial experience.

The election was, however, a triumph for the movement to democratize the Labour Party, although it highlighted further changes that had to be made to the electoral machinery. The main principle for which Tony Benn had stood was established. The whole Party, rather than just MPs, had been given the right to elect the leadership. But having been personally defeated, Tony Benn was spurned by many, especially those who, in the belief that he would become the Leader of the Labour Party, had rallied to his cause only in the hope of furthering their own careers or interests. Like every person who becomes well known, Tony Benn had for years been surrounded by endless hangers-on who took up his time, creating a life apart from his family. Yet the disappearance of this amorphous swarm of drones was, as she states, anticipated by Caroline Benn: 'It is inevitable in politics. I knew that many would go the moment the patronage potential ended, and the ones who were true friends and true socialists would stay.'

He is willing to treat so generously even the most obvious of opportunists because he is genuinely interested in people and in finding solutions to their problems. Time and time again I have seen him stop working on something others might have thought was far more important to talk at length with someone needing help. As the person most likely to be abused in the press, he also unhesitatingly gives support to those similarly attacked. So in the aftermath of the Labour Conference he fiercely opposed the demand that swept the Party for a ritual sacrifice to cleanse the leadership of the taint of 'extremism'. He opposed, therefore, the expulsion of *Militant* supporters and the blockage of Tariq Ali's application for membership. He also campaigned for Peter Tatchell, the much denigrated Labour candidate in the Bermondsey by-election.

Throughout 1982 he continued, as he had always done, to champion the causes in which he believes and to stand by his principles. This meant, as it had so often done, that he expressed unpopular views for which he was fiercely attacked. With a small group of others, while the Party's leadership appeared to vacillate, he openly attacked in Parliament the British military expedition to the Falkland Islands, calling it 'a tragic and unnecessary war'. While the British public, urged on by the popular press, revelled in the military successes, Tony Benn argued that the political and financial costs of a victory were so great that in the long term they would prove to be unacceptable.

By the time of the 1982 Labour Party Conference it was clear that Thatcher would soon capitalize on the sudden boost given to her popularity by the Falklands War and call an early General Election. Faced with what would inevitably be a quieter Conference than the previous year's, the press spent much time in analysing Tony Benn's position in the Party. The Glasgow Media Group has given a reason for this attention:

'The focus on Benn goes beyond merely the desire to inform on his actual activity or role. "Tony Benn" and the word 'Bennery" are important, particularly in the right-wing press, as a symbol of all that is supposedly unacceptable in the left. In these contexts, "Benn" becomes another word alongside "far left", "hard left" or "activist" as a way of pre-empting a real discussion of what issues are at stake or who supports them for what reasons.'[3]

At the 1982 Conference, unlike that in 1981, Tony Benn was consistently portrayed as a spent force. For example, an article on 30 September in the *Sun* began, 'Is the Ayatollah of the Labour Party dead?' Of all the photographs of the Conference appearing in national newspapers 17 per cent were of Tony Benn. They were carefully selected to show him in a thoughtful, non-smiling moment, and the accompanying headlines hammered home the message of his imminent downfall. 'UNIONS DESTROY BENN'S AUTHORITY IN PARTY LEADERSHIP' declared *The Times* on its front page alongside a photograph of a grim-faced Tony Benn. The *Daily Mirror*, using the same technique, announced 'SULKY BENN FACES THE PUSH'. Although Tony Benn easily retained his position at the top of the poll for the constituency section, the news stories concentrated on the election of additional right wingers to the NEC and the removal of Tony Benn from the chairmanship of the Home Policy Committee and from membership of six other key committees.

But in what was assumed to be the run-up to the General Election, the press had another target apart from Tony Benn. During the Conference the photographs of Foot depicted him as a likeable but shambling old man, often shown taking his dog for a walk. In contrast, Thatcher was much photographed at the Conservative Party Conference triumphantly waving both hands above her head. As the opinion polls showed a massive Tory lead, it was almost certain that the Prime Minister could have her victory whenever she chose.

For Tony Benn there was no certainty about the next election. Boundary changes had been proposed that would abolish Bristol South East, the constituency he had represented since 1950. As it was generally agreed that the proposed new constituencies would give the Conservatives a considerable advantage, the Labour Party decided to contest their introduction in the courts. The case was eventually lost, and the action only succeeded in delaying the nomination of Labour candidates in the new constituencies. Tony Benn was asked to stand by local parties in several safe Labour seats, but, ignoring the advice of many people, including Caroline Benn, that he should accept one of these offers, he refused to leave Bristol. Feeling an immeasurable debt of gratitude to the people of the city for their help and support over the years, especially during the battle against the peerage, he decided not to desert them until at an election they rejected him. He was selected for the new constituency of Bristol East, which was anything but a safe Labour seat, for the results in the earlier local government elections of the wards that made up the constituency produced a clear Conservative majority.

Yet Tony Benn fought the election campaign with all his usual enthusiasm and dedication. For just one week I followed him through what was to me an exhausting blur of walkabouts through windy shopping-centres, meetings in public halls, interviews with the press, a live appearance on television, canvassing house to house, discussions with party workers, and such unexpected events as a late-night visit to a West Indian club. Hurried meals were eaten at Temple Meads railway buffet or in the self-catering hotel-room. Working each day from early morning until long after midnight he belied his fifty-seven years. As might be expected, a few of the people he met were offensive, but the vast majority appeared impressed by his courtesy, charm and sincerity. Right up until the count on 9 June 1983, he appeared confident that against all the odds he would win. Caroline Benn recalls:

'Just before we went to the count I said, "What are you going to say afterwards?" He gave me his speech and I said, "That's great, but if you lose what are you going to say?" And he just hadn't even thought of it. So I said, "I've just written down some things that you might want to say if you lose."'

In his dignified acceptance of his defeat, Tony Benn gave his valediction, after thirty-three years, to the people of Bristol:

'First of all I should like to thank the Chartists and the suffragettes who gave every working man and woman a vote in this country. And every election is a tribute to their strength.

Secondly, I would like to thank the people of Bristol, who over a third of a century have returned me to Parliament, and to say how glad I am that I stayed, since nothing but the decision of the people of Bristol would ever have induced me to leave this city.

And third, I would like to say "Thank you" to the Labour voters, not only in this constituency, but all over the country, who stood firm with a very good programme in an election when a great deal has been thrown at them, and they have not been diverted from their faith in our policies. I hope that no Labour voter will be discouraged by this result ...

If I can say one personal word – I do not believe that politics is about personalities. And I want to make absolutely clear to those in this constituency and elsewhere that what has happened today will make absolutely no difference to my own commitment to the Labour movement, which can be discharged as well outside Parliament as inside Parliament. Thank you very much indeed.'

As a consequence of his defeat, Tony Benn was ineligible to enter the contest for the Party leadership which, following Foot's expected resignation, took place at the beginning of the 1983 Party Conference. Using the electoral college that Tony Benn had been so instrumental in establishing, the movement chose Kinnock as Leader and Roy Hattersley as his Deputy, a partnership illuminatingly referred to in the traditionally anti-Labour press as 'the dream ticket'. It was easy to see why so many of Tony Benn's political opponents were willing to conclude that his career was finished, but, like the Benns before him, he could not so easily be exiled to the wilderness. Still remaining the most popular speaker with Labour Party audiences, he was obviously needed by the Labour Party in Parliament. The first opportunity came when Varley's resignation meant that there would be a by-election at Chesterfield. Immediately the press mounted a campaign to block Tony Benn's selection, loudly proclaiming that his candidature would be an embarrassment to the new leadership and a cause of division within the Party. After his victory at the Chesterfield selection meeting, the press reacted venomously. 'BOGEY MAN BENN ROARS BACK' proclaimed the *Sun*, gleefully reporting the Liberal agent's fatuous comment: 'Labour must be bonkers.' Similarly the *Daily Express* announced, 'LABOUR GLOOM AT BENN TRIUMPH'.

A record total of seventeen candidates stood at Chesterfield, but almost all the media's attention was directed at only one – Tony Benn. In addition to the large pack of newspaper reporters, between twenty-five and thirty film units were present in Chesterfield and it has been estimated that over a million pounds was spent by the media during the by-election campaign. Virtually without exception, the national newspapers were hostile to Tony Benn and it was obviously hoped that their biased reporting would influence the outcome.

At the start of the campaign it was widely assumed that Tony Benn would be defeated. When opinion polls and the genuinely sympathetic hearing Tony Benn received wherever he went in Chesterfield made it seem likely he would win, the broadcasters and journalists turned to urging voters to prevent his victory by tactical voting. Hoping to capitalize on this, both the Liberal and Conservative candidates spoke about little other than their Labour rival. This too appeared to have but a minimal effect and so, in the final week before the election, the press in desperation flung whatever mud it could rake up. On the Sunday before Polling Day the front page of the *Sunday Times* carried a story with the headline 'BENN SET TO WIN AS POLITICS TURN ROUGH'. But it was left to its sister-paper, the *Sun*, to plumb new depths of disgraceful journalism. On 1 March 1984 – polling day – it gave a centre page to a squalid article, headlined 'BENN ON THE COUCH', in which an anonymous American psychiatrist purported to analyse Tony Benn. Among the many absurd claims were:

'He is a Messiah figure hiding behind the mask of a common man ... He is greedy for power and will do anything to satisfy his hunger ... It scares the hell out of these sort of people when they just suddenly say to themselves, "Could I be crazy?"'

(In a *World in Action* programme transmitted on 5 March, the psychiatrist used by the *Sun* was identified. He denied making the statements and declared, 'I'm disgusted. I've been lied to and misquoted. The trusting relationship one should have in working with a media-man has been blown to hell.')

It is impossible to assess what effect the media's vilification of Tony Benn had on the voters, although it certainly did help generate much public interest in his candidacy and a large television audience watched the declaration of the result, which was:

Tony Benn (Labour)	24,633
Max Payne (Liberal)	18,369
Nicholas Bourne (Conservative)	8028
The other 14 candidates	1962
Labour majority	6284

And so Tony Benn was returned to the House of Commons for the thirteenth time – a figure not exceeded by any serving Member of Parliament.

Considering the weight, if not the substance, of the opposition, it was a remarkable victory, for he succeeded in securing more votes than his predecessor, whose sudden resignation had caused the by-election. Yet the result was not a surprise for those who followed or worked with Tony Benn in the constituency. Throughout the campaign he was tireless and effective, canvassing voters, speaking at factory gates and addressing the many public meetings that were attended by a total of 13,000 people. As in all his previous elections, he refused to abuse the other candidates, or even refer to them by name. He concentrated entirely on policies and political principles, and his honest and serious campaign won him much support and many friends.

His by-election victory at Chesterfield has meant the return to Parliament of one of its ablest and most conscientious Members, who has never been afraid to speak out clearly and courageously on all matters of importance. Yet once again Tony Benn had to endure the campaign of systematic character assassination in the media that has continued unabated for over twenty years, frequently being extended to his wife and family, who have no adequate platform from which to defend themselves. Yet the Benns have all the virtues that it might be expected would be most praised. They are honest, sincere, principled and incredibly hard-working; their family life close and mutually supportive. In addition, Tony Benn, who is probably the greatest living political orator, has throughout his long career constantly striven to make the country's constitution more democratic during a period when the survival of our way of life is seen as being about the defence of democracy.

So why has Tony Benn for long been so unpopular with both the media and the anti-socialist leadership of his Party? I asked him why he thought this was so:

'What needed to be done to make the Labour Party democratic and effective did involve raising the unspoken problem of the relationship between the Parliamentary Labour Party and the Party. Because of my experience in Parliament and in Government, I was bound to support those who outside saw that as a barrier to advance. That did alienate colleagues, although they cannot say, whatever they may wish, that I did not say it all when I was in office. I remember once being interviewed by Bob MacKenzie about my book *Arguments for Socialism*, and he said, "Well why didn't you say all this when you were in office?" I replied, "Bob, look at the book. Every speech was made when I was in office." And my colleagues know that I said it all when I was in the Cabinet. But they see me as a traitor to the parliamentary class.

As far as the press is concerned, I'm a sort of traitor to my social class. They see me as coming from a comfortable family background – which I did, although without what they claim to be my aristocratic connec- tions. Then from very early on I made the media my interest. So I think they may well have attacked me because I put a spotlight on the way they worked.

You know, you do get wounded in these attacks. But there is, I hope, a certain recovery from it, in the sense that if what you are saying is right and you are seen to be sincere (and truthfully I am, for what would the point be in doing all this for gain and what would the gain be anyway?) there is in the end a certain credibility that survives. Even a defeat can deepen your credibility, if people know that you have paid a price for what you said. But it is a bit hard. I don't suppose for twenty years I've opened a popular newspaper and read any references to me that haven't been pejorative and destructive. That is an indication, I suppose, that there is thought to be a potential threat in the ideas that I am expounding.'

The reaction of the media to Tony Benn's ideas is considered by James Curran in an article published in *The Times* on 1 December 1982:

'The claim that Benn has moved left to become Leader of the Labour Party is patently unjustified. The classic route to the top of the Labour Party is the inside left track. That is precisely where Benn was situated in the late 1960s – when his record as the youngest Minister in Wilson's Cabinet made him the front runner as a future leader. Far from enhancing his position, Benn's move to the left is probably the only reason why he is not now, and probably never will be, the Leader of the Labour Party. His radicalization was activated by conviction, not self-interest.

Press portrayals of Benn as irrational and opportunist are not simply smear tactics. They appear convincing to many journalists because they offer an explanation of Benn's conversion to the left. Yet ironically, when Benn was advocating policies that journalists in the centre and left-of-centre press agreed with, he was their favourite son ... It is a measure of how far the press has moved to the right, and only to a lesser extent of how far Benn has moved to the left, that he should have been transformed in so short a time from Fleet Street protégé to folk devil.'

It is then not the man but his views which anger and perhaps frighten the media and the establishment. At a time when 'socialist' has become a word used by many only as an insult, he proclaims himself to be a socialist whose beliefs are founded on his own experiences and the certainty that it is the better way to work for others and for the common good.

The willingness to put cause before self is rarely understood by contemporaries. History is kinder, for it dismisses those whose only influence stems from the reflected glory of their positions. Although more interested in actions than in theories, Tony Benn, as a socialist, believes that changes are inevitably going to take place, regardless of the part played in them by individuals. He sees his responsibility as making sure that at the time when he can make a contribution he is there.

And his contributions have been considerable. His fight to reject the peerage changed the law, so extending the rights of constituents to elect the Member of Parliament that they prefer. His fight to have a national referendum on the Common Market changed the law so that people gained the right to be consulted about major alterations to the constitution. As a Minister he gave employees the necessary encouragement to prove that workers' co-operatives can flourish and that industry does not have to be organized by capitalists. His continuing analysis of the media has alerted people to the bias of the proprietors and limitations of most news coverage. His fight for greater democracy and more open government has revealed that unnecessary secrecy has permitted the assumption of greater powers by the Prime Minister and the Civil Service. He has shown that people should expect to have a greater influence on Governments than can be exercised solely in a General Election held once every five years. His fight to democratize the Labour Party has helped to give its members the right to be involved in determining its policies and its leaders. As a result of this process, trade unions are being urged by their members to become more democratic and less bureaucratic.

All these are important, but Tony Benn's most substantial achievement, and the one for which history will remember him, is to have ensured that, against all the odds, the Labour Party has remained true to its socialist traditions when the natural inclination of its leaders was to abandon them. It was his father who, by refusing to accept the leadership of Lloyd George, successfully defended the radical traditions of the Liberal Party. It is fitting that his son has accomplished the same for socialism within the Labour Party.

In doing this Tony Benn, like his father, refused to take the easy way. Like most politicians, he could have chosen the strict careerist route; or, as he was often advised, he could have been much more circumspect, offering discreet support to the causes in which he believed rather than taking the initiative. But he followed the far riskier course of presenting his views honestly and campaigning vigorously even when his cause was unpopular.

Like his father, he will continue to do so as long as he lives. When I asked him how he saw his future, he said:

'History is full of examples of people who fight the battles not living to see the fruits of victory. It could be so for me. It could be that the chronic failure of the Labour Party to be anything other than an incorporated, ameliorative factor in a declining capitalism will be totally inadequate when the day comes. It could be it's a little different, although not in any way that I have planned. I don't believe that I will, like de Gaulle, be called back, but it is my belief that possibly somebody will be glad that the socialist tradition had been kept alive when darkness was all around us. It is after all the majority tradition within the Labour Party. So I think that all I have been is one voice for the Conference majority when the voices of the Parliamentary Labour Party, the media and the establishment have been so very different.'

Although the establishment may wish that it was not so, Tony Benn's voice has already been heard, and what he has had to say has deeply influenced many individuals and the Labour Party. Tony Benn has not only been the prophet of socialism in Britain, he has also helped to mould its form. By his speeches, writing and actions, he has ensured that socialism in Britain is built on the traditions to which he also is an heir. It is this radical, nonconformist background that has helped to ensure that socialism is seen not only as a collection of economic theories but also as a way of organizing society to provide for 'the deeper needs of humanity'. This is the cause that the Benns have for four generations so tenaciously and so successfully pursued.

SOURCES AND REFERENCES

MAJOR SOURCES

a. *Unpublished*

The papers of William Wedgwood Benn, MP, First Viscount Stansgate, in the House of Lords Record Office. (These are referred to throughout by the appropriate file number – always prefaced by *ST* – used in the *House of Lords Record Office Memorandum No. 56.*)

The papers of Tony Benn, MP

Benn, John Williams, *The Joys of Adversity – A fragment of autobiography* (c. 1920) – abbreviated *JofA*

Craig, Irene (*née* Benn), *I Remember* (c. 1963)

Stansgate, Viscount (William Wedgwood Benn), *Victorian Boyhood* (c. 1956) – abbreviated *VB*

b. *Published*

Benn, Ernest J.P., *The Confessions of a Capitalist* (Hutchinson, 1925)

Benn, Ernest J.P., *Happier Days – Recollections and Reflections* (Benn, 1949) – abbreviated *HD*

Benn, Tony, *Arguments for Democracy*, edited by Chris Mullin (Cape, 1981) – abbreviated *AfD*

Benn, Tony, *Arguments for Socialism*, edited by Chris Mullin (Cape, 1979) – *AfS*

Benn, Tony, *Parliament, People & Power – Agenda for a Free Society* (Verso, 1982)

Benn, Tony, *The Regeneration of Britain* (Gollancz, 1965)

Benn, Tony, *Speeches* (Spokesman, 1974) – *STB*

Benn, Wedgwood, *In the Side Shows* (Hodder & Stoughton, 1919) – *ISS*

Benn, Wedgwood & Margaret, *Beckoning Horizon* (Cassell, 1934)

Freeman, Alan, *The Benn Heresy* (Pluto, 1982)

Gardiner, A.G., *John Benn and the Progressive Movement* (Benn, 1925) – *JBPM*

Jenkins, Robert, *Tony Benn – A Political Biography* (Writers & Readers, 1980)

OTHER MATERIAL

Beaverbrook, Lord, *The Decline and Fall of Lloyd George* (Collins, 1966)

Bentley, Michael, *The Liberal Mind 1914–1929* (Cambridge U.P., 1977)

Birkenhead, Earl of, *Contemporary Personalities* (Cassell, 1924)

Braithwaite, William J., *Lloyd George's Ambulance Wagon* (Chivers – Bath, 1970)

Brockway, Fenner, *Inside the Left* (George Allen & Unwin, 1942)

Castle, Barbara, *The Castle Diaries 1974–76* (Weidenfeld & Nicolson, 1980)

Cross, Colin, *The Liberals in Power (1905–1914)* (Barrie & Rockliff, 1963)

Crosland, Susan, *Tony Crosland* (Cape, 1982)

Crossman, Richard, *The Diaries of a Cabinet Minister* (Hamilton & Cape)

Douglas, James, *Parliaments Across Frontiers* (H.M.S.O., 1975)

Douglas, Roy, *The History of the Liberal Party 1895–1970* (Sidgwick & Jackson, 1971)

Glasgow University Media Group, *Really Bad News* (Writers & Readers, 1982)

Grigg, John, *Lloyd George: The People's Champion 1902–1911* (Eyre Methuen, 1978)

Hollingsworth, Mark, *Policies or Personalities?* (Unpublished dissertation – Bristol Polytechnic, 1982)

James, Robert Rhodes, *Churchill – A Study in Failure 1900–1939* (Weidenfeld & Nicolson, 1970)

James, Robert Rhodes, *Memoirs of a Conservative – J.C.C. Davidson* (Weidenfeld & Nicolson, 1969)

Jenkins, Roy, *Asquith* (Collins, 1964)

Jenkins, Roy, *Mr Balfour's Poodle* (Collins, 1968)

Kogan, David & Maurice, *The Battle for the Labour Party* (Kogan Page, 1982)

Koss, Stephen, *Asquith* (Allen Lane, 1976)

Koss, Stephen, *Nonconformity in Modern British Politics* (Batsford, 1975)

McKenna, Stephen, *Reginald McKenna 1863–1943* (Eyre & Spottiswoode, 1948)

Marquand, David, *Ramsay MacDonald* (Cape, 1977)

Masterman, Lucy, *C.F.G. Masterman* (Nicholson & Watson, 1939)

Middlemas, Keith & Barnes, John, *Baldwin – A Biography* (Weidenfeld & Nicolson, 1969)

Morgan, Kenneth & Jane, *Portrait of a Progressive* (Clarendon Press - Oxford, 1980)

Owen, Frank, *Tempestuous Journey - Lloyd George, His Life and Times* (Hutchinson, 1954)

Pimlott, Ben, *Labour and the Left in the 1930s* (Cambridge U.P., 1977)

Pollock, Ian, *Press Coverage of the Labour Party's 1981 Deputy Leadership Election Campaign* (Unpublished dissertation - University of Surrey, 1982)

Rees, Caroline, *Photography, Politics and Fleet Street* (Unpublished dissertation, 1983)

Riddell, Lord, *More Pages from My Diary 1908-1914* (Country Life, 1934)

Riddell, Lord, *War Diary 1914-1918* (Nicholson & Watson, 1933)

Rowland, Peter, *The Last Liberal Government's Unfinished Business 1911-1914* (Barrie & Jenkins, n.d.)

Samson, Charles Rumney, *Fights and Flights* (Benn, 1930)

Scott, C.P., *The Political Diaries 1911-1928* (Collins, 1970)

Spender, J.A. & Asquith, Cyril, *Life of Herbert Henry Asquith, Lord Oxford and Asquith* (Hutchinson, n.d.)

Stevenson, Frances, *Lloyd George - A Diary* (Hutchinson, 1971)

Webb, Beatrice, *Diaries 1924-1932* (Longman Green, 1956)

Wedgwood, Josiah C., *Memoirs of a Fighting Life* (Hutchinson, 1941)

Williams, Marcia, *Inside Number 10* (Weidenfeld & Nicolson, 1972)

REFERENCES

Introduction

1 Stansgate, Viscount, 'Parliament in Six Reigns', *The Listener*, 28 August 1958, p. 303
2 *AfD*, p. 130

1 Julius and John Benn - 1827-1883

1 *JBPM*, p. 28
2 *ST*/287

2 John and Wedgwood Benn

1 *1883-1903*

1 *JofA*, p. 107
2 *HD*, pp. 21-22
3 'Parliament in Six Reigns', p. 304
4 *JBPM*, pp. 475-476
5 *VB*, p. 16
6 *HD*, pp. 32-33

7 *VB*, p. 25
8 *JofA*, pp. 133–134
9 *ST*/292/2
10 *VB*, p. 29
11 *VB*, p. 35
12 *ST*/292/2

II *1903–1914*

1 *ST*/1
2 *ST*/3
3 Owen, *Tempestuous Journey*, p. 161
4 *ST*/11
5 *ST*/292/2
6 *ST*/292/2
7 Braithwaite, *Lloyd George's Ambulance Wagon*, pp. 163–164
8 *ST*/292/2
9 *ST*/292/2
10 Riddell, *More Pages from My Diary*, p. 214
11 House of Lords, Lloyd George Collection, C/6/11/15

III *1914–1918*

1 Riddell, *War Diary*, p. 10
2 An unpublished journal in the possession of Tony Benn
3 *ISS*, pp. 26–27
4 *ISS*, p. 51
5 *ST*/286
6 Samson, *Fights and Flights*, p. 164
7 Quoted in Morgan, Kenneth & Jane, *Portrait of a Progressive*, p. 53
8 House of Lords, Lloyd George Collection, E/2/19/15
9 *JBPM*, p. 446
10 All telegrams quoted in *ST*/24/1
11 *JBPM*, p. 448
12 *ST*/286
13 *ST*/24/4
14 Dated 28 February 1917, in *ST*/286
15 *ST*/286
16 *ISS*, p. 286
17 *JBPM*, p. 446
18 *ISS*, p. vi
19 *ISS*, p. 58

IV *1918–1922*

1 *ST*/40/1
2 *ST*/40/1
3 House of Lords, Lloyd George Collection, F/38/4/27
4 *ST*/40/1
5 *ST*/40/1
6 *ST*/286
7 *ST*/286
8 Quoted in Koss, *Asquith*, p. 124
9 *JBPM*, p. 453
10 *JBPM*, p. 464
11 *ST*/292/2

3 Wedgwood Benn 1922–1925

1 *ST*/287
2 Spender & Asquith, *Life of Asquith*, Vol. II, p. 346
3 *ST*/66
4 *ST*/66
5 *ST*/78
6 *ST*/78
7 *ST*/78
8 *ST*/66
9 *ST*/286
10 *ST*/287
11 *ST*/2/1
12 *ST*/85/1

4 Wedgwood and Tony Benn – 1927–1950

1 In the possession of Lady Stansgate

6 Tony Benn
I *1964–1975*

1 Williams, *Inside Number 10*, p. 317
2 *STB*, p. 202
3 *STB*, p. 141
4 *STB*, p. 265
5 *STB*, pp. 99–100
6 *STB*, pp. 143–144

7 Speech given at the Yorkshire Labour Women's Rally on 5 June 1971, *STB*, p. 193
8 In *What Went Wrong* (Spokesman, 1976), p. 90
9 The correspondence is in the possession of Tony Benn

II *1975–1984*

1 'What did a Tory MP say in the Cumberland Hotel?', *New Statesman*, Vol. 101, No 2605, 20 February 1981
2 *AfD*, p. 18
3 *Really Bad News*, p. 110

INDEX

Acland, Francis: loyal to Asquith, 77
Acland, Sir Richard, 136
Addison, Dr Christopher, 62-3, 64
Adriatic Barrage, John joins, 67-8
Aims of Industry, 179
Ali, Tariq, 204
Amery, Julian, 137
Ashcroft, Peggy, canvasses, 125
Ashton, Joe (Tony's PPS): sacked – reinstated, 191
Asquith, H.H.: becomes PM (1908), 42; offers Joint Chief Whip to Wedgwood, 57; forms Coalition Govt (1915), 58; resigns (1916), 63; and party split, 64; opposes Ll. G., 74; loses East Fife, 76; struggle with Ll. G., 77, 78, 79, 84, 89; wins Paisley, 80; defeated at Paisley, 94; and Ll. G. leadership, 95-8; accepts earldom, 99, 100; has stroke (1926) – resigns leadership, 105-6
Astor, Lady (Nancy), 102
Attlee, Clement: Leader of Labour Party, 117; PM (1945), 125; second Govt, 131; loses election, 134; and Tony's renunciation Bill, 137; resigns Party leadership, 138; on Wedgwood, 144

Baldwin, Stanley: becomes PM, 90; on Wedgwood, 99; and India, 113
Balogh, Tommy, 158
Barnardo, Dr J.T., 17
BBC and democracy, 162-3; see also broadcasting
Beaverbrook, Lord (Max Aitken), 63

Belloc, Hilaire, 48
Ben-my-Chree, Wedgwood and, 64-6
Benn, Ann (née Taylor): marries Julius, 6; invalid, 7; dies, 24
Benn, Caroline (née De Camp): meets, marries Tony, 126-7; children, 134; inheritance, 134-5; on peerage fight, 153; work in education, 156, 159; on deputy leadership (1981), 200; on hangers-on, 204; on election (1983), 206
Benn, David (son of Wedgwood): born, 112; tubercular – learns Russian – Head of BBC Yugoslav Dept, 117
Benn, Ernest John Pickstone (son of John): born (1875), 12; character, 19, 20, 26, 86; *Happier Days* by, 20; year in Paris, 24; expands publishing business, 34, 35, 72, 85, 86; election agent for Wedgwood, 46; opposition to Ll. G., 97; becomes Conservative, 101, 105; sends Wedgwood on holiday, 103; founds Individual Movt – *Confessions of a Capitalist*, 105; family holidays with, 115
Benn, Florence (née Nicholson – *later* Florence Rutherford): marries William Rutherford (1882), 15; daughter, Margaret, born, 28; dies, 31
Benn, Henry (son of Julius): works for John, 19
Benn, John (John Williams): born (1850), 6; first job (1861), 8; starts stamp and coin businesses, 9; learns furniture design, 9; arrested by beadle, 9-10; 'Pepper's Ghost', 11, 14;

219

ship campaign, 200-1, 202; and Conference (1982), 204-5; and Chesterfield election, 207-8; Tony on, 209; *Times* on, 210

prices and incomes policy, Heath's, 175, 176

Progressives on LCC, 22-3, 39

Protectionism: Joseph Chamberlain converted to, 38-9, 40; Conservatives for Protectionism, 90; *see also* Free Trade

public ownership, 181; and Tony's Russian visit, 142; National Enterprise Board, 175, 178, 179, 183, 186

Rank and File Mobilizing Cttee, 198

Redmond, John: and Home Rule Bill, 47

referendum on EEC, 182, 184; Tony proposes, 166, 169, 170

Reid, Jimmy, 168

Reformatories, Julius works for, 6-7

Roberts, Charles: supports Asquith, 89

Rodgers, William: and Limehouse Declaration, 198-9

Rogers, Herbert (Tony's agent), 147

Rolls-Royce troubles, 161, 167

Rootes Motors rescued (1967), 160

Rosebery, Lord: and LCC, 23

Royal Air Force created (1918), 69

Runciman, Walter: loses election (1918), 76; opposes Ll. G., 64, 97-8, 101

Rutherford, Margaret, 28, 31

Rutherford, William *and* Florence, *see* Benn, William *and* Florence

St Clair, Malcolm: and Bristol seat, 147, 149-50; resigns, 152

St George's in the East and Wapping: Julius moves to, 6; becomes pastor, 10; social changes, 29, 37; *see also under* Benn, John, *and* Benn, Wedgwood

Samson, Col. Charles: and seaplanes, 62

Samuel, Herbert, 52, 76

Scottish Daily News as co-operative, 181

Seeley, John, Lord Mottistone, 39

Shaftesbury, Earl of, 19

Shipbuilding Industry Bill (1967), 160

Shipbuilding Industry Board, 167

Shore, Peter, 179, 184, 186; leadership election (1980), 198

Silkin, John: and EEC, 186; leadership election (1980), 198; deputy leadership election (1981), 203

Silverman, Sidney, 136

Simmons, Percy C.: opposes Wedgwood - sues for libel, 46-8

Simon, Prof. Brian, 156

Simon, Sir John, 89, 92, 101

Sinn Fein wins seat (1918), 77

Snowden, Philip, 94; loses election (1918), 77; wife presses Wedgwood to join Labour, 103

Social Contract, 183, 189

Soper, Donald, 136

South Africa: Wedgwood - supports Boer independence, 32; visits, 36; Simonstown exercises, 183

Spurgeon, Revd C.H., 19

Stansgate, Viscount, *see* Benn, Wedgwood

Stansgate, cottages at: John buys and sells, 34-5; Wedgwood rents, 106; Wedgwood buys, 116-17

Steel, David: on Tony, 187; Lib-Lab pact (1976), 192

sterling: crisis (1965), 159; devaluation (1967), 160

Stirling, Col.: raises private army, 179

Stockwood, Mervyn, 131

Storrs, Sir Ronald, 58

Sueter, Commodore Murray, 67

Suez crisis, 138

Sutherland, Graham, 148

Tandura, Alessandro: dropped by parachute, 69-70

Tatchell, Peter, 204

Taverne, Dick: stands for Democratic Labour Party, 174

teetotalism, 20, 83

Ten Year Industrial Strategy for Britain (Francis Cripps), 186

Thatcher, Margaret: leads Tories, 187
Thames floods Benns' house, 110-11
Thomas, George, 137
Thomson, George: resigns from front bench, 170
Thorne, George, 96, 97
Toynbee, Arnold: on Tony's peerage fight, 148
trade unions: in media, 174; and moderation, 188; press attacks, 189; and deputy leadership campaign (1981), 202-3
Trade Unions for Labour Victory, 199
tramways: John's promotion of, 23, 29, 37; social effects of, 37; libel against John, 49, 50
transport, Tony spokesman for, 142
Trevelyan, C.P., 91, 96
Tribune Group, 199
Turks and Chanak crisis, 87

Ungoed-Thomas, Sir Lynn, 144, 146
unemployment, growth of, 161, 164
Upper Clyde Shipbuilders (UCS): rescued, 164; work-in (1971), 168-9
USSR: Wedgwood visits, 105; Tony visits - impressed by public ownership, 142

Vansittart, Lord, 129

'wage question' (1903), Wedgwood on, 38
Wapping, Julius pastor in, 10; *see also* St George's in the East
Wales, Prince of (*later* Edward VIII): and National Appeal Fund, 55
Walker, General: raises private army, 179
Wedgwood family: distant relatives, 12

Wedgwood, Josiah, 89, 91
Wembley Conferences: (1980), 197; (1981), 198
Westminster Palace Hotel, John lives in, 28, 32, 33
Wilkins, William ('Will'), 146, 148
Williams, John de Kewer: converts Julius, 6; pastor in Hackney, 12, 16
Williams, Marcia: on Tony, 157
Williams, Shirley: and Limehouse Declaration, 198-9
Wilson, Harold: resigns from Govt, 134; stands for leadership, 143; Party Leader, 151; and 'scientific revolution', 154-5; repudiates Tony on workers in media (1972), 174; forms Govt, 177; attacks Tony on NEB, 179; and Cabinet collective responsibility, 180-1, 182-6, 190; on Tony, 187; and Honours list, 190; resigns, 191
Wilson, Sir Matthew 'Scatters', 56, 59
Windle, Dick, 132
'winter of discontent', 194
women, equal opportunities for: Tony on, 167-8
workers' control: Tony on, 165; in media, 174; co-operatives, 181, 185, 189
Workers Weekly threatened over seditious libel, 92
World War I declared, 55
World War II: declared, 119; VE day, 125
Wood, MacKinnon, 51, 76

Young, Hilton: joins Tories, 101

Zander, Michael, 149
Zinoviev letter, 95